Pirates of the Caribbean

Axis of Hope

By the same author

Pirates of the Caribbean
Axis of Hope

Tariq Ali

VERSO

London • New York

First published by Verso 2006
This edition published by Verso 2008
Copyright © Tariq Ali 2008
Appendix Two copyright © Henri Maler 2004. First published as 'Venezuela:
Le Monde vacille entre "d'une part" et "d'autre part"' on www.acrimed.org, 20
August 2004; Appendices Three and Four copyright © Editora Abril, Cuba
2004. First published in *Our Chávez*, 2004.

1 3 5 7 9 10 8 6 4 2

Verso
UK: 6 Meard Street, London W1F 0EG
USA: 180 Varick Street, New York, NY 10014-4606
www.versobooks.com

Verso is the imprint of New Left Books

ISBN-13: 978-1-84467-248-6

British Library Cataloguing in Publication Data
A catalogue record for this book is available from the British Library

Library of Congress Cataloging-in-Publication Data
A catalog record for this book is available from the Library of Congress

Typeset in Fournier by Hewer Text UK Ltd, Edinburgh
Printed in the USA by Maple Vail

For
Eduardo Galeano,
whose pen, like Bolívar's sword, seeks to displace
an Empire and unite a continent

Tariq Ali is a veteran pirate. He has written more than a dozen books on world history and politics, six novels and scripts for the stage and screen. He is an editor of *New Left Review* and lives in London.

Contents

Preface

This book is the result of numerous trips to Latin America over the last few years. I have been to Venezuela and Brazil on several occasions over the last six years, witnessed the disintegration of the Argentine economy first hand and visited Cuba for the first time in 2005. These trips convinced me that there is reason for hope. South America is the continent where an essentially social-democratic alternative to neo-liberal capitalism is rising from below and infecting politics everywhere. And what a relief it is compared to the religious revivalism elsewhere (including the United States).

It was Colin Robinson's idea that I write this book. Friends in London and the US, Brazil, Argentina, Cuba and Venezuela were supportive and they have all helped in different ways: Max Arvelaiz, Atilio Boron, Rosa Elizalde, Forrest Hylton, Deborah James, Alex Main and Emir Sader.

A very special debt is owed to Richard Gott – a friend and comrade since 1966 – whose classic study *Guerrilla Movements in Latin America*, his regular despatches from Bolívar's continent to the *Guardian* and the Penguin Latin America Library that he edited, helped to educate an entire generation. His latest books on Cuba and Venezuela continue in that tradition. It would have been tiresome if he, too, had sold out to the New Order. But he remains a pirate.

Marcus Rediker's spirited defence of pirates, *Villains of All Nations*, was another inspiration. He quoted a 1724 work by Captain Charles Johnson, in which he referred to pirates as 'marine heroes, the scourge of tyrants and avarice, and the brave asserters of Liberty.' One can overdo this line of argument, but I still hope that 'We Are All Pirates' becomes a regular chant on global justice marches.

Thanks are due to Tom Penn, Giles O'Bryen and Sebastien Budgen at Verso's London HQ, who offered useful editorial advice, and also to colleagues old and new at the *New Left Review* – Perry Anderson, Robin Blackburn, Mike Davis, Jacob Stevens, Susan Watkins and Tony Wood, as supportive as always, without necessarily being uncritical.

In a book of this sort it is essential to stress that none of the above-mentioned should be held responsible for my polemical excesses. Nobody ever is except myself. Long years ago, the British conservative political philosopher, Michael Oakeshott, referred to politics as 'a conversation not an argument'. Some of us who hailed from a different political tradition found it difficult to accept such a view – and this book, please be reassured, is definitely an argument.

And now to more important matters. The choice of font for a book is never easy. A great deal has to be taken into account. Does it need 'sexing up' or the opposite? I thought Garamond a bit too Sixties and noisy for a book that needed toning down. Quadraat, in polar contrast, was too post-modern. The grey scaling doesn't work as well as it should and as for the triangular-shaped top serifs, the less said the better. Georgia was unacceptable. There was, of course, the Motra (modern-traditionalist) hybridity of Martin Majoor and his Scala and Scala Sans typeface, but it was too arty and commercial. Having rejected these alternatives, I returned to the safety of Fournier, an old favourite, designed by the great French typographer, Pierre Simón Fournier (1712–1768), whose turbulent design transformed typography but who, alas, missed the French Revolution.

Tariq Ali
July 2006

Chapter 1

The Age of Disinformation

Where injustice speaks with the voices
of justice and of power
where injustice speaks with the voices
of benevolence and of reason
where injustice speaks with the voices
of moderation and of experience
help us not to become bitter

And if we do despair
help us to see that we are desperate
and if we do become bitter
help us to see that we are becoming bitter
and if we shrink with fear
help us to know that it is fear
despair and bitterness and fear

So that we do not fall
into the error
of thinking
we have had a new revelation
and found the great way out
or the way in
and that alone had changed us.

Erich Fried, 'Prayer at Night' (1978)

What determines and influences our consciousness; how we think, behave and act? The spirit of the age? How should that be defined? The pressures and processes of everyday life as experienced within the specific social structures of a dominant counter-revolutionary state and its allies is the answer favoured by this author. How else can one explain the mass conversions that marked the end of the twentieth century as hordes of politicians, academics, intellectuals, novelists and journalists, not to mention bandwagon careerists, collectively ingested the Washington Consensus (hereafter WC). Their sharpened instincts realised that the decisive trend in political and cultural life was conformity. They metamorphosed, hoarding all their ideas in a single enclosure. All this engendered its own psychology and language. The pillars of the new global order were viewed as almost divine institutions whose authority derived from the mere fact of their existence: a global corporation is beneficial because it is a global corporation and it is a global corporation because it is beneficial. In reality, this logic had to be imposed by NATO's eastward expansion and a network of US military bases in a hundred and twenty-one countries.

The crisis and collapse of all non-capitalist alternatives coupled with the end of the cold and hot wars between the United States and the Communist world (1917–91) had a profound impact on many people who had been till then, broadly speaking, aligned to the Left. Even those who had few or no illusions about the Soviet model of socialism were strongly affected by its collapse. Just as after the Restoration in eighteenth-century France very few could publicly declare 'I am a man of 1794' – Stendhal was a remarkable exception, choosing the year of the royal executions as decisive for the infant republic – so for many in Europe after 1991 it was no longer possible to say 'Despite everything, I remain a person of 1917'. In the latter case this would soon lead some to other conclusions: 'I never could have been a New Deal woman' or 'I always thought Labour in 1945 was wrong to nationalise the mines and railways' or 'The French obsession with the State is a hangover from Vichy' or 'Perhaps it's not such a bad thing that the Left lost the Spanish and Greek civil wars', and so on.

In contrast to Europe, Australia and the USA, there were fewer penitents in South America. A substantial layer of activists and intellectuals refused to turn their backs on the Cuban Revolution. More importantly, even those sharply critical of Castro refused to applaud his would-be-assassins in Washington or Miami. There were famous exceptions, of course, Carlos Fuentes and Mario Vargas Llosa among them. The same, alas, cannot be said of most Latin Americanists in the Western academies or doing service in the global media army. They 'matured' and crumbled or, to put it bluntly, sold out. If you can't re-learn, you won't earn.

In the West, the triumph of Capitalism appeared to be definitive. The WC became hegemonic. The two principal ideas of the New Order were: (a) the new model capitalism as the 'sole' way of organising humankind from now till the planet imploded, and (b) the West's flagrant violation of national sovereignty in the name of imposing its own brand of 'human rights'. These ideas and the domestic and foreign policies based on them have spread like a contagious fever over the last two decades. Betrayed illusions and discarded hopes led to an embittered view of the past, fuelling personal ambitions. The individual took precedence over the community. The fittest prospered.

The result of the first idea has seen a hollowing out of democratic institutions and the continued decay of the political-party system. While this is more pronounced in the West, it can also be seen in India, Brazil and South Africa. Drained of political differences, the parties have become empty shells, mechanisms designed to help the political elite share both power and money. The parties have fewer and fewer members but are kept going by a tiny network of professionals, political equivalents of their peers who staff the advertising industry. In the last century Herbert Marcuse was widely mocked for predicting that trends in modern capitalism were creating a consumerist culture in which humans, too, were being mass-produced and which was leading inexorably towards a passive and atomised society. The collapse of Communism turbo-charged the process.

After 1991 any talk of political resistance, even on the level of ideas, had become widely regarded as mad, dissonant, perverse, living-in-the-past. The great longing now, on the part of many once on the left, was to belong and this was such a powerful impulse that many intelligent men and women who had once looked to Moscow and Beijing or Prinkipo and Coyoacan or Havana, Hanoi and Managua, and in some extreme cases Pyongyang and Tirana, now became converts to the New Order.[1]

---

1. The Cuban writer, Abel Prieto, now Minister of Culture in his country, has a similar explanation: 'The continued existence of Cuban Revolution reminds them of what they were when they were young and what they have given up. For this reason, the Cuban cause is disturbing, specially because it appears like a ghost that shames them and tells them that they have capitulated.' The Cuban case is special. Personally, I would feel very ashamed if I had ever been a worshipper of Kim Il Sung. The two trips I made to Pyongyang in the Seventies left me with a strong feeling of disgust for the regime. A Kim Il Sung fanatic at the time was Jon Halliday who was surprised that I had even managed to get into the country. He assured me that he was not 'a hundred per center' but he was certainly close to 95 per cent. I look forward to a mea culpa in the shape of a biography of Kim and Son by him, though I hope, just for old time's sake, he will not rely exclusively on South Korean intelligence documents.

Individual psychology is, of course, not unimportant in explaining a total transformation of a person's political opinions but in this case the phenomenon was so widespread that it can only be seen as marking a major retreat by an entire social layer.[2] Observing the changed social and political landscape they ceased to think. Capitalism, which many had once regarded as an incurable cancer, was now perceived as the only available cure.[3] What does this represent, if not an abject prostration before the difficulties and dangers of history?

The new faith is, as we know, an old one. Capitalism had existed for five hundred years. This – the very fact that it had survived all its crises whereas actually-existing socialism had lasted a mere seventy years and collapsed when confronted by its first major challenge – gave it an antique quality compared to the upstart social experiments that had ended in disaster. And so it came about that WC supporters became semi-religious in their devotions. What they supported became immutable and infallible; all problems would cease once the entire world had been properly converted. All heresies needed to be expelled from it so that it became self-consistent. Any challenge to this view was to be ruled out of court.

And yet if one looks deeply into the minds of the new converts all that can be seen is an empty space with borrowed furniture. Many want to repress this fact, but nothing up there belongs to them. It is the baggage of the New Order and it influences everything: their beliefs, their gestures, their unctuousness, even how they dress. In some cases the old body-language and the punctilious prose is preserved; bloodshot eyes light up and clenched fists are raised to celebrate a glorious new imperial

---

2. The examples are too numerous and on a global scale would require an encyclopaedia. I have provided a pen-portrait of one of them in Appendix One because of the role he plays in the narrative.

3. This applies principally to politics and popular culture, in which fantasy, mysticism, irrationality, an over-reliance on psychological perceptions, lifestyle and reality TV shows all flourished.

war or coup. Since the war has been a disaster and the coup has collapsed in ignominy, the show of self-confidence is little more than an embarrassed mix of pretence and bluster. Insignificant in themselves, what such people represent is the polluted tip of the iceberg. It is the latter that needs to be uncovered.

A single Empire, but numerous 24-hour news channels dominate the world we live in; all of them bar two (al-Jazeera and Venezuela's Telesur) share the same agenda.[4] The concentration of media power in the hands of half a dozen global tycoons is designed more to promote 'regime change' than freedom of speech or thought. The disinformation corporations (including the state-controlled networks such as the BBC and ABC) form an important layer of the imperial scaffolding that girdles the world. The friend/enemy, believer/heretic dichotomy promoted by the White House and the WC dominates mainstream media coverage. Writing in different times, the Austrian satirist and critic Karl

---

4. And in times of war, when the control of information becomes crucial in order to maintain a grip over public opinion, any attempt to provide images that challenge the dominant order is taken very seriously. During the bombing of Yugoslavia, NATO justified the assault on the TV station in Belgrade on the grounds that it was 'broadcasting propaganda'. Arguments such as this are dangerous because they provide ammunition to terrorists who might utilise them to bomb CNN or the BBC. In Afghanistan and Iraq, the United States bombed the al-Jazeera studios and as a senior al-Jazeera correspondent was reporting the occupation of Baghdad, he was targeted by US helicopters and killed. Earlier al-Jazeera had provided the US with details of their offices in Baghdad to prevent an 'accidental bombing'. Instead it was done deliberately and in public view. Footage of this can be seen in the Canadian documentary, 'Control Room'. A gifted al-Jazeera journalist, Taysir Alluni, who interviewed Osama Bin Laden a month after 9/11 was arrested and charged as a 'terrorist' in Spain, the country of his birth. He is currently in the high-security prison of Alcala-Meco, serving a seven-year sentence. Few doubt his innocence and the only evidence is that he obtained a journalistic scoop. Had a senior US or Spanish journalist been offered the chance of interviewing OBL it is unlikely that they would have refused. 'They hate our freedoms' is the slogan of the Bush/Blair toadies, but when it comes to defending the freedom of a journalist doing his job, the 'defenders of freedom' fall silent. The journalist was of Arab origin working for an 'enemy' TV channel. Who cares?

Kraus once commented that 'if the reporter has killed our imagination with *his* truth, he threatens our life with his lies'.[5]

A single image, decontextualised and repeated often enough, has often proved sufficient to convince the citizens of our humanitarian-imperial world that it is time for another war. Images of this sort dominated media coverage in the run-up to the wars on Yugoslavia and Afghanistan, but no up-to-date pictures were available for Iraq in 2002 – the earlier ones depicting the effects of napalm and poison gas in a Kurdish village were sparingly used, since they were over two decades old and some older viewers might have recalled that the Iraqi despot was at the time a valued Western ally, as were the bearded 'freedom-fighters' in Afghanistan. In the absence of the image, lies had to suffice; they did so even when they had been conclusively exposed as such.

And peacetime? The times when it was ideologically necessary to demonstrate the importance of diversity, dissent, a vibrant public opinion, oppositional politics to the deprived citizens of the Soviet Union and Eastern Europe are long gone. China has demonstrated that a dynamic capitalism does not require even a rudimentary democracy. Today, the New Order requires socio-economic-political conformity, and news management becomes more important than it was for most of the previous century.[6]

---

5. Karl Kraus, *In These Great Times: A Karl Kraus Reader*, edited by Harry Zohn, Manchester, 1976, p. 78.
6. A revealing example of the conformity that the New Order induces was the comment of a decaying media guard-dog on George Clooney's thoughtful film, *Goodnight, and Good Luck*. Shamed, presumably, by the virtual absence of a consistently critical media and his own tiny role in its decline, BBC culture man Mark Lawson wrote in an article headed 'Unfair and Unbalanced' (*Guardian*, 10 February, 2006): 'Clooney wants journalists to switch from a two-hands approach to a single jabbing punch on such issues as Iraq and oil. But what about viewers who back Bush and the drilling barons? Do they just switch off or turn to Fox News, an existing rightwing application of the Murrow-Clooney rules that scarcely encourages other such experiments? None of this is to suggest that "objectivity" and "balance" are uncontentious or even achievable aims. All

Given that the new rules apply to all aspects of imperial politics and strategy, how could reportage of the changing world remain immune? For the overwhelming majority of journalists in the West, leave alone the minority directly linked to the intelligence agencies, there is one principal criterion for evaluating a regime: not its human rights record, but whether or not the state concerned is a friend or an enemy of the WC. Washington's allies can bomb cities, torture people, commit war crimes; this is either portrayed as unfortunate but necessary or else the victims are blamed for what is being done to them. Palestine and Chechnya, Iraq and Afghanistan, are the most obvious examples.

Rarely has the proclaimed ideology of the West come into such sharp conflict with reality as in 2002, during the US/EU-backed coup d'état in Venezuela, where the elected President, Hugo Chávez, was regarded as disloyal to US interests in the region. (Venezuela is the largest oil producer in Latin America.) The temporary overthrow of an elected President was so loudly cheered by the politicians and media watch-dogs of the New Order that one might have been forgiven for imagining that we were back in the times of colonial suppressions of native uprisings. Virtually the

---

6. reporting has a stance: even a piece that divides the time between the three main parties by stopwatch implicitly accepts the political status quo while posing as impartial. Equally, Murrow's Blitz reporting, though it met most standards of journalistic excellence, was neither objective nor balanced; it worked from the assumption that Hitler dropping bombs on London was wrong. But the point is that, except in instances of coup or genocide, balance is a better ambition for broadcast journalism than partisanship because it is less subject to personal or cultural prejudices and leaves the historical record in better order. So, for all its intelligence and elegance as a movie, *Good Night, and Good Luck* is not the DVD that trainee journalists should be given on their birthdays . . . In a culture in which the pronouncements of the media are met by almost as much scepticism as those of politicians, the answer, surely, is not more editorialising but more reporting. *Good Night, and Good Luck*: good film, but bad logic.'

Good boy, Mark. Possibly trainee journalists should only be given DVDs in how to interview celebrities, please their superiors and by so doing build their careers. Journalism as commodity in the world of the market.

same commentary appeared in most of the mainstream press and TV channels. As we shall see, the short life of this particular coup froze the media operation at the overture stage: another week and the hallelujahs would have become deafening. The episode was revealing on many levels and will be discussed in greater detail elsewhere in this book. Here it is only necessary to study the widespread disinformation campaign in the WC media networks.

The coverage of the coup in the transatlantic press – *The Economist* and *Financial Times* – was predictably tendentious, often displaying a preference for fantasy and wish-fulfilment rather than reporting social-political reality. The two respective correspondents in Caracas were Philip Gunson (who also doubles up as the Caracas stringer of the *Miami Herald* and an all-purpose anti-Chávez hack wherever required) and Andrew Webb-Vidal. This pair stationed themselves permanently in the posterior of the Venezuelan oligarchy and its political parties. Viewing everything from this advantaged position, these two reptilian journalists became the principal keepers of the oligarchic flame in the Western media. Gunson's radical past as a partisan of the Sandinista Revolution in Nicaragua and his disenchantment that followed its collapse soured his vision of Venezuela. Embittered and cynical, he now became a whole-hearted opponent of the Bolivarian process, slightly shame-faced during the early years but more and more rabid as Chávez grew in stature and strength. Webb-Vidal – less intelligent, but more biased – developed a tone, a method and the journalistic ethics of denunciatory articles that was oddly reminiscent of *Pravda* during the Brezhnev epoch.[7]

---

7. *Pravda* was the official organ of the Communist Party of the Soviet Union known for its shrill reductionism. Leonid Brezhnev was the First Secretary of the CPSU for too many decades. The uniformity of much of the Western media today recalls that earlier epoch. Just as the *Pravda* line was faithfully echoed in the pro-Soviet press throughout the world, today the Washington Consensus line, honed to a fine art by *The Economist*, *Financial Times* and the *Washington Post*, is loyally reproduced on each continent.

This sordid bard of a discredited social order made no secret of his oligarchic sympathies and the *Financial Times* saw no reason to question this 'objectivity'.

It was when the Chávez government attempted to take charge of the state-controlled oil giant, Petróleos de Venezuela – whose senior executives and trade-union leaders had been put in their positions by the previous administration's totally discredited politicians and who had refused point-blank to work with the new government – that the Venezuelan oligarchy and its political cronies realised the preservation of their futures and bank-balances required rapid action. The appointment of a new Board of Directors was the signal for the oil workers' union (closely attached to the defeated Acción Democrática party) to go on strike. The oligarchs and their friends in Washington and Madrid were convinced that without the flow of oil the economy would collapse, leading to mass unrest and permitting the use of time-honoured methods to remove a weakened Chávez government.

So when, exactly a year before it invaded Iraq, the United States green-lighted the coup in Venezuela, the oligarchs were openly thrilled. A former President of the Chamber of Commerce, dilapidated even by Venezuelan standards, was dressed up as a presidential stooge. A few tame generals then ordered the arrest of Hugo Chávez and he was taken to a military base. So far, so bad. As the news spread, anger grew in the *barrios* that surround Caracas and the poor decided to march to the Presidential Palace, the Miraflores. Simultaneously another, equally significant event was taking place in the palace. With the Western media ready and waiting to introduce the bent president to the world as the saviour of Venezuelan democracy (the *New York Times* had defended the coup as enhancing democracy) a general came out of the palace and spoke to the military band. He informed them that a new president was about to emerge, and that they should play the national anthem as per usual. The soldiers questioned his orders. Angered by the disobedience, the general turned to the young bugler, an 18-year-old soldier, and instructed him to blow the bugle when he saw the new president. 'Excuse me General, but which president do you speak of? We know of only one. Hugo Chávez.' A furious general told the bugler to obey orders. At this point the bugler handed his instrument to the general and said: 'You seem to be very keen on playing the bugle. Here it is. You play it.' This was a soldier who can proudly tell his children: 'I did not obey orders.' The combination of a popular upsurge and the threat of a soldiers' mutiny saw the triumphal return of Chávez. The people of the *barrios* had marched down to the city to defend their Bolivarian government. They did so because they knew that Chávez had been removed for helping them; because they understood that a complex gestation had begun in Venezuela, which was trying to free the country from Washington's domination; and because they believed that even weaknesses of the Bolivarians were better than the strengths of the Opposition. A year after the failed coup that was certainly my impression from talking to a variety of people from different social backgrounds, some of whom were no supporters of Chávez.

The instincts of the young bugler were thus much more in tune with the majority of his fellow-citizens in Venezuela than those of the media folk who had been programmed to respond positively to a blatantly anti-democratic coup, which they proceeded to do without any sense of shame. Within the country itself, the two major daily newspapers had no sympathy whatsoever for Chávez (one of them was used to being bribed or clandestinely subsidised by previous governments; it had offered the same terms to the Bolivarians but had been refused). It was the Spanish-language CNN and, in a much more open way, Gustavo Cisneros' channels which backed the coup. In Cisneros, the Venezuelan oligarchy had found its purest representative. The Latin American billionaire, a would-be Murdoch or Berlusconi, was centrally involved in the coup. Like his equivalents elsewhere, he thought first of his own interests. He served the old political parties only because they served his needs, and showed his appreciation of their servility by using the odd Finance Minister as a personal bagman. He liked to half-pretend that all this was not for personal gain but for his continent's good.[8] But why should he devote his energies to his continent unless there was money to be made? He had owned Venevisión, the largest private channel in Venezuela, since 1961, long before the world had moved in his direction. And now it could be used as a weapon against the barbarians who threatened the power of money. In recent years Venevisión became well known for its endless attacks on the Bolivarians as 'mobs' and 'monkeys', the latter term reflecting the traditional Creole attitude to their dark-skinned cousins. How they chuckled in the leafy suburbs of Eastern Caracas at this display of wit.[9]

The most sophisticated media technology is now put in the service of the primitive and simplistic needs of the system, delivering whatever is required, including coups d'état and scabrous replacements for elected presidents. The Mexican elections of July 2006 are a case in point. While the bulk of the global media networks was announcing a victory for the right-wing, neo-liberal candidate, Felipe Calderón, a small, but effective independent media team was patiently analysing what was taking place in the country; it soon became obvious that its concerns

---

8. 'From the 1980s he has extended his empire across Latin America to include Chile's Chilevisión and Colombia's Caracol TV, with a major stake in DirecTV Latin America, whose satellite beams a diet of sport, game-shows, telenovellas and predigested news to twenty Latin American countries. He also has a lucrative share in Univisión, the main Spanish-language channel for the United States, and a joint Latin American internet connection venture with AOL-TimeWarner.' Richard Gott, 'Venezuela's Murdoch', *New Left Review*, 39, May–June 2006.

9. Seeking to restore his reputation after the coup's defeat, Cisneros approached an old novelist, Carlos Fuentes, and persuaded him to write a glowing introduction to a hagiography in which the Mexican writer canonises Cisneros as the voice of modernity engaged in battle against a barbarian *caudillo*. The age of disinformation requires conformity on every level, but for a writer of Fuentes' calibre to permit himself to be used in this fashion is despicable.

were justified. The team was helped by reporters from Mexico's independent daily *La Jornada*, who were convinced that, as in 1988, the establishment had stolen another general election.

Within twenty-four hours of the preliminary election results being declared, Al Giordano of 'Narco News', in the first of three carefully researched reports (whose quality was much higher than anything published in the Western press), challenged the disinformation by alerting cyberspace to the corrupt practices taking place in the country:

Today, in Mexico, begins a 'recount' of votes cast in Sunday's presidential election . . . in which the umpires are refusing to recount the votes.

Election authorities of the Federal Electoral Institute (IFE, in its Spanish initials) closed ranks on Tuesday with the National Action Party (PAN) of President Vicente Fox and candidate Felipe Calderón to oppose the actual recounting the votes. This, on the heels of Tuesday's 'discovery' of 2.5 million votes hidden by IFE since Sunday's election, added to a growing body of evidence – and corresponding public distrust in the institutions – that a gargantuan electoral fraud has been perpetrated.

The partial 'recount' began at 8 a.m. on Wednesday, in Mexico's 300 election districts – each with an average of 400 polling places and 140,000 votes to tabulate – and sparks are already flying over the struggle to conduct an authentic count in the sunlight of public scrutiny. Attorneys and party bosses of the PAN – whose triumphalism has turned to visible panic in recent hours – have orders from headquarters to universally oppose the reopening of any ballot boxes and subsequent public accounting of the actual number of votes cast for each candidate. On the other side, representatives of the Democratic Revolution Party (PRD) of candidate Andrés Manuel López Obrador and many outraged citizens armed with video cameras have besieged the 300 recount locales demanding an actual ballot-by-ballot recount . . .

One of the major problems for IFE and the Fox adminis-tration is that if they were to allow the bread-and-butter recount that the public demands, the ugly truth would come out that an unknown number of ballot boxes have 'disappeared' in the past two days. The ballots from three precincts in the city of Nezahuacoyotl – a López Obrador stronghold – were discovered yesterday in the municipal garbage dump. The results from two of those precincts have been missing, since Sunday, from IFE's vote tallies. An IFE official, ambushed by television reporters, exacerbated the crime yesterday when she blamed the Mexican military: the Armed Forces, not IFE, are supposedly guarding the ballots, she said, in defense of her bureaucracy. This, sources close to the military told Narco News, produced significant anger among the military generals and troops who – if the public does not believe or accept IFE's final decision – will be called upon to quell the national rebellion that follows.[10]

The massive scale of the fraud could not be covered up, and the more serious Western correspondents had to accept that a great deal of chicanery had taken place, especially when a million and a half supporters of the Opposition Democratic Revolution Party gath-ered in Mexico City on 15 July 2006 and pledged to struggle until every single vote had been recounted. The ensuing panic in the more 'enlightened' wing of the Mexican elite was expressed by a State Department favourite, Jorge Castañeda in the *Miami Herald*, suggesting that the Mexican establishment had something to fear.

Castañeda denounced the demand for a total recount as totally unacceptable, despite all the information that is already available to observers. His article was a plea to the United States to accept

10. Narco News can be accessed on www.narconews.com.

Calderón at any cost, and an appeal to Calderón himself to steal elements of his opponent's programme to separate López Obrador from his mass base. This as an alternative to a proper and total recount. Castañeda then explained why Washington should rejoice at having so narrowly escaped a 'populist' President in Mexico:

> The United States should count its blessings. Calderón's apparent victory spared Washington a major conundrum. I say 'apparent' because, according to some, it is still in doubt. But after two full tallies, numerous exit polls and quick counts all pointing in the same direction, it seems inconceivable that Mexico's Electoral Court of Appeals would either cancel the election or overturn the IFE's decision. López Obrador is perhaps not another Hugo Chávez. But he certainly could be taken for another Luis Echeverría, the country's president between 1970 and 1976, who was just recently indicted for crimes against humanity for the Tlatelolco massacre in 1968, when he was interior minister.[11] And López Obrador never clarified his stance on Chávez or Cuba, for that matter: what he really thought about the way both countries were governed. He is showing his true colors by not only refusing to accept the IFE's decision – he of course has the right to challenge it in the courts – but also contesting it in the streets and denouncing the IFE and Fox as traitors to democracy and the architects of electoral fraud.

So Washington would do well to recall, as many have said before, that it is one thing to have Evo Morales in the

---

11. On 2 October 1968, tens of thousands of students and workers (and their wives and children) came together in a rally in the Plaza de las Tres Culturas, Tlatelolco, Mexico City. At sunset, army and police began firing live rounds into the crowd, killing demonstrators and passers-by alike, an operation that continued into the night as the security forces 'mopped up' in surrounding houses and apartments. Estimates of deaths range from 200–300 to several thousand.

Andes or Hugo Chávez along the Orinoco and quite another to have a populist on the border.[12]

Despite this appeal a number of Western correspondents refused to give Calderón the benefit of the doubt. They remained critical of the proceedings – which they had certainly not been when the 2002 coup against Hugo Chávez was in motion in Venezuela. Then, the *Financial Times*' Andrew Webb-Vidal sent the following overheated despatch from the Venezuelan capital, a model of disinformation and propaganda that was to be exploded by the events that transpired forty-eight hours later, on 14 July:

The military revolt under way in Venezuela last night caps a week of political tensions marked by demonstrations, strikes, government interruptions of television news reports and, finally, pitched battles in the streets. President Hugo Chávez, who was believed to be inside the presidential palace, was dubbed 'a traitor of the nation' by a group of high-ranking officers from all four branches of the military.

The tensions were sparked by Mr Chávez's televised dismissal of senior managers at state-owned Petróleos de Venezuela (PDVSA), who had called for a slowdown of operations at the company to protest against his recent appointments at the company.

For a broad array of businesses, unions, civil groups and opposition parties, the live, on-air dismissal was the culmination of a series of actions by Mr Chávez that they perceived as intolerable and unbearable. In response they launched a crippling, indefinite strike. Analysts say the country landed in this state of open, civil rebellion because of a fundamental clash between Venezuelans' perception of the people they thought they were going to get in government and those they actually had.

---

12. *Miami Herald*, 12 July 2006.

Mr Chávez, a charismatic former army commander who led a failed coup in 1992, was elected in a landslide election three years ago, riding in on the desires of a population intent on banishing the corruption-tainted parties of the past.

'Venezuelans saw Chávez as a punisher of the ills of the past, and a leader of the nation with a traditional, Latin American populist message,' says Luis Leon, director of polling company Datanálisis. 'But, gradually, after he was elected, Chávez turned out to be something else. He really thinks he is a revolutionary, he has never believed in the democratic system, he simply used it to give apparent legitimacy to his ideas.'

Under what he calls his 'Bolivarian Revolution', Mr Chávez has attempted to put his personal stamp on an eclectic mix of greater state intervention in the economy, constitutional reform and radical rhetoric. He has infused these moves with frequent references to Simón Bolívar, Latin America's 19th century liberation hero, for whom his movement is named, and Cuba's Fidel Castro, a close associate.

In practice, despite the rhetoric and windfall revenue from strong oil prices, opinion polls suggest that, after three years, a majority of Venezuelans consider Mr Chávez's government to have been roundly unsuccessful in finding solutions to reversing the country's economic decline and tackling rising crime.

In addition, Mr Chávez has shown himself to be overbearing and autocratic, with critics, such as Teodoro Petkoff, a former planning minister and editor of the influential daily *Tal Cual*, saying he has run the country as if he were a 'sergeant-major in a military barracks'. An example of Mr Chávez's militaristic style has been his confrontational relationship with the local media, particularly television.[13]

---

13. *Financial Times*, 12 April 2002. For a pen-portrait of Petkoff, see Appendix One: 'Teodoro Petkoff: A Man For All Seasons'.

The next day, Webb-Vidal's piece was supplemented by a contribution from fellow-hack Richard Lapper. Headlined 'End of Autocratic Regime', it was an improvement neither in prose style nor objectivity:

> Marked by violence, ousted President Hugo Chávez's exit from the Miraflores government palace early yesterday proved to be a virtual mirror image of his entry into Venezuelan politics. Just as he burst on to the scene in an attempted coup a decade earlier, it was a coup that removed him.
>
> Mr Chávez's forced resignation came after a group of high-ranking officers led a revolt against him after the president's supporters opened fire on a 150,000-strong anti-government demonstration, killing 13 and injuring more than 100.
>
> The undignified end of Mr Chávez's three-year autocratic regime marked the climax of a rebellion of the armed forces in the space of four hours. But while it was the military that had the last word, it was the mounting disenchantment of a broad – and somewhat unusual – alliance of labour, business and civic leaders, and their escalating demands, that was the real force behind the ousting of Mr Chávez.
>
> Discontent among business groups had been simmering since the end of last year, when the president decreed a package of 49 radical economic laws that increased the role of the state in the economy . . . [14]

The *Financial Times* reporters – and, it needs to be stressed, all those newspapers and TV networks and political toadies big and

14. *Financial Times*, 13 April 2002. The most detailed and effective rebuttal of the allegation that pro-Chávez groups opened fire is contained in Gregory Wilpert's study, *Changing Venezuela By Taking Power*, London and New York, 2007.

small[15] that followed the WC lead (CNN/BBC, *El País/Le Monde*) in reflecting the views of the defeated politicians and the coup-makers – either underplayed or ignored the following facts:

(a) That mass disgust with the violence, ineptitude and corruption of the old dyarchic regime was the basis of the Bolivarian victories, with the result that Hugo Chávez was elected president; that he had won a referendum on the country's new constitution by an overwhelming majority and in the face of opposition by all the oligarchic parties; (b) that the 'political tensions' were the direct result of a refusal by the defeated political parties to accept the right of an elected government to implement its programme and were reminiscent of the 'middle-class revolt by patriotic Chileans' against Allende on 11 September 1973 that had been masterminded by Henry Kissinger and the CIA; (c) the men who dubbed Chávez 'a traitor to the nation' were simultaneously attempting to circumvent Venezuelan democracy and were acting in concert with the Spanish and US embassies in Caracas; (d) the polling company quoted is well known for its close links to the discredited political parties; (e) that 85 per cent of the media is privately-owned, had opposed Chávez with a venom, often deploying *ad hominem* and racist slurs that would not be – and are not – tolerated by any Western government (Webb-Vidal, whose newspaper defended the Blair government's assault on the BBC, is an odd champion of media 'freedom').

Despite all this, not a single Venezuelan newspaper or TV station has been taken over or punished by the Chávez administration.

---

15. One of the more vocal, if insignificant, toads was Denis McShane, then an underling at the Foreign Office and never shy of self-promotion. He supported the coup in public and referred to Chávez as a 'ranting demagogue'. Removed from the government for extra-curricular reasons, McShane often appears on BBC programmes on Venezuela. More recently he has been heard informing British Latin American specialists and academics that their help is vital because 'Tony Blair is very disturbed about the turn to the left in Latin America'. The BBC greeted the coup by describing Chávez 'not so much a democrat as an autocrat'. That's fine then, and what the Venezuelans vote for is irrelevant.

A few days later, when the coup debacle had run its course, Webb-Vidal's political twin Phil Gunson was forced to concede in *The Economist* that:

> . . . within hours, the coup began to unravel. The original plan for a broad civilian-military junta was jettisoned even before Mr Chávez surrendered to the army. In its place Pedro Carmona, the leader of the business lobby, was installed as president, with a cabinet of conservative fanatics which excluded labour. Mr Carmona was persuaded to decree the immediate closure of the National Assembly and the Supreme Court, and tore up Mr Chávez's constitution, which had been approved by a large majority in a referendum in December 1999. Swaddled like a chrysalis within the original plot, this 'coup within the coup' angered many who had worked to unseat Mr Chávez.
>
> Even so, it was astonishing that Mr Chávez, who on April 12th seemingly lacked all military support, should be swept back to his palace by the armed forces two days later. But Mr Carmona, though backed by many generals and admirals, lacked support from middle-ranking officers who control troops. And the conservatives underestimated the fervour and anger of Mr Chávez's remaining supporters. Opinion polls show support for Mr Chávez having plunged to 30%. But his hardcore sympathisers in Caracas's numerous shantytowns poured onto the streets over the weekend, looting and rioting. In all, some 50 people were killed in the four days of mayhem. Lastly, the conservatives had failed to take elementary precautions to secure their hold on power. An uprising led by the paratroop division (of which Mr Chávez is a former commander) and the presidential guard was enough to overthrow Mr Carmona.

But, Gunson insinuated:

Mr Chávez may be back in office, but his country has changed
since last week. The coup revealed that the opposition was
right when it insisted that most military officers are institu-
tionalists, who have not signed up for Mr Chávez's 'Bolivarian
revolution'. Most of those who supported his restoration did so
not because they share his ideology but because they believe in
the rule of law. 'We rose up against the government, not the
constitution,' said General Efrain Vasquez, when he withdrew
his support for Mr Carmona on April 14th (though he was later
detained for his role in the coup).

Mr Chávez's restoration may have come with strings
attached. There are three points on which the army may
try to hold the president to account. First, there is control
of the oil industry, the issue which triggered the general strike.
Secondly, the army wants him to disarm the 'Bolivarian
circles', an embryonic civilian militia, some of whose thuggish
members fired on the opposition march. Then there is Mr
Chávez's seemingly benevolent attitude towards Colombia's
guerrillas. The army wants tighter border security.[16]

The twin apologia for the coup-makers is quoted in full because it
expressed the wisdom of the State Department and the EU. If only
the 'heterogeneous coalition' representing the oligarchy as a
whole had prevailed then all would have been well. Condoleezza
Rice, then National Security Advisor in the White House,
publicly expressed the hope that the coup had taught Chávez
'a lesson' and that he would behave properly in the future. In fact,
both Ms Rice and her friends in the financial press were indulging
in a great deal of wishful thinking. The failure of the coup had
little to do with the military top brass, but the realisation by the
bulk of the officer corps in the Venezuelan Army that ordinary

---

16. *The Economist*, 18 April 2002, 'Hugo Chávez has survived for now, but power
lies with the Army.'

soldiers were threatening mutiny unless Chávez was restored to the Presidency. This, coupled with a mass uprising, made the coup unviable and, contrary to the hopes of the West and its journalists, strengthened Chávez and ensured his electoral triumphs in the years that followed. Gunson's notion that low ratings in opinion polls (he does not enlighten us as to which company carried these out and in which districts) led the politicians to underestimate hardcore support for Chávez is highly entertaining given that both Bush and his English bloodhound Blair were on 30 per cent or less in 2005–6. Would this justify a coup by the Joint Chiefs of Staff? And if such a coup were to take place because of differences on Iraq, would the 'hardcore' poor blacks of Washington DC surround the White House to re-instate the great Thinker President? Unaskable questions for the watchdogs of imperial interests. But though their total blindness to the racial dimension of Venezuelan politics speaks for itself, it would be unfair to single out the twins in Caracas.[17] Their scribblings were repeated with little variation in the *Independent*, *Le Monde*, *Libération*, *El País* and the bulk of the US media. The German press was marginally more restrained and two Berlin newspapers reported US involvement in the coup from the very beginning.

Le Monde, once a model of serious reporting from every continent, has degenerated beyond recognition. After 11 September 2001, its Publisher Jean-Marie Colombani wrote an emotional editorial titled 'We Are All Americans'. And this was certainly

---

17. '[In Venezuela under the diarchy] the ideal of racial equality has been eroded by intensified practices of segregation and discrimination, including apparently trivial ones that show how racial boundaries are being redrawn (such as the exclusion of darker-skinned Venezuelans from upper-middle-class discothequés). The same polarising process, with similar racialised expressions, is taking place in other Latin American countries, such as Peru, where the Supreme Court recently judged in favour of the right of a club that had excluded dark-skinned Peruvians.' Fernando Coronil, 'Toward a Critique of Globalcentrism: Speculations on Capitalism's Nature' in *Millennial Capitalism*, edited by Jean and John Comaroff, Durham, NC, 2001.

the case well before September that year, with *Le Monde* adopting an Atlanticist posture during the years of Jospin and the socialist government. It had backed NATO's war against Yugoslavia and published very few dissenting voices. Its attitude to the Bolivarian victories in Venezuela was coloured by the same prejudices as those revealed by Acrimed, the most sophisticated critical media website in Europe, whose founder Henri Maler stings hard.[18]

Another marginally less crude version of the same offensive is the frequently drawn comparison between 'bad' Latin Americans (Castro, Chávez and now, Morales) and 'good' Latin Americans (Lula, Bachelet, Garcia and Fox) with Nestor Kirchner currently hovering between the two categories. I experienced this first-hand during a visit to Brazil in 2005 when a public lecture at the Federal University of Rio led to an editorial rebuke from the leader-writer of the country's leading liberal daily, *Folha de São Paulo*, for the crime of contrasting the reforms in Venezuela to the neo-liberal desert in Brazil.[19]

---

18. www.acrimed.org. *Libération* was not much different. It seems barely necessary to recall that during this period an ex-Trotskyist edited *Le Monde*, while a former Maoist edited *Libération*. One almost detected a sense of disappointment in both papers when the French government refused to back the invasion of Iraq. Most of their journalists were ready to join the hurrahs of their US colleagues. Good relations were restored when President Chirac convinced Bush to overthrow the elected President of Haiti. *Libération* reported the event with joy, denouncing the toppled Haitian leader in a language that combined chauvinism and racism. For an Acrimed offering on *Le Monde* coverage of Venezuela, see Appendix Two.

19. *Folha de São Paulo*, 21 September 2005. An editorial titled 'Esquerda Obtusa' accused me of expressing 'ranco antidemocratico' which had to be denounced because of my supposed influence on sections of the Brazilian Left. My response was published in the newspaper a week later (30 September 2005) and triggered off an interesting debate. I received over two hundred e-mails from different parts of Brazil which suggested that, whatever else, the Venezuelan experience was being hotly debated in the country at large. I wrote:

What I argued at the Conference of the Federal University of Rio was that many politicians (including Lula) respect anti-democratic institutions:

The source of this relentless outpouring of propaganda is hardly a secret. Will it be able to impose its will and re-impose a fierce and ferocious epilogue on a turbulent continent? And why so much fear and hostility to the new movements and the governments that want an alternative to the WC? Presumably

---

19.   IMF, World Bank, US Treasury Department, WTO. These are the institutions of the Washington Consensus: unelected in every case and their key personnel appointed or approved by the United States. Does democracy today mean a neo-liberal economy with the primacy of consumption, speculation as the hub of economic activity and the entry of private capital into hitherto inviolate domains of collective provision? If this is what democracy will tolerate then what we have is the dictatorship of capital. Is it possible in this neo-liberal world to challenge this consensus? Or is any such challenge a sign of 'populism' or 'dictatorship'? Is diversity reflected in the fact that all of Rupert Murdoch's 247 editors in different parts of the world supported the war in Iraq?

The events in Venezuela are important not because that path can be followed in every other Latin America country. Each country has its own specificity, its own traditions, its own institutions. But the importance of Venezuela lies in the fact that the Bolívarians have reinvigorated and rejuvenated democracy. The Bolívarian constitution gives the people the right to recall a President. No other state in the Americas has such a clause.

The views expressed in your editorial parrot those of the Venezuelan oligarchy and its political parties, who have been regularly defeated in national and local elections and the referendum. It was the former US President Jimmy Carter who declared that the referendum in Venezuela was totally democratic. Chávez put his trust in the people by empowering them and they responded generously. The opposition and its supporters will only discredit themselves further by denying this fact.

However loud their cries (and those of their media apologists at home and abroad) of anguish, in reality the whole country knows what happened. Chávez defeated his opponents democratically and for the fourth time in a row. And this has happened despite the total hostility of the privately owned media: the two daily newspapers, *Universal* and *Nacional* as well as Gustavo Cisneros' TV channels and CNN made no attempt to mask their crude support for the opposition. Some foreign correspondents in Caracas have convinced themselves that Chávez is an oppressive *caudillo* and, like your editorialist, they are desperate to translate their own fantasies into reality . . .

Could Lula and the PT learn something from this experience? They could. In Venezuela, a million children from the shanty-towns

Washington's partisans had imagined something different. A
paradiso, a marketised globe, unchallenged, unchallengeable.
The overwhelming triumph of capitalism during the last decades
of the twentieth century blinded its supporters, old and new, to
any other possibility. The world-spirit had been tamed. It was the
end of history. Radical ideas were binned and the works on which
they were based consigned to a public bonfire. Golden centuries
lay ahead. That the warriors of the IMF/World Bank were
enthused by this vision was one thing; but the zeitgeist deeply
affected many former opponents of Capital's rule. Overcome by a
combination of fatigue and a fear of the unknown, they began to
paint its new victories in glorious primary colours, in more
extravagant language than that used 150 years ago by Gladstone,
who more disparagingly described imperial successes as the
'intoxicating growth and augmentation of all our wealth and
power'.

The post-1989 disillusionment, cynicism and an embittered
view of the past affected every continent without exception. And
those who now adopted the victors' view of history came from all

---

19.   and the poorest villages now obtain a free education; 1.2 million illiterate
             adults have been taught to read and write; secondary education has been
             made available to 250,000 children whose social status excluded them from
             this privilege during the ancien régime; three new university campuses
             were functioning by 2003 and six more are due to be completed by the end
             of 2006.

             As far as healthcare is concerned, the 10,000 Cuban doctors, who were
             sent to help the country, have transformed the situation in the poor
             districts, where 11,000 neighbourhood clinics have been established and
             the health budget has tripled. Add to this the financial support provided to
             small businesses, the new homes being built for the poor, an Agrarian
             Reform Law that was enacted and pushed through despite the resistance,
             legal and violent, by the landlords. By the end of last year 2,262,467
             hectares has been distributed to 116,899 families. The reasons for Chávez'
             popularity become obvious . . .

             It is ridiculous to suggest that Venezuela is on the brink of a totalitarian
             tragedy. It is the opposition that has attempted to take the country in that
             direction . . . (*Folha de São Paolo*, 30 September 2005).

social classes and political backgrounds: left social-democrats, Eurocommunists, ex-Trotskyists, pristine pure sectarians in their prime and now transferring the same vice to serve older causes, Maoists once prone to street-violence, Marxist theorists, staunch anti-imperialists who in their zeal had defended the Ethiopian Dergue and the disastrous Soviet intervention in Afghanistan, former anarchists – representatives of all these species could be found serving virtually every neo-liberal government – in Europe and North America, South Africa and Brazil, China and Australia and the Muslim world – or, where this was not possible, applauding wildly from the sidelines. They still believed in the class struggle, but had changed sides.[20] They had not understood that the historical graph never rises consistently. It is a broken and contradictory line that can fall to zero and then rise again, suddenly and without warning.

Politicians and academics, novelists and playwrights, film-makers and journalists united to celebrate each new triumph of the WC. Nor should it be forgotten that in those heady post-1991 days news of victories came thick and fast. The more recent the convert, the stronger the ardour with which the New World Order was defended. There was an intense longing to break decisively with the past and to demonstrate this as publicly as possible in self-righteous tones, without a blush of shame. What better way but to denounce the opponents of 'humanitarian wars' (the colonial whip that is one of the more savage and hypocritical heirlooms from previous centuries) as reactionary enemies of civilization and all anti-capitalist alternatives as paving the way to totalitarianism? Having convinced themselves that no other roads were possible or desirable, they remodelled their lives and work to

---

20. Interestingly, amongst the larger countries, India alone was more or less immune to the disease, possibly because a majority of the dominant left intellectuals close to the parliamentary and extra-parliamentary factions of the Left in India retained a mass base, which helped to steady their nerves after the collapse of Communism in the Soviet Union and China.

meet the requirements of the New Order. A few even found themselves unable to condemn torture as long as it was being carried out in the interests of humanity and civilization. Others discovered that old-fashioned colonialism was not such a bad thing after all and defended imperial occupations of sovereign states and the creation of new Western protectorates in the Balkans or the Hindu Kush. And all the while they insisted that they were the true voices of reason. Yes, they had joined the ranks of the imperial armies as propagandists; yes, they had supported wars and occupations, but no other choice was on offer. Were there other choices, then, when Montaigne derided European racism, Toussaint led a successful revolt against slavery, Mark Twain denounced the imperial occupation of the Philippines, or Marcel Proust mocked the biblical pretensions of Zionism?

The Left, the anti-war movement, the handful of tough-minded journalists still permitted a voice in the mainstream media, the 'idiots' who attended the festivals of the World Social Forum, the 'Islamo-fascists' all derided the coarse cynicism of the neo-imperialist folk and their role as treacherous turncoats. Thus described, rage injected venom into their opportunism. Not a few soft-spoken, snivelling journalists and academics were transformed overnight into warriors for the imperial cause, desperate to please their new masters and, as a result, often more boorish and belligerent than those they served. A similar constellation of characters had emerged after epochal defeats in previous centuries. Leveller ideologues had hitched their carts to the Stuart Restoration; Jacobin militants had celebrated the defeat at Waterloo; Bolshevik supporters in the West had become apologists for a succession of Empires. In many cases, these by no means unintelligent people expended much of their energy in the primitive and petty task of self-justification, which meant that their most recent productions displayed no signs of intellectual hunger. In the new milieu in which they found themselves there were always more experienced time-servers, more established and more con-

sistent defenders of the status quo. To make themselves heard
they had to work harder than more traditional conformists: they
had a past to expunge. Some succeeded. Were they all devious
and insincere? I don't think so. The conversions, in most cases,
were genuine enough, albeit a few continued to convince themselves that they remained 'on the democratic left' or were the
'only real left'. Why this insistence? Perhaps to admit a total
break would mean placing their life's work on a funeral pyre.
Vanity forbade such excesses.

The bandwagon careerists who clambered aboard the 1990s war
chariot had been hasty in assuming that because they were
finished, everything else was too. The earth had been stolen,
surveillance satellites littered the sky, but free thought and
dissidence had not completely disappeared. Nowhere was this
more the case than in the late President Monroe's imperial
backyard. Illusions about the civilizing function of a bloody
Empire and the rancid rhetoric of WC politicians were being
destroyed on the battlefields of Iraq and in the mountains of
Afghanistan and subsequently in Lebanon. The glimmer of an
actual political alternative, however, was visible only in Latin
America. There, new social movements had thrown up new
political leaders. They were insisting that, despite the fall of
the Soviet Union, the world was still confronted with old choices.
Either a revamped global capitalism with new wars and new
impoverishment, chaos, anarchy or a rethought and revived
socialism, democratic in character and capable of serving the
needs of the poor. These leaders were determined to rescue the
stranded ship 'Utopia', to initiate more egalitarian, redistributive
policies and to involve the poor in the political life of their
countries. For proclaiming these modest goals they were traduced
and vilified. Their real crime is to challenge the certainties of the
New Order, to disregard the 'Forbidden' signs of the WC. An ally
of that consensus can crush its opponents, torture and kill political
prisoners, ban all rival parties, sell half a country's assets for

private gain and still obtain the 'international community's' seal of approval. But if a government challenges the priorities of the global system in the name of an invigorated democracy and an ultra-democratic consititution and, worst of all, continues to be re-elected by its stubborn citizenry it will be vilified and attacked. For refusing to concur with the WC it is accused of 'totalitarian-ism' and orders go out that it must be crushed politically, ideologically and, if necessary, by force of arms. This is the world in which we live today, a world described with telling scorn by Harold Pinter.[21]

This was the world in which Hugo Chávez Frías was elected President of Venezuela for the first time in February 1998. The majority that turned out to vote for him was angry and deter-mined. The mass of Venezuelans had felt unrepresented for ten years; it had been luxuriously betrayed by the traditional parties; dissenters had been imprisoned, tortured and killed. The oligar-chy – complacent, self-satisfied and convinced of its impregna-bility – decided to be frivolous and selected Irene Sáez, a former Miss Universe, as its candidate. As the elections drew closer she was dumped in favour of the more charismatic, if less pretty, Christian Democrat, Henrique Salas Romer, a competent ex-Governor of Carabobo state. He, too, lost. Fewer excuses might have been necessary if the oligarchy had remained loyal to Miss Venezuela.

Electing Chávez (he won 56.2 per cent of the vote) was the revenge of the dispossessed. Till this occurred, Latin America had virtually been ignored by Washington. True, Cuba was still there but with the stranglehold of sanctions in place, the consensus was to wait till Fidel Castro was dead before making a new move. For the rest, the dictatorships had been carefully remodelled into representative democracies: Brazil, Argentina and Chile were

21. Harold Pinter, 'Art, Truth and Politics', The Nobel Prize Lecture, Nobel Foundation, 2005.

pledged to the pursuit of neo-liberalism. Political freedom and the market, de-linked for many decades because of the Cold War, could now be brought together and harmonised. The world stopped paying attention to South America. From the Mexican peso crisis of 1994–5 onwards, however, a series of financial blow-outs – East and Southeast Asia, Russia, Brazil, Argentina – revealed the hollowness of the neo-liberal project.

The majority of Venezuelans opposed the economic policies then in force, which consisted of a frontal assault on the poor and the less privileged in order to shore up a swollen, parasitical oligarchy and a corrupt, reactionary civilian and oil-industry bureaucracy. They opposed the use that was made of the country's oil reserves. They hated the arrogance of the Vene-zuelan elite, which utilised wealth and a lighter skin-colour to sustain itself at the expense of the poor, dark-skinned majority. They condemned this same elite's blind mimicry of all the values – social, political, imperial, cultural, economic – held dear by its US counterparts. None of this is a secret.

By 1998, it was clear that this oligarchy had failed. That is why the people elected Hugo Chávez. They wanted an end to corruption and privilege and subordination to the WC. Only when it became clear that Chávez was serious and determined to make modest, but important changes to the country's social structure was the tocsin sounded in Washington. Imperial satraps dedicated to making money and/or building political, ideological, academic or journalistic careers, hate any disruptions from below. The WC's new converts, it is worth restressing, are often the most vituperative against anything that smells of their own past. Nowhere has the embittered bigotry emanating from this quarter been more evident than in its actions and propaganda against the Bolivarian Republic of Venezuela.

Thus it was that the election displacement of the traditional oligarchy's favoured politicians met with loud protests from an unruly gang of media commentators, united by their prejudices against Chávez, whose advent to power was viewed as an insane aberration, disrupting the soothing and monotonous rhythms of the market in ideas. This was the view promoted by the US State Department and repeated endlessly by its media appendages. The changes in Venezuelan society were regarded as a regression to the bad old days, a first step on the road to totalitarianism; the embedded journalists of the New World Order were not interested in contextualising what was taking place in the country. For some there was no reason to maintain even a pretence of objectivity. Others, once partisans of the Cuban Revolution and the Nicaraguan guerrillas, had tired of struggle and changed sides, as we have seen.[22]

The debates around the Venezuelan Constitution and the set of six democratic victories won by the Bolivarians would have been impossible had it not been for the wave of mass disillusionment that had swept the country after the repeated failures of the social democrats of Acción Democrática (AD) and the Christian Democrats of COPEI (Comité de Organización Política Electoral Independiente) who had begun to resemble the nineteenth-century 'Yellows' and 'Blues' – liberals and conservatives who competed for power from 1847–70 but offered no real choice to the people. While there were moist-eyed references to the old politicians and their innate sense of decency, none of the mourners saw fit to remind readers and viewers of the events that had led to the Bolivarian triumph. The Venezuelan poor were tired of listening to promises, tired of World Bank economics. Hunger had made them feverish. They wanted something different, even

---

22. A senior Sandinista commandante, Humberto Ortega, a stern upholder of 'scientific socialism' in the early 1980s, developed a 'society as soccer stadium' view and confided to an interviewer in 1996: 'There's a hierarchy. A hundred thousand people can squeeze into the stadium, but only five hundred can sit in the boxes. No matter how much you love the people, you can't fit them all in the boxes.' Quoted in Eduardo Galeano, *Upside Down: A Primer for the Looking-Glass World*, New York, 2000, p. 310.

if it was slightly peppery. They got Hugo Chávez. A country virtually unknown to most of the world began to be viewed as a role model. This revival of hope and the emergence of a modest alternative to the status quo alarmed Washington. Hence the systematic disinformation by the corporate media networks. Hence this book.

Chapter 2

Imperial Vapours

But the great white monkey has got hold of the keys of this world, and the black-eyed Mexican has to serve the great white monkey, in order to live. He has to learn the tricks of the great white monkey-show: time of the day, coin of money, machines that start at a second, work that is meaningless and yet is paid for with exactitude, in exact coin. A whole existence of monkey-tricks and monkey-virtues. The strange monkey-virtue of charity, the white monkeys nosing round to help. To save! Could any trick be more unnatural? Yet it is one of the tricks of the great white monkey.

D. H. Lawrence, *Mornings in Mexico* (1924)

Sometimes it seems to me that America went off the track somewhere — back around the time of the Civil War or pretty soon afterwards. Instead of going ahead and developing along the line in which the country started out, it got shunted off in another direction — and now we look around and see we've gone places we didn't mean to go. Suddenly we realize that America has turned into something ugly — and vicious — and corroded at the heart of its power with easy wealth and graft and special privilege . . . And the worst of it is the intellectual dishonesty which all this corruption has bred. People are afraid to think straight — afraid to face themselves — afraid to look at things and see them as they are . . .

Thomas Wolfe, *You Can't Go Home Again* (1934)

Looking down on the world from the imperial grandeur of the Oval Office in the fall of 2001, the Cheney–Bush team was confident of its ability to utilise the September events to re-model the world. The Pentagon's Admiral Cebrowski summed up the linkage of capitalism to war: 'the dangers against which US forces must be arrayed derive precisely from countries and regions that are "disconnected" from the prevailing trends of globalisation'. Half a decade later, what is the balance sheet for Washington?

On the credit side, if China represents a future economic challenge, politically at least it remains as mute as Russia, India and Eastern Europe.[1] In Western Europe, after a few flutters on Iraq, the EU is firmly back on side. Chirac now sounds more belligerent than Bush on the Middle East, and the German military are busy doing Washington's work in Afghanistan.

On the debit side, American control of the Middle East is slipping. Since 2005 the position of the US in the region has weakened. The shift has not been uniform, with at least one front moving in the opposite direction, with a successful intervention in the Lebanon in 2004 wrecked by the Israeli onslaught of summer

---

1. The only Asian exception here has been the Himalayan kingdom of Nepal, held together for decades by a corrupt monarch and a rigid caste system, where a classical democratic revolution almost toppled the monarchy: the aftershocks were felt in Delhi and further afield in Washington. The compromise settlement appears to be extremely unstable.

2006, and probably not salvageable by the UN. But elsewhere the tide of events is running against Washington.

In Iran and Palestine, elections in 2006 humiliated those on whom the 'international community' had counted as pliable instruments or interlocutors, propelling more radical forces into power. In Iraq, the resistance has inflicted a steady train of blows on the US occupation, preventing any stabilisation of the collaborator regime and sapping support for the war in America itself. In Afghanistan, guerrillas are on the move again and Washington is busy wooing Taliban factions close to Pakistani military intelligence. Further revelations of torture by US and British forces, and plunder of local resources by the invaders and their agents, have intensified popular hatred of the West across the Arab world. American forces are over-stretched, and the belief of troops in their mission is declining. Establishment voices at home are beginning to express fears that a debacle comparable to – or even worse than – Vietnam may be looming. But outcomes across the whole theatre of conflict still remain uncertain, and are unlikely to be all of a piece.

And then there is Latin America. When two fronts unite, there is always the possibility of success. The public defiance of the United States by Hugo Chávez has brought him huge popularity in much of the Middle East, as well as other parts of the globe. Interviewed for an hour by Faisal al-Qasim on al-Jazeera television's flagship programme 'The Opposite Direction', Chávez's crisp responses and his no-nonsense attitude to imperial policies was watched by 26 million people. Several thousand e-mails arrived in response and the bulk of them, according to a senior al-Jazeera journalist, posed a single question: when will the Arab world produce a leader like Chávez?

The question was posed despite the fact that new forces and faces are emerging in the world of Islam that have something in common. Muqtada, Haniya, Nasrallah, Ahmadinejad: each has risen by organising the urban poor in their localities – Gaza and

Jenin, Beirut and Sidon, Baghdad and Basra, Tehran and Shiraz. It is in the slums that Hamas, Hezbollah, the Sadr brigades and the Basji have their roots. The contrast with the Hariris, Chalabis, Karzais, Allawis, on whom the West relies – overseas million-aires, crooked bankers, CIA bagmen – could not be starker. A radical wind is blowing from the alleys and shacks of the latter-day wretched of the earth, surrounded by the fabulous wealth of petroleum.

The limits of this radicalism, so long as it remains captured by the Koran, are clear enough. The impulses of charity and solidarity are infinitely better than those of imperial greed and comprador submission, but so long as what they offer is social alleviation rather than reconstruction, they are sooner or later liable to recuperation by the existing order. Leaders comparable to figures like Chávez or Morales have yet to emerge, with a vision capable of transcending national or communal divisions, a sense of continental unity and – most importantly – an egalitarian, redistributive, socio-economic strategy.

If the wave of rebellions and social movements spreading unevenly across the South American continent draws on long-standing insurrectionary traditions there, it can also be directly attributed to the economic dislocations created by the Washing-ton Consensus. In several states the traditional mechanisms of control have been weakened, leading to the release of energies that have helped to create a new political space. If the collisions taking place are a result of the turbo-charged capitalism of the present epoch, a number of old questions confront the new leaders who have been thrown up out of the crisis. Can present-day contradictions between what exists and what is necessary be wished away or will they have to be fought out to the end? Washington's unmasked response to these queries is clear. There can be no blurring of boundaries: the enemies of globalisation must be taken on and defeated, by political-economic measures where possible, by force where necessary.

Latin America was the first laboratory for the Hayekian experiments that finally produced the Consensus. The Chicago boys who pioneered neo-liberal economics used Chile after the Pinochet coup of 1973 to test their theories. It was easier to do so after a bloody political cleansing had already taken place. The Chilean working class and its two principal parties had been crushed, their leading cadres killed or 'disappeared'. A few Western journalists began to sing in praise of the New Order in Santiago, writing lyrically about all the consumer goods on offer after the years of 'socialist austerity' and 'greyness'. What they preferred to ignore was that the majority of Chileans could only window-shop. Chile had 'worked' because tens of thousands of people were killed. It is only recently that a new generation has emerged unmarked by the Pinochet experience. The school students who marched throughout Chile in June 2006, to be greeted with tear-gas and baton charges, were raising demands that effectively challenge neo-liberal orthodoxy. It usually takes a long time, usually over a decade, for a crushed people to recover – and not just in Latin America. Look at Britain.

The movements of today differ from each other and vary from country to country, leave alone the past. In the years following the Cuban Revolution, attempts were made throughout the world to mimic its success by creating armed groups and imagining that these would automatically win mass support. The counter-revolution was more successful. The Left suffered tragic defeats in almost every country, which included the capture and execution of Che Guevara in Bolivia in 1967. A few years later the same fate befell Salvador Allende in Chile. The Tupamaros were savagely crushed in Uruguay and their leader Raúl Sendic and his comrades subjected to inhuman tortures. In Argentina, the military junta decreed the extermination of its opponents. Since all this was openly supported by the US intelligence agencies, nobody in those days called for 'humanitarian interventions' or 'regime change'.

Two decades later, the Zapatistas in Mexico became a new source of inspiration. Intelligently they chose to build a base in

Chiapas, where they had the support of the majority of the people – a support that had been won by demonstrating their ability to defend the poor. In other words the Zapatistas took arms to defend local power. Obviously, they could not do so nationally and it would have been suicidal to try, but some of their Western supporters attempted to theorise this weakness by the inane slogan of 'It is possible to change the world without taking power', a plea, in reality, to abstain from politics. Elsewhere, Brazil's Landless Worker's Movement (MST) – and the mass social movements against the privatisation of water and electricity in Bolivia and Peru – created the basis for political victories against neo-liberalism, not all of which have yet come to fruition.

Evo Morales' triumph in Bolivia, at the head of the Movement Toward Socialism (MAS), was the dramatic outcome of these and other struggles in that country. But if victories in Venezuela and Bolivia have rekindled hope beyond the shores of South America, with each government trying to implement serious social reforms in health, poverty alleviation, education, land, shelter, and so on, any continent-wide generalisations would be premature. Colombia returned Uribe to power, one of the few victories for Washington in the region.[2] Chile and Brazil, with Bachelet

---

2. 'While media outlets such as the *Christian Science Monitor* declared that Colombians "gladly came out to vote for him," the reality is that only a small minority actually cast ballots for Uribe. The Colombian president garnered only 27 per cent of the country's eligible vote, while other first round winners in recent elections in the region performed significantly better. For example, 42 per cent of Bolivia's eligible voters cast a ballot for Evo Morales in 2005 and 46 per cent of Uruguayans turned out for Tabaré Vázquez a year earlier. Also in 2004, 42 per cent of Venezuela's eligible voters came out in support of President Hugo Chávez in that country's recall referendum. In fact, the only recent victorious South American presidential candidate to receive as low a percentage of the electoral vote as Uribe did last week was none other than Uribe himself four years ago. In 2002, only 24 per cent of Colombia's eligible voters turned out in support of Washington's closest regional ally.' Garry Leech, 'Putting Uribe's "Mandate" Into Perspective', Colombia Journal Online (www.colombiajournal.org), 2 June 2006.

and Lula in office, are the alternative that the West prefers to Castro, Chávez and Morales.[3] In terms of class polarities (or income distribution) Chile remains amongst the top ten. One in five of its citizens still live below the poverty line; 50 per cent of the overall income is retained by 10 per cent of the population. The remaining half is shared by 90 per cent of the population with peasants, workers and women suffering the most. Wages, even when adjusted for inflation, are still below the level reached in 1972 under President Allende, despite a 60 per cent increase in labour productivity. Michelle Bachelet, a single mother, is undoubtedly a highly respected politician in Chile but, like her predecessors, is trapped by the Washington Consensus and unlikely to break with the elite strategy established by Pinochet unless a mass social movement from below compels her to do so. Isolated from its own continent since the Pinochet coup of 1973, Chile remains heavily dependent on the North American market and has been regressing towards becoming a primary-export economy heavily dependent on copper.

The Brazilian tragedy requires a modern Euripides, who could take us from the honourable suicide of the general-turned-democrat Getúlio Vargas to the blood that trickles down from self-inflicted wounds by the worker-president Lula da Silva. It seems highly likely that Lula will be re-elected President of Brazil in 2006, but that should not detract from what is happening to the country.

---

3. In a recent essay, a former Mexican Foreign Minister, currently in search of a new role in life, noting the new developments in Latin America, explained to the US foreign policy elite that there were 'two lefts' in Latin America: 'One is modern, open-minded, reformist, and internationalist, and it springs, paradoxically from the hard-core left of the past. The other, born of the great tradition of Latin American populism, is nationalist, strident and close-minded. The first is well aware of its past mistakes . . . and has changed accordingly. The second, unfortunately, has not.' Jorge. G. Castaneda, 'Latin America's Left Turn' in *Foreign Policy*, May/June 2006. Chávez, in jocular mood, expressed the same truth during a conversation with Lula: 'Your problem is that the Americans will never try and get rid of you'.

There is an irony in the fact that both supporters in Washington and Europe and opponents at home are united in seeing
Lula as a tropical Tony Blair.[4] Like his English equivalent, he is
ready to please on virtually any level, surrounded by advisers and
cronies totally loyal to the WC and corrupt to the core. It is true
that, till now, he has refused to participate in US plans to isolate
Venezuela (so, incidentally, has his more right-wing fellow-
globaliser Uribe in Colombia) but in 2004 Brazilian troops
(together with Chilean and Argentine units) were speedily
despatched to help occupy Haiti after a US-French force had
toppled a democratically elected President, who was punished not
for his vices, but for resisting the privatisation of water and
demanding a return of the money Haiti had paid in reparations to
France in the past to compensate for the loss the French had
sustained when slavery was abolished in 1805, payments that had
bled Haiti dry for decades.[5]

The abandonment by Lula's Workers' Party (PT) of its
traditional programme in favour of neo-liberal capitalism was a
matter of choice. Like social-democratic parties elsewhere, the PT
leadership decided that coming to power was more important than
adherence to the programme that would help them to the
Presidency. Lula's entire campaign combined a direct appeal to
the poor which included constant references to his own class
background and his determination to create a better society with
repeated reassurances to the IMF/World Bank that, if elected, he
would not alter the system set in place by his predecessor. And so,
indeed, he became a tropical Blair to Fernando Henriques

---

4. The irony becomes heavier if one recalls how soon after the New Labour
victory in Britain, one of its architects, Peter Mandelson (currently an EU
commissioner after being removed twice from the British government for
misusing his position) visited Brazil and in order to situate himself as close to
Cardoso as possible, quite gratuitously attacked Lula and the Workers' Party
(PT) as beyond the pale of the new politics.

5. See Peter Hallward, 'Option Zero in Haiti', *New Left Review*, 27, May–June
2004, pp. 23–47.

Cardoso's Thatcher.[6] Soon even the veneer of dignity had disappeared.

The fact that 60 per cent of the active population is either unemployed or works in 'informal' employment (short-term work in bad conditions) creates a new situation both in Brazil and elsewhere in the world. This process, central to the functioning of neo-liberal capitalism, virtually precludes trade unions, reduces the power of institutions strong enough to make politicians accountable and tends to institutionalise apathy. Money politics now play as big a role in the parties of the 'centre-left' (as the former social-democratic, socialist and Communist parties now like to style themselves) as on the Right, and corruption scandals are common all over the globe.[7] The new system also generated a

---

6. A useful analysis of the political economy of Brazil under the PT administration is by Lecio Morais and Alfredo Saad-Filho, 'Lula and the Continuity of Neo-Liberalism in Brazil', *Historical Materialism*, 13:1, pp. 3–32.

7. They take on a special character in Brazil where gangsterism against radical politicians, trade unions and landless peasants has been going on for several decades. In 2002, the murder of Celso Daniel, a popular 51-year-old PT politician, respected for his integrity and honesty and thrice elected mayor of Santo André in greater São Paulo, shocked the whole country. What created an even bigger scandal was that the Daniel family refused to accept that this was a case of mistaken identity or that he had been killed by mistake. Their fingers pointed in the direction of the PT establishment. Why? Because according to Celso Daniel's brother, the doctor João Francisco Daniel, Celso was murdered because of his opposition to the growing corruption inside the PT and that he had prepared a report on corruption in the local district of Santo André.

João stated that his brother had been part of a corruption scam in Santo André designed to raise money for the PT. According to him those involved included local government dignitaries and businessmen in the transportation sector, as well as key PT notables like José Dirceu and Gilberto Carvalho, Lula's personal secretary. According to João, some members of the scheme began to divert funds illegally marked for the Workers' Party to their own personal accounts. When Celso Daniel discovered this he prepared a report exposing the scam. He was killed. The report disappeared. All this rings true. The fact that Daniel himself raised money in this fashion for the PT is sad, but reflects the state of the country. According to the pro-Lula *Financial Times* (27 March 2006): 'Public prosecutors believe Mr Daniel's kidnap and

high degree of volatility amongst the poor and it is this that
creates the basis for a radical populism.[8]

The political establishment is aware of this, but there is now no
fundamental difference between the PT leaders and the opposition
that challenges them. The differences that existed are buried in the
past. The constraints imposed by the globalised order, once
accepted by all sides, make democracy superfluous. Lula's opponent, Dr Geraldo Alckmin, is a former Governor of São Paulo
state and a technocrat to the core. With a palpable sense of relief,
the *Financial Times* noted that:

> When you speak to the men responsible for drawing up the
> candidates' programme for government, it is sometimes diffi-
> cult to tell them apart.
>
> Marco Aurélio Garcia, from the president's camp, reels
> off a shortlist of priorities: social inclusion through job
> creation; economic development through continued stability
> and investment in infrastructure; political reform; and ad-
> vances in education, especially concentrated on science and
> technology.

---

7. murder was a contract killing and say government officials have interfered in
   investigations to preserve the notion that it was "a common crime". They are
   convinced that Mr Daniel was silenced because he sought to shut down a
   corruption scheme channelling funds to Mr Lula da Silva's leftwing Workers'
   Party (PT). "This is nitroglycerine," says Bolívar Lamounier, a political
   consultant in São Paulo. "If a connection is established between the murder
   and the PT's finances, the whole political landscape will change." '
   Subsequent developments appeared to establish the connection. In December
   2005, José Adalberto Vieira da Silva, an aide to José Guimarães Neto, who at
   the time of the episode, was Ceará state deputy (in northeastern Brazil), was
   literally caught with his knickers in a twist: wads of dollars were found in his
   underwear during a random airport search – it was PT money designed to buy
   votes in parliament.
8. For a serious study of populism, by one of the world's foremost experts on
   the subject, see Ernesto Laclau, *On Populist Reason*, London and New York,
   2005.

José Carlos Meirelles, for Mr Alckmin, has a similar list: a vigorous education programme focused on primary schooling and further education in science and technology; growth through investment in infrastructure; political reform; and reduction of bureaucracy and the cost of government.

It would be easy to conclude that they have similar ideas about how to achieve their aims.

'We have to keep inflation low, our accounts balanced, and continue efforts to reduce our vulnerability to external shocks,' says Mr Garcia. 'Fundamentally, our idea is to continue with current economic policy.'

Although the PT denies it, continuing with current policy means maintaining policies introduced by the previous, PSDB, government: using tight monetary policy to combat inflation, and supposedly tight fiscal policy – cutting spending on investment, though allowing current expenditure to increase – to attack the high level of government debt, currently equal to 50 per cent of gross domestic product and a big impediment to investment.

Mr Meirelles, too, sometimes finds it hard to disagree with his opponents' policies. 'The Lula government has shown some good ideas,' he says. 'But there is no management.'[9]

Argentina is an interesting case study. Its collapse was a message to the world at large, not just Latin America. If you follow the dictates of Washington blindly this is what could happen to you as well. Not many have learnt that lesson (certainly not Brazil or India) but it should be studied and understood by social movements and those working for change. Here was a country whose leaders and many of its intellectuals thought they were a cut above the rest of Latin America. The elite certainly felt closer to Europe than its own

---

9. *Financial Times*, 4 July 2006.

neighbours. Menem's government had kept the peso pegged to the dollar throughout the 1990s, and when the crash came in December 2001 the devastation was total. In Buenos Aires in early 2003, some friends kept me up past midnight one evening so that I could see with my own eyes the invasion of the city centre by children from the relatively less well-off suburbs. Like locusts, they arrived in formation. They wore plastic gloves and carried old plastic bags. Unconcerned by passersby, they systematically set about scavenging the dustbins for comestibles and anything else that might be of use. This had not been seen in Argentina before the collapse, but was common in many parts of the world. It was the shock generated by a total social breakdown that radicalised people and led to a degree of self-organisation hitherto not seen on this scale in the Americas. The popular assemblies in Buenos Aires (one of which I attended) were, at their peak, extremely moving and powerful gatherings, demonstrating by their very existence the possibility of living in a different way and with different priorities.[10]

Kirchner's electoral victory, and his attempts to find a third way between Chávez and Lula, were made possible only because of what happened to the country when its politics and economy were destroyed by the refusal of the Argentinian elite to break from the Washington Consensus. Venezuela's emergence as a pole of attraction for the Latin American poor has also helped. In an attempt to prevent the Bolivarian infection from reaching epidemic proportions, the United States has marginally decreased its pressure on other countries to conform a hundred per cent to imperial requirements. 'Differences with friends' in Condoleezza Rice's phrase, are only tolerated because the choice is worse. It brings back memories of the Alliance for Progress set up by Washington in 1961 after the Cuban Revolution. The Alliance

---

10. Naomi Klein, in particular, has written well about this process. Her script for the documentary film *The Take*, directed by Avi Lewis, is a snapshot of Argentina in which people have been forced to turn to self-organisation and empower themselves.

proposed social reforms to impede any repeats of Cuba. Much of what they proposed is now being implemented by Chávez and Morales but is forbidden by Washington. Kirchner's repayment scheme of 30 cents on every dollar that it owed on the $100 billion loan has saved Argentina a great deal of money and reduced the country's indebtedness, whereas a total default could easily have led to sanctions. However, given that this loan had helped wreck the country, he should have defaulted and demanded reparations from the IMF and World Bank for what they had done to Argentina. 'We need desperately to recreate a *national* bourgeoisie', Kirchner is reported to have half-joked in despair.

However the fact that he could unilaterally decide to pay 30 per cent of the loan reflects the impact that the rebirth of a Latin American Left is having on the continent. And elsewhere. Demonstrators in the Philippines carry portraits of Chávez; peasants in West Bengal turn out in tens of thousands to greet the Latin American leader in Calcutta; Hezbollah leaders in South Lebanon refer to him as 'our brother Chávez'. The Bolivarians have re-ignited hope and demonstrated the possibility of change to an imprisoned world.

From the United States' point of view, the problem with Chávez was always that he meant business on two crucial fronts. Where Simón Bolívar had taken on the might of the Spanish Empire in the eighteenth century and fought for independence, the Venezuelan who took the Liberator's name for a new movement was determined to do the same vis-à-vis the United States. New Bolivarianism combines continental nationalism and social-democratic reforms fuelled by oil revenues. It is this mixture that has created a hostility and tension between the two sides. The political contradiction can only be resolved by empowering the poor, by the spread and advancement of education, health and shelter for all; in other words, by reversing the priorities of the Washington Consensus. Not an easy task, but it has begun, and this modest beginning opens up new avenues to discuss and determine whether it is possible to build a society free of poverty, of booms and slumps, free from wild speculators and their speculations and from the out-of-control market forces that dominate the world economy, while at the same time enhancing democracy. It is for posing these questions as a prologue that the Bolivarians are being denounced in extravagant language by the apologists of the New Order all over the world.

Chapter 3

The Fierce Bull and the Cunning Donkeys

. . . The United States, which seemed predestined by Providence to rain down misery on the Americas in the name of liberty . . .

Simón Bolívar, 'Letter to Patrick Campbell' (1829)

And Manuel Ladera explained why he had said that there was no need to say any more: 'There you have the history of Venezuela: a fierce bull, its eyes covered and ringed through the nose, led to the slaughterhouse by a cunning little donkey.'

To which Marcos replied, 'There, you see. That's what I call customfitting the shoe. In the school in Ciudad Bolívar they wanted to stick in my head what was written about Venezuela's history, and I was never able to understand it, and now I understand it completely.'

Rómulo Gallegos, *Canaima* (1935)

It is the sixth largest country in Latin America and the richest in terms of natural resources. The late Venezuelan philosopher and educator Mariano Picon Salas once compared his country's map to 'the skin of a bull dried in the tropical sun and so oddly cut that some pieces have remained stuck to it'. Its not the only thing that has remained stuck to the country. For most of the twentieth century the Venezuelan Army played a key role in buttressing and defending oligarchic interests either directly or via competing networks of politicians. During the teenage years of the Republic, the military regime of Juan Vicente Gómez sold the country's oil to favoured foreign companies and failed to keep a record of the royalties it received in return.[1] There are no statistics on oil company profits (loot might be a more accurate description) between 1914 and 1936.

Gómez – one of the many continental dictators on whom García Márquez is reputed to have based *The Autumn of the Patriarch* – was an astute operator who managed to balance the interests of the oil companies and the local elites that gradually developed into an oligarchy and established an iron grip on the country. Gómez had seized power in 1908 and kept it (with the

---

1. For this and much else Fernando Coronil's magisterial work, *The Magical State: Nature, Money and Modernity in Venezuela*, Chicago, 1997, is an invaluable source.

exception of two brief interludes) until 1935. In 1902 three
European powers – Germany, Britain and Italy – had laid siege
to the country (still recovering from a gruelling civil war) in a
combined assault, bombed the port city of Puerto Cabello and
threatened a permanent occupation if the foreign debt was not
paid. Imperial powers in those days were nothing if not direct.
Timely US mediation averted the danger and a deal was done. In
1930, to mark the centenary of Simón Bolívar's death, Venezuela
paid off its entire foreign debt.

The democratic interlude (1935–48) which saw the country's
leading novelist, Rómulo Gallegos, elected as President came as a
relief and his commitment to liberal modernism was never in
doubt. Gallegos' politico-cultural pedigree was distinguished.
Doña Barbara (1929) and *Canaima* (1935), his two most powerful
novels, evoke the spirit of Sarmiento's *Facundo* and da Cunha's
Rebellion in the Backlands, two late nineteenth-century classics
which saw the struggles in Argentina and Brazil as ones between
native/indigenous barbarism and the modernising civilizations
inherited from old Europe. But as Fernando Coronil convincingly
argues, the structure of the Venezuelan state rested strictly on the
diarchy, and 'modern democracy' and 'primitive dictatorship'
were different sides of the same coin. Whatever else changed, the
oil-based oligarchy grew in strength as did the contrast between
extreme poverty and extreme wealth.

In 1952 Pérez Jiménez, backed by Washington, had toppled
Gallegos' elected government and embarked on a 'modernisation'
that led to uneven development, increased poverty and the total
destruction of the character of old Caracas.[2] The old tiled-roof
town that had existed for over three hundred and fifty years had
gone. Jiménez plundered the resources of the state to get rich
quick (without sharing it equitably with the rest of the military or
political elite) and squandered too much money on fancy building

---

2. Coronil, op. cit.

projects. One of these, a brand new Officer's Club, excited some serious advertising prose from *Time* magazine on 28 February 1955:

> Nothing in Venezuela – or outside of it, for that matter – can compete with the palatial Círculo de las Fuerzas Armadas, the social club for military officers and top governmental officials. It has a hotel (television in every room), restaurants, bar, cocktail lounge, nightclub, two swimming pools, stable, gymnasium, fencing court, bowling alleys, library and theatre. Some notably sumptuous touches: marble floors, blue Polaroid windows, Gobelin tapestries, Sèvres vases, Tiffany clocks, a glass-walled conservatory housing a living, blooming chunk of the Venezuelan jungle. To the grander dances at the club, some colonels' wives wear $1,500 Balmain gowns.[3]

It was not Balmain gowns that elevated Venezuela to the status of Washington's favourite backyard state. The actual reasons were far more prosaic and perfectly comprehensible: the new regime gave US corporations more privileges than its predecessor. During the Jiménez regime reduced taxes alone lost Venezuela 4,508 million bolívars. Half of Standard Oil's annual profits were provided by its Venezuelan subsidiary and during a seven-year period (1950–7) amounted to $3.79 billion.[4] The size of the profits was boosted by the low-wages-no-strikes policy of the dictatorship. And to keep things that way the FBI and CIA were invited to carry out regular 'surveillance' of the workforce and help root out 'subversives'.

Nothing was left to chance and a carefully planned right-wing migration from Spain, Italy and Portugal was organised to help

---

3. In 2004, together with other visiting pirates attending a conference I was a guest at a dinner hosted by Hugo Chávez at the Officer's Club. Its kitsch splendour was still in evidence. The company was stimulating, but the food reminded one of mid-Sixties Britain.
4. Coronil, op. cit.

displace and control local workers. This was different from the turn-of-the-century immigration to Latin America, which had crossed the Atlantic with the radical traditions of the early European labour movements largely intact. The Venezuelan dictator used the new migrants to combat the growing militancy of the native workforce and the new Europeans were staunch in their support of Jiménez. In 1955 he was awarded the Legion of Merit medal by the US government.

The image of Caracas presented in US magazines was that of a brash, bustling, modern city whose blinding-white skyscrapers sparkled against the green Andean backdrop, but Villanueva's stunning University City with its murals by Leger and others was, alas, not the norm. Even as the skyscrapers were going up, accompanied by an orgy of self-congratulation, there were voices that advised caution and warned that the earthquake-prone city was losing its character, that it would soon become shabby and smudged. Gabriel García Márquez described it as 'an apocalyptic, unreal, inhuman city', but nobody was listening.

Corruption grew apace with the skyscrapers. The increasing disparity in wealth between rich and poor was the trigger for growing popular protests which erupted in spontaneous street demonstrations and sometimes physical attacks on the architecture of privilege that typified the Jiménez era. Fearful that these tensions might result in bloodshed, the Venezuelan Church unleashed a broadside in the form of a pastoral letter signed by the Archbishop of Caracas. While accepting the statistical rise in per capita income, the Archbishop denounced the low wages, the assault on workers' rights, the absence of social services for the poor, and challenged anyone in the country 'to affirm that this wealth is distributed in such a way that it will reach all Venezuelans, since an immense mass of our people live in conditions which cannot be regarded as human'. The Church's decision to break publicly was an indication of the lack of stability and cohesion of the regime.

Jiménez had gone too far. It was time for him to be retired. The business elite linked forces with the traditional parties and a summit in New York between the Chamber of Commerce leaders and those of Democratic Action (AD), the Democratic Republican Union (URD) and the Social Christian Party (COPEI) agreed on a transition to a new government. The other side of the coin had begun to be polished. It was named the Patriotic Junta. Contacts with the military were established by this new alliance and revealed growing officer discontent with Jiménez, a direct result of his insatiable greed (he would later be found guilty of embezzling $200 million while in office). The politicians and businessmen encouraged military insurrections. A few took place and were brutally crushed. This increased the dictator's isolation, and a combination of strikes and street demonstrations emboldened the chiefs of the armed services to confront him. As is often the case in these situations, he was abandoned during his last days by those closest to him. In January 1958 he was removed and given safe passage to the United States. It was the Army High Command that had tightened the noose: without it, the Patriotic Junta would have floundered.

The politicians now agreed a formal division of the loot:

Rather than quarrel over the spoils of power, they arranged to share them amongst themselves. AD's Rómulo Betancourt and COPEI's Rafael Caldera devised a plan, the Pact of Punto Fijo, to keep democracy within strict bounds and make it difficult for other parties to participate in it. The deal practically ensured that AD or COPEI would triumph in elections, henceforward obviating the need for the military to act as a ballast for the status quo, and thwarting a vibrant Left that had been instrumental in helping to bring down Pérez Jiménez. The democratic Left remained an energetic opponent well into the 1970s, but could not overcome its own internal divisions or AD's grip on the trade unions. From 1969 onwards, when AD

started swapping power with COPEI, an apparently impreg-
nable institutional dyarchy was in place, excluding all outsiders
and implementing only such reforms as reinforced the power of
the ruling parties.[5]

Oil revenues helped to polish the façade, but the social
structure of the country was untouched. Profits and poverty rose
together. In 1988, after three decades of COPEI/AD governments, the poverty level was 38.5 per cent and the yearly inflation
rate was 40.3 per cent. Trouble was inevitable. It arrived a year
later.

27 February 1989: a luminous day in Venezuelan history. On the
streets of Garenas, a small provincial town in the northern state of
Miranda, there commenced a series of spontaneous mass protests by
the people against the measures taken by an Acción Democrática
government that, like its Second International siblings in Europe,
had exhausted its own ideological universe. On the face of it these
manifestations seemed to be relatively minor. Neither the government, semi-paralysed by a partial police strike, nor the workers and
the poor who had come out to voice their anger had any idea of the
profound impact the next forty-eight hours would have on the
country's future. Few of the protestors envisioned a different
future. They were motivated simply by a desire to preserve the
gains they had won. They were aware that the oligarchy perceived
them as shabby, insignificant and miserable creatures. Time,
perhaps, to demonstrate how deadly their collective power could
become. It is also worth recording that what became known as the
Caracazo was the first genuine mass revolt by the poor against neo-
liberal capitalism, pre-dating Seattle by a decade.

The reasons for the anger, which had been building up slowly
against the AD regime headed by Carlos Andrés Pérez during his

---

5. Jeremy Adelman, 'Andean Impasses', *New Left Review*, 18, November–December 2002, pp. 41–72.

second stint in office (1989–93), are not difficult to fathom. AD was once the most powerful social-democratic party in Latin America and, in terms of members in proportion to the population, the largest affiliate of the Socialist International. In his first term as president (1974–9) during the oilboom years, Pérez's speeches were laced with honey and hope. He had railed against the World Bank, describing the economists on its payroll in colourful language as 'genocide workers in the pay of economic totalitarianism' and referring to the IMF as a 'neutron bomb that killed people, but left buildings standing'. The rhetoric was popular, but it was the acts that followed which strengthened his support amongst the poor: the nationalisations of Shell, Exxon, US Steel.

Ten years later he once again waged a vigorous electoral campaign. He declared that he was doing so to turn history around so it could serve the poor. His re-election would make history and once again he denounced the global financial institutions in extravagant language: once again the IMF was described as *la bomba solo-mata-gente* (a bomb that only kills people). It worked. He won 53 per cent of the votes. Nearly two dozen heads of state, including Fidel Castro and Daniel Ortega, attended the lavish inauguration ceremonies where, once again, Pérez pledged to make history. Amongst those who voted him into power, very few were aware that, even while he spoke, his advisers were reassuring the 'bomb that only kills people' not to take the rhetoric seriously. Within weeks of his election, he had shifted into reverse gear. Making history, he now explained, had really meant making *el gran viraje* (a great volte-face). His incapacity to deliver what he had promised might have been accepted, but the austerity measures he delivered were the exact opposite: price controls were lifted, subsidies were savagely cut and it was the poor who bore the brunt of the 'reforms'.

This was the pound of flesh demanded by the IMF in return for the 4.5 billion-dollar loan they had put on the table. The 'structural readjustment' required was at the expense of those who had voted him into power. They now began to hate him for his deedless words. Carlos Andrés Pérez had dominated Venezuelan politics for so long that he thought there were no earth-born clouds that could not be dispersed. He ignored the early signs of unrest. Politicians inebriated with power imagine they are invulnerable, untouchable. In this respect, Pérez was no different from his colleagues elsewhere in the world. His problem lay in the antiquated social structure of the country where the poor in the shanty towns were ignored and left seething with anger. The political parties put on their friendliest faces and expressed great sympathy for the suffering of the poor, but they did nothing. The only institution they could not completely control was the Army.

Ten days prior to the *Caracazo*, Pérez had caved in abjectly to the International Monetary Fund and agreed to implement the measures demanded by that body (usually described as 'reforms' by the media apologists of the Washington Consensus) in return for financing the country's external debt. The IMF was not singling out Venezuela for special treatment. This was a policy it implemented across the globe (with the exception of the United States) without fear of its victims and with the favour and support of the elite networks that were always the principal beneficiaries.

In those early days of neo-liberal restructuring, the rhetoric deployed by its pioneers utilised words like 'progress', 'trickle-down', 'modernisation', 'reform' and, occasionally, 'revolution' in order to mask the destruction of the real progress that had been achieved in some areas of everyday life and for a significant minority, during the twentieth century. To their enormous credit the poor of Venezuela, without the benefit of advice from renegade intellectuals to the effect that this was a new hegemonic project and, as such, unchallengeable, understood instinctively what all this was really about. They lost little time in organising a show of strength against the new government that they had hitherto regarded as their own. They felt betrayed and, as is often the case in these crises, the people in the streets demonstrated that they were made of sterner stuff and were more clear-eyed than their political leaders.

Within a few hours the anger that had lit the streets in Guarenas began to infect large swathes of metropolitan Caracas; it triggered off a series of embryonic uprisings in Caricuao, La Guara, Maracay, Valencia, Barquisimeto, Guayana, Merida and Maracaibo. What the government feared the most was that the revolt might affect the regions where the oil terminals were situated and thus affect the flow of oil. But instead of offering concessions, especially on the contentious issue of public transport and the price of gasoline, the regime opted for a fatal choice.

On 28 February 1989, Pérez declared a 'state of emergency', suspending all the clauses in the Constitution related to civil liberties. All public assemblies were banned. The Venezuelan military was in control. Their first act was to impose a twelve-hour curfew that compelled citizens to stay at home from 6 p.m. to 6 a.m. Over the next four weeks the generals ordered the soldiery, in most cases fresh recruits between the ages of 16–20, to assault the poor neighbourhoods, inspire fear through acts of terror and, if necessary, shoot to kill. Plan Avila, a set of measures prepared in the Sixties to deal with the armed-struggle factions (including that of sub-Comandante Teodoro Petkoff) in the countryside, was now put into action against an unarmed urban population.

The massacres that followed led, according to unofficial estimates, to the loss of three thousand lives, including those of many women and children. In some cases, the dead lay on sidewalks outside their tiny dwellings where the bullets had found them. The global response was muted. It had not yet become fashionable to describe a massacre as genocide and threaten 'humanitarian intervention'. How could a massacre carried out to further the cause of neo-liberal capitalism be anything more than 'conservative rioters resisting reforms firmly dealt with to preserve law and order'?

The government admitted to only 276 dead, without providing any figures for the injured or disappeared. The unofficial view in Caracas was that several hundreds had been killed. Later enquiries uncovered many more deaths, but it was not till ten years later, in November 1999, that a judgement of the Inter-American Court of Human Rights confirmed this view:

> However, this list [of officially admitted deaths] was invalidated by the subsequent appearance of mass graves . . . two non-governmental organizations that carried out investigations in situ, as well as international experts, agreed that most of the deaths were due to indiscriminate firing by agents of the Venezuelan State, while others resulted from extrajudicial executions. They also agreed that the members of the armed forces opened fire against crowds and against homes, which caused the death of many children and innocent people who were not taking part in criminal acts.[6]

Repression on its own cannot usually crush an organised mass movement, capable of an underground existence, that can re-emerge and strike again some years later. But it would be foolish to imagine that state repression is not effective in suppressing a spontaneous upheaval. It needs to do this precisely in order to prevent the emergence of an effective political organisation from utilising mass spontaneity for its own ends. The entire continent was teeming with examples of class contradictions reaching a climax, but incapable of resolution. That the repression would work in the short term was obvious, but Pérez went into an over-kill mode that was totally counter-productive. Not even he could have imagined that one of the repercussions of the *Caracazo* would be the beginnings of a debate within the officer corps of the Venezuelan Army which would lead several years later to *El Bolivarian Viraje*.

---

6. Inter-American Commission on Human Rights, www.cidh.oas.org.

The one institution not totally under the control of Venezuela's political elite was the Army. A group of young officers, enraged by the use of recently recruited soldiers to crush the *Caracazo*, began to meet more frequently in secret. A young colonel named Hugo Chávez, much addicted to the example of Simón Bolívar and the writings of Simón Rodríguez, usually led the discussions. The founding moment of radical Bolivarian groups in the Army and Air Force was in the late Seventies when, mostly young lieutenants, they met informally and discussed the state of the country and the Armed Forces.[7] Older officers who had links with some of the armed-struggle groups of the Sixties had contacted their younger colleagues. The older men were members of the clandestine organisation ARMA (Acción Revolucionaria de Militares Activos/Revolutionary Action of Active Soldiers). In 1978, one of these, Squadron Leader William Izarra Caldera, contacted Lieutenant Luis Reyes Reyes, who offered to put him in touch with his friends, but 'I was exaggerating', Reyes later confessed, 'because I only had one friend who shared these ideas: Hugo Chávez. Some time later, the three of us met in Palo Grande, a rich neighbourhood in Caracas. What this gentleman outlined for us then was a broad civic and military movement.'

Four years later both Chávez and Reyes were organising likeminded officers in small discussion groups in the Army and Air Force. They no longer confined their discussions to corruption inside the Armed Forces, but began to discuss the problems confronting Venezuelan society as a whole. As they grew in size and influence they began the dangerous phase of establishing contacts with civilian groups. The first organisation contacted, Reyes explained, was 'Radical Cause (R Cause), a leftwing party that sold out to neoliberalism and is now one of the worst . . . [at that time] we worked with members of R Cause in Guayana.

---

7. There were many similarities to the Free Officers groups inside the Egyptian and Iraqi armies during the Fifties of the last century.

They had set up a good work team there with iron and steel workers' unions.'

The groups soon became infiltrated and military intelligence began a careful campaign of repression. When informed that there was organised dissent in the Army, President Carlos Andrés Pérez inquired what the ranks of the officers concerned were and when informed that they were majors he brushed the danger aside. As they rose higher they could be bribed into submission. But some of them were being carefully watched. A few members of the group died in mysterious circumstances. Others were regularly transferred, but the High Command was not able to destroy the movement. Why?

> Do you know what worked to our advantage at the time? There was a huge internal power struggle in the Armed Forces that distracted them. They were fighting amongst themselves to decide who would command the army, who was such and such a party's favourite, who was going to win the elections and how each of them would stand. They probably thought that the young and restless officers would forget all about it when they were promoted . . . Later some university professors started to attend our meetings . . . [8]

Chávez's 1992 attempt to topple the regime that had ordered the killings of its own citizens was not a thunderbolt from a cloudless sky, but the planning went awry and the rebels were

---

8. Luis Reyes Reyes, Governor of Lara State, was interviewed in 2004 by Cuban journalists Rosa Miriam Elizalde and Luis Baez. This and other interviews were published in *Our Chávez: Unpublished Accounts*, Havana, 2004. The interview with Reyes is particularly fascinating because of the details he provides of the organisation inside the Armed Forces in the Eighties and Nineties. His account of the radical anger inside the Army and Air Force provides a useful antidote to the accounts in the Western media that portray Chávez as an isolated power-hungry *caudillo*. The complete interview, which includes Reyes' account of the April 2002 putsch, is published as Appendix Three.

easily isolated. The attempt was seen by some as a Venezuelan version of Fidel Castro's 1953 attack on the Moncada Barracks, but it was, in fact, far more serious. Its military objectives had been achieved, but it was politically unsuccessful in that it failed to provoke the mass uprising that was its declared aim. Astonishingly, Chávez went on television and accepted personal responsibility for the attempt and the defeat. In a country where nobody accepts any responsibility for anything, this alone had a huge impact on the population. Hoisting high the flag of revolt against the IMF so that it was visible to the country at large was to leave a mark on many people. Opinion polls showed that 60 per cent of the country was sympathetic to the failed uprising.

Chávez and his fellow rebels ended up in prison, defeated but defiant. A year and a half later they were freed. The only reason they were not treated more severely is because of their popularity. Observing these events from afar was an old man in Havana. Soon after Chávez was released he received an invitation to give a lecture on Bolívar at the Great Hall in the University of Havana. In 1994, as he arrived to deliver his talk the Venezuelan was slightly disconcerted, but also greatly excited, to see a familiar bearded face waiting for him at the airport. That was his first meeting with Fidel Castro, regarded even by Latin Americans who disagree with him as a figure in the tradition of Bolívar, Martí and Sandino. The Cuban leader, on his part, wanted to inspect and question Chávez closely so that he could determine whether the young Venezuelan was made of strong enough timber to accomplish the tasks that lay ahead.

In his speech in Havana that year, Chávez explained what the two Simóns – Bolívar and Rodríguez – had taught him: do not serve the interests of others, make your own political and economic revolution and unite this continent against all Empires:

> Bolívar said: 'Political gangrene cannot be cured with palliatives' and Venezuela is totally and utterly infected with

gangrene. A green mango will ripen, but a rotten mango never ripens; the seed of a rotten mango must be saved and planted so that a new plant may grow. That is happening in Venezuela today. There is no way the system can cure itself . . . 60 per cent of Venezuelans live in a critical state of poverty.

It's unbelievable, but it's true: in twenty years in Venezuela more than 200 thousand million dollars just evaporated. So, where is the money? President Castro asked me. In the foreign bank accounts of almost everyone who has been in power in Venezuela, civilians and soldiers, who filled their pockets, protected by the power they held . . .

The coming century, in our opinion, is a century of hope; it is our century, it is the century when the Bolivarian dream will be reborn . . .[9]

Fidel Castro may not have shown it publicly on that occasion, but he told colleagues in private that he was greatly impressed by Chávez. He had certainly read a great deal, but Castro appreciated the uniqueness and complexity of the Venezuelan. There was no doubt: he was an original. Venezuela's politicians were less astute. Arrogant, complacent, self-centred and light-skinned, they could not take Chávez seriously. No lessons were to be learnt by them, with the surprising exception of the 77-year-old COPEI Senator-for-life Rafael Caldera. Regarded by many of his factional rivals as a political corpse, he had resuscitated himself with remarkable vigour. A week after the defeated 1992 uprising, the veteran fixer had struck a discordant note in a parliament dominated by demagogy and rabid attacks on the profane officers who had dared to challenge the sacred rites of democracy. Caldera had noticed the lack of any action by the people to defend this particular democracy and had explained the reasons to his surprised colleagues:

9. *Granma*, 15 December 1994.

It is difficult to ask the people to burn for freedom and democracy while they think freedom and democracy are not able to feed them and impede the exorbitant increase in the cost of subsistence; when it has not been able to deal effectively with the blight of corruption. The *golpe* [coup d'état] should be censured and condemned, but it would be disingenuous for us, without giving attention to their aims, to think that we are dealing with merely a few ambitious officers precipitously launching an adventure on their own account.[10]

Most of Caldera's colleagues, however, appeared genetically incapable of dealing with the source of mass anger and, to make matters worse, the Pérez government accepted new IMF instructions to implement an even more severe round of 'structural adjustment measures'. But the attempted coup had shaken the government. A year later, Pérez was threatened with impeachment by his own party unless he agreed to leave voluntarily. The charge was corruption. His mistress Cecilia Matos had established herself as his principal intermediary with the business elite and 'devil's excrement' had polluted the hands of both sides. All of this was public knowledge and had added to the anger. Pérez was finally removed in May 1993, but the death agony of the old order could not be prolonged indefinitely. Rafael Caldera was wheeled on to the stage at the head of a seventeen-party coalition. One of his new ministers, committed to continuing the measures that had already resulted in death and rebellion, was Teodoro Petkoff, the former guerrilla leader who had followed the example of many former Communists in Russia and Eastern Europe and changed sides. The new 'government of impotents', as it was christened by the street, fully justified the sobriquet. Just over a month after the

---

10. Quoted in David Hellinger's 'Political Overview' in *Venezuelan Politics in the Chávez Era: Class, Polarization and Conflict*, edited by Steve Ellner and Daniel Hellinger, Boulder, 2003, p. 32.

ritual swearing-in of Caldera and his cabinet of not-so-cunning donkeys, the Venezuelan economy collapsed. To prevent a total collapse of the banking system, foreign loans and local funds acquired from taxes and privatisations were utilised and in a single year 12 per cent of the country's GDP (5.6 billion dollars) was spent on propping up ten banks. While this was taking place the speculators' wing of the Patriotic Junta was, as always, busy spiriting capital abroad to offshore accounts. The symbiosis between money and politics helped ensure that the economy and the traditional politicians would sink in tandem.

Under Rafael Caldera and his government (with Teodoro Petkoff comfortably accommodated as Minister of the Central Office for Co-ordination and Planning) the poverty figures had jumped to 66.7 per cent by 1995.[11] This is the background that explains the subsequent electoral triumph of Chávez. His participation in the 1992 rebellion was viewed by a majority of Venezuelans as a quixotic attempt to bring down a corrupt and indefensible system. It had made him a national hero, especially but not exclusively amongst the poor. As he began his long campaign for the Presidency, Chávez began to speak of the need for a 'Bolivarian Revolution' that would end the corruption and the serial treachery of the two-party system. Radical social and political reforms – land redistribution and a new constitution – were required for a structural transformation of the political system and the everyday life of the people. If the entire establishment had become corrupted and cronyism was rampant on every level, a clean sweep was the only way to take the nation forward.

His opponents, backed by the entire media – not a single major newspaper or television network supported Chávez – failed to

---

11. Julia Buxton's sobering essay 'Economic Policy and the Rise of Hugo Chávez' in Ellner and Hellinger, op. cit., provides a useful assessment of the state of the economy under the dyarchy and the early Chávez years.

understand the charge that lay behind the Bolivarian appeal to the
less privileged citizens. By declaring their unity against a common
enemy, the political parties were displaying attitudes that were
primitive, oppressive and, from their own point of view, irrational. Primitive because they refused to take the challenge of a
mestizo seriously; oppressive because, backed by Church and
Washington, they assumed a divine right to rule the country;
irrational because they put their own narrow, factional interests
above those of the country as a whole. They underestimated
Chávez, whose appeal had become irresistible and who out-
manoeuvred them on every front.

In December 1998 the Bolivarians carried the Presidency with
56 per cent of the votes. The oligarchic parties – AD and COPEI
– were defeated. The following year a new constitution was
adopted with massive public support. In 2000, Chávez was re-
elected for a six-year term. His majority had increased to 59 per
cent. It seemed likely that he would be re-elected once again in
2006 and for the same reasons.

The Bolivarians were triumphant, but cautious. They did not
change the foundations of the system. This was deliberate, as
Chávez explained publicly on many occasions. We were no
longer in the twentieth century. This was not the epoch of
proletarian revolutions, but the beginnings of a process of
'rethinking socialism'. Ironically, the very Western politicians
and journalists tied to their coat-tails, who would have screamed
'murder' had Chávez mobilised support to carry out a full-
blooded revolution, were now critical of him for not doing
enough to improve the conditions of the people. When the
Bolivarians took power, the conditions in Venezuela were truly
grim: two-fifths of the population lived in squalor, while one-
tenth shared half the country's national income. Nowhere was the
contrast more visible than in Caracas. The opulent suburbs where
the rich lived and from where they had sucked more and more
money from the system over the preceding twenty years con-

trasted badly with the shanty towns on the hills where the ordinary people lived, a large majority that was poor, ignored, brutalised and left to stew in its misery. It was angry and, on occasions, its rage overpowered the fatalism and despair. Here lay the heart of the Bolivarian movement.

While it is perfectly true that during the first period in office, the Bolivarians remained prisoners of macro-economic policies and were unable to bring immediate benefits to those who needed them the most, the partial solutions that began to be implemented after 2002 were extremely important. They improved the lives of millions of poor people by providing them with education and better healthcare. These achievements cannot be measured simply in cash terms and those who dismiss or ridicule them have, in most cases, little awareness of the social crisis that had gripped Venezuela or the reasons for the popularity of the process. By the middle of the second year of the Bolivarian process, it is estimated that there was a capital flight of eight billion dollars, accompanied by the formation of a shadowy alliance between pro-US military commanders in the Army, the Chamber of Commerce and the AD/COPEI networks, in order to try and topple the regime by a coup d'état. Defeated by the people in the elections, these defenders of 'democracy' against 'authoritarianism' were now planning a military takeover of the country.

The sharp foreign policy turn taken by Chávez immediately after he took office greatly angered Washington. The Bolivarian Republic developed close ties with Cuba and began to send vital aid to help break the economic isolation of that country; it refused to boycott Iraq and attacked the UN sanctions regime; it unequivocally denounced the terrorist attacks of 9/11 on the US but was equally opposed to the invasion of Afghanistan; it revived Simón Bolívar's call for a Federation of South American States, not now against Spain, but against the USA. These policies were not designed to appease Washington or the Venezuelan elite. It was impossible that Chávez would make radical foreign policy changes but somehow remain loyal to the Washington Consensus on the domestic front. They knew, better than some of their new liberal friends, that a high-voltage foreign policy can only be sustained by mass support and that this requires an equally radical domestic policy, just as neo-conservative social policies at home are easily tied to imperial adventurism abroad. What was impressive, as always, was the ideological power at Washington's disposal to enforce its taboos and prejudices with a ruthless and vindictive zeal. This was done via an impressive network: intelligence agencies, tame journalists, pliant academics and voluntary converts to the imperial cause helped to set the scene for more drastic interventions.[12]

---

12. Who, apart from a few diehards like myself, could have imagined that the venerated *New York Review of Books*, the bible of the global *bien pensant*, would have sought to play a part in this sordid enterprise? Robert Silvers, the *NYRB* editor, is a longstanding member of the Council of Foreign Relations (a liberal adjunct of the State Department). Within months of Chávez's victory he decided to go on the offensive. The choice of writers was limitless. He could have approached Carlos Fuentes or Mario Vargas Llosa, or lesser known imperial blowhards from South America. Astutely, Silvers went for a less obvious choice. He approached the Nobel laureate V. S. Naipaul, an old-fashioned conservative with a pungent pen. Brought up in Trinidad, a boat-ride away from Venezuela, Naipaul knew the country and had close friends in Caracas. He was approached and agreed to ponder the proposal. He was still undecided when he began to receive recently unclassified and possibly semi-classified US intelligence documents on Venezuela. Precisely because he is a conservative of the old school, Naipaul was angered at being taken for granted and instrumentalised in such a crude fashion. He refused to bite the Silvers' bullet and a few sharp words were exchanged. This was the second occasion on which Silvers, in Naipaul's view, had violated journalistic ethics. The first offence had taken place when Naipaul was in Teheran during bad times, but that is another story. The *NYRB* delayed its report from Venezuela for a few years. A second-rate surrogate in the shape of the ever-reliable Alma Guillermoprieto was despatched to Caracas, where her prejudices were reinforced by the *Miami Herald* stringer and *Economist* man, Phil Gunson. What this episode reveals is the spectrum of domestic support – extending from the *NYRB* to Fox TV – that had been garnered by Washington. Unlike Iraq, where the imperial establishment was seriously divided, as far as the South American backyard was concerned there was no leeway for dissent. Never again would the US be caught by surprise as it had been in Cuba. But it had been unprepared for Venezuela and this necessitated a unified propaganda campaign to ready public opinion for the measures that might need to be taken.

There were three concerted attempts to defeat Chávez, the first two extra-parliamentary, the third seeing the frustrated politicians utilising clauses from a constitution they had mightily opposed. The first showdown, as discussed in Chapter One, came in April 2002. The coup had been carefully planned for several months: a public demonstration was designed to provoke a confrontation with the government and the resulting clashes used as the pretext for a military coup. Triumphant senior officers, who obviously had no idea that this would be one of the most short-lived coups in history, admitted as much on the actual day they were in power. Admiral Carlos Molina boasted on television that 'the fall of President Chávez has been in the planning since a year ago and in some sectors even further back than that. Nonetheless, all of the ideas and currents for getting rid of this doomed government converged, just as it turned out.' A fellow *golpista*, Colonel Julio Rodríguez, was equally frank, informing a journalist: 'Twelve months ago a firm movement began to be organised in all seriousness, that fortunately was realised on this day.' But sadly for the Colonel, it was not extended too much beyond that day.[13]

The very fact that the coup had been planned for over a year makes it impossible to take US denials of its involvement seriously. Two months prior to the coup, the Director of the CIA calmly informed a Senate Committee on Intelligence that if Chávez did not change his ways 'he would not finish his term'. And how did three US warships enter Venezuelan waters without authorisation and drop anchor close to the island where Chávez was being held captive? Is it credible that Otto 'Third' Reich, a former US

13. Quoted in Gregory Wilpert, *Changing Venezuela By Taking Power*, London and New York, 2007. Wilpert's account of the coup is the most thorough that I have read and backs up with a wealth of facts the case made in the Irish documentary film, *The Revolution Will Not Be Televised*. Wilpert's exemplary reportage can be accessed on www.venezuelanalysis.com, a website which regularly dissects *escualido* writing at home and abroad. See also his essay, 'Collision in Venezuela', *New Left Review*, 21, May–June 2003, pp. 101–16.

Ambassador in Caracas, a lobbyist for Mobil Oil and 'Assistant Secretary of State for Western Hemisphere Affairs' in the Bush administration, had no knowledge of what his friends were planning in Venezuela? Whether the conspirators met in the US or Spanish Embassies is not relevant. Both countries were involved in the plot.[14]

A green light from Washington, however, could not guarantee a pair of safe hands in Caracas. The chosen one, Pedro Carmona Estanga, a corrupt businessman hurriedly sworn in on 13 April 2002 as Venezuelan President had, on a trip to Madrid, been measured for a custom-fitted presidential sash in a fashionable store.[15] He wore this proudly, fingering the silk, as he appeared on television to disband parliament, suspend the constitution, close down the Supreme Court and dismiss the elected governors of the provinces, measures that took 'Third' Reich by surprise and made some of Carmona's useful idiots such as Teodoro Petkoff squeal with pain. They were for toppling Chávez – but this was far too crude for their delicate sensibilities. Mercifully these debates did not last too long.[16]

---

14. After the electoral defeat of José Maria Aznar in 2004, his minions in the Spanish Foreign Ministry destroyed the evidence, but forgot to change or destroy the hard disks on the Ministry computers. These revealed the extent of Aznar's duplicity and shocked the new Socialist Prime Minister Zapatero. He instructed his Foreign Minister to publicly apologise to Chávez, much to the irritation of the right-wing press in Spain. Relations were normalised. Months later a former Spanish Prime Minister, Felipe González, visited Caracas as a lobbyist for business interests and assured Chávez that he, González, had been totally opposed to the coup. Whether Chávez questioned him on the consistently biased commentaries in the Gonzalista daily, *El País*, is not known.

15. Carmona personally ordered the ceremonial sash from a Madrid tailor's shop specializing in military uniforms. It was discovered among the objects he left behind and stands as evidence supporting the charges against him. Manuel Viturro de la Torre was the Spanish ambassador in Caracas and travelled to Miraflores with US Ambassador Shapiro for a meeting with Carmona on 13 April.

16. See Appendix One for a pen-portrait of Teodoro Petkoff, guerrilla fighter, reformed Communist, minister in a Christian Democrat neo-liberal government, fierce journalist and a port-of-call for all anti-Bolívarian foreign journalists.

With Chávez apparently defeated, the different factions involved in the coup began to fight over how the spoils should be
divided. The pampered bureaucrats of the AD oil workers
demanded salary rises and a place in the new cabinet. Carmona,
a talentless and egocentric mediocrity, refused point blank and
began to pack his 'government' with discredited COPEI apparatchiks. When Chávez's daughter smuggled out a message to the
Cuban leader and the Venezuelan people making it clear he had
never resigned, the inhabitants of the hillside ranchitos above
Caracas poured down into the streets below, burning cars, looting
stores and threatening to occupy the city and the Miraflores
Palace unless their elected President was returned. Their entry on
the political stage galvanised the poor throughout the country and
the military barracks in downtown Caracas emptied as soldiers
joined the crowds, waving their rifles and berets as the populace
surrounded the Presidential Palace. The plotters lost their nerve,
dumped a hapless Carmona on the night of 13 April and released
Chávez. Only then did Washington disavow the coup – on the
very same morning that the paper of record had claimed that the
military action enhanced democracy:

> With yesterday's resignation of President Hugo Chávez,
> Venezuelan democracy is no longer threatened by a would-
> be dictator. Mr. Chávez, a ruinous demagogue, stepped down
> after the military intervened and handed power to a respected
> business leader, Pedro Carmona . . .
>
>   This week's crisis began with a general strike against
> replacing professional managers at the state oil company with
> political cronies. It took a grave turn Thursday when armed
> Chávez supporters fired on peaceful strikers, killing at least 14
> and injuring hundreds. Mr. Chávez's response was character-
> istic. He forced five private television stations off the air for
> showing pictures of the massacre. Early yesterday he was
> compelled to resign by military commanders unwilling to order

their troops to fire on fellow Venezuelans to keep him in power. He is being held at a military base and may face charges in Thursday's killings.[17]

The source of the disinformation was hardly a secret and the canard that Chávez supporters fired on 'peaceful strikers', which was repeated verbatim by the globalised media networks, has often been rebutted and disproved – but as Hitler's favourite spin doctor once remarked, a lie repeated often enough becomes the truth. He claimed he had learnt this from British imperial propagandists during and after the First World War.

In Venezuela itself, on 11 April 2002, just a few hours before Chávez was arrested, Vice-Admiral Victor Ramirez, a leading coup-maker, appeared on a live TV broadcast on Venevisión, publicly thanking 'civil society' for its help in unleashing a dictatorship: 'We had a deadly weapon: the media. And now that I have the opportunity, let me congratulate you.' Simultaneously in Spain, viewers watching TVE heard a Venezuelan journalist, Patricia Poleo, reporting from Caracas. They must have been impressed by her investigative skills when she informed them with a knowing smile: 'I believe the next President is going to be Pedro Carmona.' During the two days he was 'in power', Carmona offered young Patricia (whose father Rafael Poleo had filed the story of the coup on the front page of *El Universal* under the headline: 'One Step Forward', which was a tiny bit more restrained than the 'Giant Leap Forward for Humanity' tone of the private TV stations) a job. He suggested she should become the boss of Venezuela's central information bureau. Her father harboured grand ambitions of becoming the Karl Rove of the dictatorship, but these sweet dreams came to nought.

---

17. *New York Times*, 13 April 2002.

Given that the Opposition virtually monopolised newsprint and 95 per cent of the air-waves, and had been indulging in a non-stop hate campaign ever since Chávez was elected, the Admiral's expression of gratitude was hardly a surprise. In a forensic critique of the Venezuelan media, Maurice Lemoine, a senior editor of *Le Monde Diplomatique*, dissected its role in the crisis:

> After Chávez came to power in 1998, the five main privately owned channels – Venevisión, Radio Caracas Televisión (RCTV), Globovisión and CMT – and nine of the 10 major national newspapers, including *El Universal*, *El Nacional*, *Tal Cual*, *El Impulso*, *El Nuevo País*, and *El Mundo*, have taken over the role of the traditional political parties, which were damaged by the president's electoral victories. Their monopoly on information has put them in a strong position. They give the opposition support, only rarely reporting government statements and never mentioning its large majority, despite that majority's confirmation at the ballot box. They have always described the working class districts as no-go areas inhabited by dangerous classes of ignorant people and delinquents. No doubt considering them unphotogenic, they ignore working class leaders and organisations . . .
>
> The 'information' that has been published has verged on the surreal. For example, 'sources from the intelligence services have uncovered agreements entered into with elements linked to Hezbollah on the Venezuelan island of Margarita, who are controlled by the Iranian embassy. You will remember that when Chávez was campaigning, a certain Moukhdad was extremely generous. That debt had to be repaid, and now Iran is to make Venezuela an operational base, in exchange for training Venezuelans in Iranian organisations for the defence of the Islamic Revolution. Terrorism is in our midst' . . .
>
> On 21 March *El Nacional* ran the headline: 'Hugo Chávez admits to being the head of a criminal network.' Next day *Tal*

Cual referred to 'the feeling of nausea provoked by the aggressive words he uses to try to frighten Venezuelans'. The president was insulted, compared with Idi Amin, Mussolini or Hitler, called a fascist, dictator or tyrant, and subjected to a spate of attacks. In any other country actions would have been brought for libel. 'An ongoing and disrespectful attack,' was how the minister of trade, Adina Bastidas, put it. 'They accuse me of funding the planting of bombs in the streets. And I cannot defend myself. If you attack them, they complain to the United States!'

Chávez responded to this media bombardment, sometimes using strong language, especially during his weekly broadcast 'Aló presidente!' on the only state-controlled television channel. But his regime in no way resembles a dictatorship, and his diatribes have not been followed by measures to control the flow of information. Since Chávez took office, not a single journalist has been imprisoned, and the government has not shut down any media. Yet it is accused of 'flouting freedom of information' and of 'attacking social communicators' . . .[18]

Despite the failure of the coup, sections of the Opposition still could not allow themselves to accept the reasons for their defeat. They blamed Carmona for failing to satisfy the interests of every group that had been involved in the attempted coup; they blamed 'cowardly' generals for not having got rid of Chávez when they had the chance; they blamed Washington for not having kidnapped Chávez and tried him for 'crimes against humanity'. They had developed so many bogus theories about the dictatorship Chávez was planning to inflict on them and had got so used to regarding him as a lowly *mestizo* or a monkey (as the private TV channels sometimes referred to the elected President) that it was

18. Maurice Lemoine, *Le Monde Diplomatique*, August 2002.

difficult for them to acknowledge the very real popularity that Chávez enjoyed in the country.[19]

Since it was only tactical blunders, or so they thought, that had cost them their big opportunity on 11–12 April 2002, they began to put other destabilisation plans into effect. In December 2002 the pampered bureaucracy of the Oil Workers' trade union, fearful of losing its position and privileges, joined with middle-class professional unions – teachers, doctors, engineers, etc. – to declare a lock-out, whose aim was straightforwardly political: to bring down the Bolivarian government. In Havana it was difficult not to compare all this to the destabilising and sustained strikes by the truckers and middle classes in Chile in 1972–3 against the late Salvador Allende. In Santiago the strikes preceded the coup. In Caracas they tried to remedy its failure. In both cases the United States was actively engaged.[20]

---

19. This view was cogently expressed by the ubiquitous Phil Gunson as he denounced the Irish documentary *The Revolution Will Not Be Televised* in, of all places, the pages of *Vertigo*, a quarterly magazine 'For Worldwide Independent Film and Video'. Rod Stoneman, who as Chief Executive had commissioned the documentary on behalf of the Irish Film Board alerted me to Vol. 2, no. 7, Autumn/Winter 2004. Here Gunson wrote of Chávez: '. . . he is a fairly standard Latin American military demagogue, who openly disavows representative democracy (despite having used it to achieve power) and is now busily installing a dictatorship . . . his "wealth distribution" is neither more nor less than the cynical and clientelistic (sic) purchase of a military/civilian power base . . . polls have consistently shown that a majority would vote for a change in government . . .' This was virtually a carbon-copy of the stated views of Rice, Rumsfeld, Otto 'Third' Reich and the rest of the gang that had funded, trained and armed the Contras in Nicaragua. They, at least, had remained consistent. As we shall see, Gunson and his friends in Caracas were proved wrong by subsequent events.
20. Philip Agee, a senior CIA officer in Latin America during the Sixties, broke ranks and wrote *Inside the Company*, a devastating exposure of the violence, terror and torture used by the CIA against its opponents in every Latin American country. Agee, now based in Cuba, wrote of the destabilisation in Venezuela:

     'The program of political intervention in Venezuela is one more of various in the world principally directed by the Department of State (DS), the

The plan was not a big secret. By stopping the production of oil and other commodities (including beer) and then closing down the country's schools and hospitals, those backing the strike hoped that the resulting chaos would detach the majority of the country from Chávez and force him to resign or at the very least announce immediate elections. They were, as ever, confident that they would win these and return to power. They certainly did succeed in creating chaos, but once again these plans backfired. Had the donkeys completely lost their cunning? The certainties of the light-skinned ones – their right to power being the most im-

20. Agency for International Development (AID), the Central Intelligence Agency (CIA), and the National Endowment for Democracy (NED) along with its four associated foundations. These are the International Republican Institute (IRI) of the Republican Party; the National Democratic Institute (NDI) of the Democratic Party; the Center for International Private Enterprise (CIPE) of the US Chamber of Commerce; and the American Center for International Labor Solidarity (ACILS) of the American Federation of Labor-Congress of Industrial Organizations (AFL-CIO), the main US national union confederation. In addition, the program has the support of an international network of affiliated organizations.

'The various organizations carry out their operations through AID officials at the U.S. Embassy in Caracas and through three "private" offices in Caracas under the Embassy's control: the IRI (established in 2000), the NDI (2001), and a contractor of AID, a U.S. consulting firm called Development Alternatives, Inc. (DAI) (2002). These three offices develop operations with dozens of Venezuelan beneficiaries to which they contribute money originating from the State Department, AID, NED, and, although no proof is yet available, most probably the CIA. The operations of the first three are detailed extensively in hundreds of official documents acquired by U.S. journalist Jeremy Bigwood through demands under the Freedom of Information Act, a law that requires the declassification and release of government documents, although many are censored when released.' www.venezuelanalysis.com, 9 November 2005.

The most detailed analysis of US involvement is 'US Intervention in Venezuela: A Clear and Present Danger' by Deborah James, Global Exchange 2006. The document can be read on:

http://www.globalexchange.org/countries/americas/venezuela/USVZrelations.pdf. Both Agee and James acknowledge the work of Eva Gollinger who, with Jeremy Bigwood, was determined to uncover the truth. See Gollinger's *The Chávez Code: Cracking US Intervention in Venezuela*, Havana, 2005.

portant of these – had been destroyed. In their desperation they were lashing out in every direction, regardless of consequence. What else can explain the mountain of blunders so carefully thrown up by the AD/COPEI and its allies that, when it crumbled, its builders were covered by the debris? The Opposition and its friends abroad still refused to give up. The third attempt came two years after the coup, but this time they chose a constitutional weapon in the shape of a recall referendum, sanctioned by the Bolivarian Constitution. No Western or any other democracy (excepting Switzerland) enshrines this right – to remove an elected President by means of a referendum – in a constitution.

Over the last five years, during several trips to Venezuela, I have had a number of conversations with Hugo Chávez at the Miraflores Palace. The subjects covered include his dreams for Latin America, his assessment of the United States, the crisis in the Middle East and, especially, Iraq and Palestine as well as the odd discussion on literature. During one such conversation on the eve of the August 2004 referendum he spoke of his reactions to the 2002 coup and the management strike:

After the initial shock, I was confident that the coup could not succeed. Once my daughter got the message out that I had not 'resigned', but had been removed by a treacherous anti-democratic coup, it was only a matter of time. But I must tell you that I was more worried during the strike because here it was not my person that was at risk but the poor of Venezuela, the people on whom we depended for our support. The Opposition was openly saying that the kids in the shanty towns, unemployed and angry, would rise up against us if they were deprived of beer. Of course they hoped the people would rebel and accept the price being demanded of them for a return to normality. The Venezuelan people have already paid too much for what has been done in their name. Two factors helped sustain my morale. The first was the support we retained in the country. I remember one day I got fed up of sitting in this place. I decided to go to the barrios on the hills and with one guard and two comrades I drove out to listen to people and breathe better air. The response moved me greatly. A woman came up to me and said: 'Chávez, follow me, I want to show you something.' I followed her to her tiny dwelling. Inside the room her children and husband were waiting for the soup to be cooked. 'Look at what I'm using for fuel', she said to me. 'The back of our bed. Tomorrow I'll burn the legs, the day after the table, then the chairs and the doors. We will survive, but don't give up now.' On my way out the kids from the gangs came and shook hands. 'We can live without beer. You make sure you screw these . . .' People were very angry, but they knew who was responsible and we were getting similar reports from all over the country. The middle classes hurt themselves a great deal by that strike.

The failure of the strike to dent the support for our Revolution was the most important thing, but then we had to go on the offensive. How? I spoke with Fidel who is a friend and a comrade. His advice during the coup was also very astute. 'Don't do anything rash', he told me, 'this continent does not need another Allende. Be very careful.' Now the Cuban comrades opened their doors wide. Within a fortnight ten thousand Cuban doctors, with field hospitals and Cuban medicines arrived in Venezuela. They set up clinics and began to treat people within twenty-four hours. Health facilities in this country have been the preserve of the well-off and often people in the barrios had to travel long distances for a doctor to even see them. Now they were being treated close to their homes. Our medical profession was angered by this as were the Opposition leaders. They said openly that these Cuban doctors were 'terrorists' who had been sent to carry out violence. They really discredited themselves here because even their own supporters knew this was nonsense. Then our doctors refused to accept patients from these clinics to their hospitals. When this happened I instructed all the military hospitals to accept everyone recommended by the clinics. So in this struggle, too, we were successful. And teachers also began to arrive from Cuba and other parts of Latin America and alternative schools were started, as substitutes for those closed down by the middle-class strike.

Both the coup and the strike were bad things but these two attempts to destroy us also taught us many lessons. I think we gained more than our opponents as a result. Now they have pushed through this referendum. Many of us are convinced that hundreds if not thousands of signatures collected are fraudulent, but this is a constitutional right which we gave the people. We will stand by it. I'm not sure, but I think we will win. Most people see this for what it is . . . having failed in the coup and the strike they are trying this but it's better. They should have used this method in 2002. If they fail? Fidel is convinced they will try assassination. If they do they could provoke a civil war . . .

Just under a million Venezuelan children from the shanty towns and the poorest villages now obtain a free education; 1.2 million illiterate adults have been taught to read and write; secondary education has been made available to 250,000 children whose social status excluded them from this privilege during the *ancien régime*; three new university campuses were functioning by 2003 and six more are due to be completed by 2006.

As far as healthcare is concerned, the 14,000 Cuban doctors sent to help the country have transformed the situation in the poor districts, where 11,000 neighbourhood clinics have been established and the health budget has tripled. Add to this the financial support provided to small businesses, the new homes being built for the poor, an Agrarian Reform Law that was enacted and pushed through despite resistance, legal and violent, by the landlords. By the end of 2003, just over 2,262,467 hectares had been redistributed to 116,899 families.

The bizarre argument advanced in a hostile editorial in *The Economist* (as in Gunson's article in *Vertigo*) during the week of the referendum, namely, that all this was done to win votes, is extraordinarily obtuse. Here the defenders of the global elite confuse their own machinations with reality. In the globalised world, where there are no basic differences between competing political factions of the elite, politics is exclusively about power; a world in which Clinton and Bush's billionaire backers, or the financiers who supported first Thatcher, then Blair, can cross sides with ease.

The Bolivarian currents in Latin America are important pre- cisely because they pose a challenge to traditional cacique politics. That is why they are loathed by the elites and their media propagandists. If Chávez had simply been interested in power he could have easily done a deal with the local oligarchy and won the support of the global financial press. The Bolivarians wanted power precisely so that real reforms could be implemented.[21]

When it happened in August 2004, the turn-out for the referendum was over 60 per cent. Chávez's victory of 58 per cent, with 42 per cent against, had repercussions beyond the borders of Venezuela. The referendum results were seen in Latin America as a triumph of the poor against the rich. Chávez had put his trust in the people by empowering them and they responded generously. Aware that its electoral processes are the most carefully scrutinised events in the world, the Venezuelan govern- ment permitted observers from everywhere, including the Carter

---

21. Richard Gott's *Hugo Chávez and the Bolívarian Revolution*, London and New York, 2005 is the most detailed and useful study of the changes in Venezuela. Gott was the first European journalist to draw attention to the significance of Hugo Chávez in a prescient piece of reporting for the *London Review of Books* ('Robinson's Footprints', *London Review of Books*, 17 February 2000).

Center in the United States. While tame hacks, blinded by prejudice, were incapable of accepting the results, the former US President, Jimmy Carter, declared that this was one of the freest elections he had ever seen. For this he was vilified by the Opposition and abused and spat at in a restaurant in the wealthy section of Caracas.[22]

The Opposition discredited itself further by challenging the results, but failed in the attempt. However loud their cries of anguish (and those of their media apologists at home and abroad), in reality the whole country knew what had happened. Chávez had defeated his opponents democratically for the fourth time in a row. Democracy in Venezuela, under the banner of the Bolivarian revolutionaries, had broken through the corrupt two-party system favoured by the oligarchy and its friends in the West. And this happened in the face of total hostility from the privately owned media.

A wave of demoralisation washed through the Opposition and its global supporters after their defeat in the referendum. If only, in Brecht's words, they could have dissolved the Venezuelan people and elected a new one. The stubborn popular support for Chávez could no longer be denied inside the country and even

---

22. Someone at *The Economist* must have realised that they could not simply publish Gunson, whose credibility was temporarily exhausted. A signed article by a woman from the Carter Center on the referendum was published stating clearly that the results were free and fair. The *Financial Times* did not follow suit. But soon after it was back to business as usual. Having convinced themselves that Chávez is an oppressive *caudillo*, and desperate to translate their own fantasies into reality, their reports bordered on science fiction: as in their earlier reporting of the 2002 coup, two of the worst offenders were both still embedded deep in the posterior of the oligarchy, as if sub-consciously mimicking the British prime minister's relationship to the incumbent in the White House. They provide no evidence of political prisoners, leave alone Guantanamo-style detentions or Abu Ghraib-style tortures or the removal of TV executives and newspaper editors (which happened without too much of a fuss in Blair's Britain and was actually supported in three separate articles in the *Financial Times*) or the new laws permitting detention without trial.

elsewhere it was obvious that the Venezuelan Opposition was totally discredited, a spent force. The donkeys had lost their cunning. The fierce bull had once again emerged triumphant.

A despairing and bankrupt Opposition now decided it would boycott the parliamentary elections due the following year. Since the Bolivarians had disappointed the Opposition by refusing to be authoritarian, the only way the old dyarchs could attempt to censure the government was to withdraw from the democratic process. Whether they contest the presidential election in December 2006 or allow Chávez to be returned unopposed remains an open question. Till now only Teodoro Petkoff has declared his intention of standing against Chávez and even though he is only on 3 per cent it is to be hoped that he will not withdraw under pressure from his friends in the Opposition. The political health of Venezuelan democracy requires debate and discussion, not coups or assassinations.

Opinion polls indicate that support for Chávez has grown to 70 per cent, but the task of a serious political opposition is to present an alternative to the electorate.[23] With the total support of the

---

23. 'Still in Diapers: How Primero Justicia Has Blown its Greatest Opportunity' by Julia Buxton. Posted on 2 December 2005 on www.vicuk.org, the Venezuelan Information Centre website. As Buxton, one of the few objective academics in this field, observes, even one of the more intelligent and less embittered Opposition leaders appears to have fallen in with the bankrupts who are too scared of losing again:

'Of all the key opposition figures, Julio Borges, leader of the Primero Justicia party, had perhaps the best chance of offering a credible alternative to Hugo Chávez in the 2006 presidential election. Although his platform of economic liberalisation does not have resonance among the majority of the Venezuelan electorate, which resisted the country's only previous attempt to move toward a neoliberal model in 1989, Borges does have the capacity to connect with ordinary people. Over the last few months, the PJ leader has toured the country, meeting with ordinary Venezuelans and performing a task central to the relegitimisation of the Venezuelan opposition – listening to the people. Borges is also young and cognisant of the most pressing issues facing Venezuelans, specifically problems of personal security and lack of access to the justice system. His greatest advantage is that he is not associated with AD and COPEI, the two traditionally dominant parties that controlled the Venezuelan

privately owned media the views of the old elite are permanently available to the public. Why then even consider a boycott? Or is it the case that the only form of democracy that is considered workable in these great times is a consensual dyarchy: AD/ COPEI, Democrat/Republican, New Labour/Conservative, SPD/CD, PT/PFL . . . and so on, backed by a corporate media and a political establishment that brooks no real change. That is why the challenge to this form of politics in Venezuela and Bolivia results in carefully manufactured outrage by the global elites, their politicians and their media.

The recklessness of the Venezuelan Opposition found a sinister echo amongst their supporters in the United States. On 22 August 2005, Pat Robertson, the Christian fundamentalist preacher, a former candidate for the Republican presidential nomination in 1988 and a staunch supporter of the current administration, calmly informed over a million viewers on his television show 'The 700 Club' that, in his view, the Venezuelan President should be 'taken out':

> He has destroyed the Venezuelan economy, and he's going to make that a launching pad for Communist infiltration and Muslim extremism all over the continent. You know, I don't know about this doctrine of assassination, but if he thinks we're trying to assassinate him, I think that we really ought to go ahead and do it. It's a whole lot cheaper than starting a war . . . and I don't think any oil shipments will stop. This man is a terrific danger, and this is in our sphere of influence . . .
>
> Without question, this is a dangerous enemy to our south, controlling a huge pool of oil, that could hurt us very badly.

23. political system and state institutions for forty years until their entrenched control was swept away after Chávez's landslide election victory of 1998. While it is widely expected that Chávez will triumph in 2006, there is always the possibility that an economic downturn, intra-Chavista rifts or a shift in popular evaluations of the government will create a small space for a political alternative to develop over the year. Borges was positioned to fill this space.'

We have the ability to take him out, and I think the time has come that we exercise that ability. We don't need another $200 billion war to get rid of one, you know, strong-arm dictator. It's a whole lot easier to have some of the covert operatives do the job and then get it over with . . .

To this, the State Department issued a mild demurral that this was 'not US policy'. If the less sophisticated on the Latin America desk in Foggy Bottom or Langley assumed that terror threats would cow the Venezuelan leader they were making a mistake. Chávez's response came some weeks later in New York where, in a characteristically feisty speech at the United Nations summit, he broke ranks to denounce the US/UN nexus. The *Washington Post* correspondent compared his appearance to that of Fidel Castro's 'fiery condemnation of American imperialism' in 1960 and wrote:

Chávez generated the loudest burst of applause for a world leader at the summit with his unbridled attack on what he characterized as American militarism and capitalism. He even offered a proposal to move the United Nations to Jerusalem or a city in the developing world . . .

In his Thursday address, Chávez railed against the Bush administration for failing to protect poor residents of New Orleans who were caught in the flooding that followed Hurricane Katrina. He also accused the United States of abetting 'international terrorism' by failing to arrest television evangelist Pat Robertson for saying that the United States should consider assassinating Chávez.

'The only place where a person can ask for another head of state to be assassinated is the United States, which is what happened recently with the Reverend Pat Robertson, a very close friend of the White House,' Chávez said. 'He publicly asked for my assassination and he's still walking the streets.'

Chávez, passing the five-minute limit for speakers, grew
irritated when a U.N. official slipped him a note requesting that
he wrap it up. Turning toward the president of the General
Assembly, Jan Eliasson of Sweden, he said: 'I think the
president of the United States spoke for twenty minutes here
yesterday. I would ask your indulgence to let me finish my
statement.'

U.N. experts and foreign envoys said Chávez, like Castro,
was able to capitalize on a reservoir of resentment of American
power in the world body. 'Obviously people are pleased with
what he said, but they cannot express themselves as frankly as
he does,' said one Arab ambassador, who spoke on condition of
anonymity because he did not want to offend the United
States . . .

The applause for Chávez was recognition of the 'sheer
entertainment factor' of his undiplomatic speech, said Nancy
Soderberg, a former senior U.S. diplomat at the United
Nations. 'Those speeches get so boring . . .'[24]

Not content with words alone, the Venezuelan government
offered cheap oil to US citizens after the New Orleans disaster.
They offered 40 per cent discounts on 49 million gallons of
heating fuel for poor people in Massachusetts, Maine, Rhode
Island, Pennsylvania, New York, Delaware, and offered the same
to Vermont and Connecticut.[25] The importance of this offer is that

---

24. Colum Lynch, 'Chávez Stirs Things Up at the U.N.', *Washington Post*, 17
    September 2005, p. A14. Readers can judge for themselves whether the applause
    was because of the 'sheer entertainment factor' or the political approach or both.
    The complete text is contained in Appendix Three.
25. As Medea Benjamin of Global Exchange commented in 'US Intervention in
    Venezuela', www.politicalaffairs.net, 3 June 2006: 'How bizarre that Texas
    Republican Congressman Joe Barton has launched an investigation into this
    humanitarian offering, instead of investigating the US multinational oil
    companies that posted over $100 billion in corporate profits last year due to
    soaring gasoline prices.'

it reveals a sharp awareness of the necessity to appeal directly to US citizens. This is one of the big differences between the political strategy of the new movements in Latin America and the Islamist rebellions elsewhere.

Mass disgust with the violence, ineptitude and corruption of the old regime was the basis of Chávez's initial triumph. It has been the reform programme of the Bolivarian government that explains its successive electoral victories. Chávez's refusal to play the oligarchic game is the reason for the virulence of the Opposition and its media henchmen. The transition to a different type of state has begun, but its future will rest on its ability to transform the living standards of the poor and by inaugurating the process of economic redistribution at the level of the economy.

That the Bolivarians have turned the traditional politics of the country upside down is beyond dispute. That the oligarchy has lost political power is significant since it was used shamelessly to promote clientelism of the crudest variety; however, the economic bases of the traditional elites have not been touched. They could rise again but, fortunately for Hugo Chávez and his supporters, the gods have not blessed the Opposition with too much intelligence. Years of prolonged rule seem to have affected their brain tissue. The next ten years will be decisive. If Chávez succeeds in transforming Venezuela and creating the foundations of a regional Bolivarian alternative, the future will be stormy and could become a nightmare for those who dreamt of an unchallenged neo-liberal paradise. For this to happen, democratic and republican institutions will have to be rebuilt, strengthened and developed as a real alternative to neo-liberal democracy, while simultaneously continent-wide structures need to be created as an alternative to the networks of the Northern global market and corruption consistently challenged. Once upon a time the national bourgeoisies of the continent (how odd this sounds today) provided a limited basis for challenging imperial domination, but thanks to the deindustrialisation in Brazil and Mexico and

Argentina and Chile, the new elites are subaltern by choice. The social movements from below that challenge the New Order need political instruments. In Venezuela and Bolivia they found them. In Brazil and Mexico the search is still on.

Chapter 4

Bolivia Again

I was conceived in a night of suffering
The rain and the wind were my cradle
No one pities my suffering
Cursed be my birth
Cursed the world
Cursed myself

(Indigenous lament)

In every republic there are two different dispositions, that of the
populace and that of the upper class . . . all legislation favourable to
liberty is brought about by the clash between them.

Niccolò Machiavelli

With the smoke and with the fire, many people muffled and silent
On a street, on a corner,
In the high city, pondering the future in search of a past . . .

Jaime Saenz, 'The City' (1970)

The memory I retain of La Paz is that of a melancholic city. I was there in the first half of 1967.[1] The airport was a tiny wooden shed. I had to wait a long time before I got through: the Pakistani passport (which I then carried) had become an object of curiosity. It was not that they thought it a forgery but simply the fact that none of the immigration police had ever heard of Pakistan. Did it really exist? I assured them that it did and offered to point it out on a world map. None could be found. A few phone calls were made to check my story, but it was the Bolivian visa firmly stamped in my passport that finally convinced them I was not from outer space. I was the first Pakistani to visit Bolivia, but soon I understood from the looks in my direction that for many Creoles I was just another Indian. That did not bother me in the slightest. Little did they know that I was a red Indian.

What struck me after a day of wandering through the streets

---

1. A detailed account of my Bolivia journey is contained in *Streetfighting Years: An Autobiography of the Sixties*, London and New York, 2004. I was part of a group that included Perry Anderson and Robin Blackburn: we had been despatched by Bertrand Russell to attend the trial of the French writer Régis Debray in Camiri. Che was still alive, but the guerrillas were encircled and escape routes were being sealed off, although we preferred not to take these reports seriously at the time. The choice of country had not been so wrong. It was the bad timing and the mode of struggle chosen that had proved catastrophic. Only a few years later Che, isolated in his last tragic months, had become an icon for the Bolivian peasants.

was that the indigenous people rarely smiled. A month or so prior to making this trip I had spent six weeks in war-torn North Vietnam where we were regularly bombed and I had seen death and destruction every day, but when the bombs stopped at night or there was a respite for a day or two the Vietnamese would crack jokes and laugh. Despite the horrors of war they knew it was their country.

It was not like that in Bolivia. Here, in La Paz, the Aymara people appeared to be occupied from without and within. Were they resigned to their fate? Was it all God's will? I remembered interviewing poverty-stricken peasants in the mountain villages of Northern Pakistan in the mid-Sixties and whenever I asked, 'Why do you tolerate this?' the reply, invariably, was to look up towards the heavens, shrug their shoulders and refer to the will of Allah. But this was a city. The indigenous people lived here. The disparities in living standards between them and the minority Creole population were horrendous. Surely they could not be as fatalistic as isolated peasant communities in South Asia?

One evening, a few leftist Bolivian friends took us to an Aymara social gathering in a La Paz suburb. There was music and drink and dancing. We were introduced as friends from afar. I saw shining eyes and shy smiles and suddenly I was overcome by an irresistible urge to tell them about what was happening in Vietnam and how the resistance was organised. My Spanish, leave alone Aymar, was non-existent. For the first and last time in my life I mimed a speech with gestures and a few words they would understand. The response was warm and the chants of 'Vietnam Sí, Yanqui No' reached the streets outside. News that the police were about to raid the location meant we had to leave in a hurry.

Poverty reigned supreme. At that time, over 85 per cent of the roads in Bolivia were unpaved and there was no electricity or running water in most of the villages or poor urban dwellings. These figures had not been greatly reduced at the beginning of the twenty-first century. In 2000 over 70 per cent of the roads were still rough and only 25 per cent of households had electricity.

What was this country that had been named after the Liberator? From the moment Bolívar and Sucre agreed that Upper Peru would become Bolivia, political and economic power remained, for most of the country's history, in the hands of a hereditary Creole elite in its various guises, regularly reinforced by European migrants.[2] All changed and nothing changed. But all had to be changed, given that 55 per cent out of a population of 9 million are indigenous, 30 per cent are *mestizo* (mixed Amerindian and white ancestry) and only 15 per cent are Creole; a fact that should have provoked more reflection than it did before the dramatic election of Evo Morales as President in 2005. This marks a new phase in Bolivia's turbulent history; prior to this no indigenous leader had even come close to power, leave alone taken the Presidency.

The country's social, anthropological and political history belies claims of its universal status as a 'backwater'. Economic underdevelopment, which produced a pyramid with poor peasants and over-exploited workers as its base and a tiny rich elite at the summit, was not after all a disease peculiar to Bolivia. But in this case it produced one of the most militant labour movements in South America and a potent mixture of radical-liberal-socialist-communist-trotskyist-nationalist currents that influenced the country's history for most of the last century. This accelerated the processes that led to the 1952 revolution, a flawed but serious attempt to break loose from capitalism and imperialism that culminated in the heroic but tragically doomed expedition of Che Guevara in 1966–7. The 1952 revolution appears not to merit much attention in the standard histories of Latin America or of

2. In La Paz in 1967, walking with the Italian publisher G. Feltrinelli on the pavement in front of the Hotel Sucre we paused to watch a military band marching down the street. It was the tune that caught our respective ears: they were playing the Horst Wessel song.

global revolutionary upheavals.[3] And yet it was a vitally important process, which shaped the political course of the country and its institutions in the decades that lay ahead.

The disastrous Chaco War with Paraguay of 1932–5 weakened and discredited the Bolivian elite, whose core consisted of tin millionaires who dominated the country's social and political life without any direct involvement in running the state. In 1936 a general strike combined with the disenchantment of young army officers to produce a so-called 'military socialist' regime which nationalised the operations of the Standard Oil Company, favoured the growth of trade unions and proclaimed the abolition of the *ponguaje*, the semi-feudal tribute paid by the Indian peasants. In 1939 the government of the radical Colonel Germán Busch attempted to control the tin companies that dominated the export sector of the Bolivian economy. Before he was able to implement these schemes Busch died in mysterious circumstances, and the regime of a conservative general was installed. In December of 1942 a strike led to troops firing on tin miners in Catavi – a massacre not unlike the *Caracazo* of 1989 and similar slaughters by the state elsewhere in the continent throughout the twentieth century.

The newly-formed Movimiento Nacionalista Revolucionaria (MNR) led a protest campaign against this massacre and established itself as a powerful force in Bolivian politics. Between 1943 and 1946 MNR participation in the government of Major Gualberto Villarroel allowed them to consolidate their support among the trade unions and in particular among the tin miners.

After the overthrow of Villarroel in 1946 the MNR was the object of persecution by successive governments until April 1952,

---

3. For instance, *The Penguin History of Latin America* (1992) by Edwin Williamson contains much that is useful, but Bolivia is not even awarded a separate chapter in the section headed 'the Twentieth Century' despite the fact that what took place there during the first half of the century was in some ways far more challenging than events elsewhere on the continent, with the single exception of the Cuban Revolution in 1959.

when a popular uprising led to the creation of a new government dominated by the MNR. Whereas previous changes of regime had reflected struggles inside the Army, this time the workers of La Paz and the mining districts, supported by some sections of the *carabineros*, the military police, fought and defeated the Army. By this time the MNR was under pressure from both Communists and Trotskyists, who had won some of the most militant workers to their ranks. The new MNR government nationalised the major tin mines and established a limited form of self-management within them, while the Confederation of Bolivian Workers (COB) was given the right to nominate four ministerial posts. Moreover, the workers' defeat of the Army helped to spark off a revolt by peasants who drove away or killed some large landlords; the MNR government legalised peasant seizures of land in the Agrarian Law of 1953. However, neither the nationalisation of the mines nor the agrarian reform were followed up by any general assault on capitalist social relations. When the Trotskyists and Communists objected to the limited nature of nationalisation, the MNR sought to attack their influence in the COB and the Army was reorganized as a check to the power of the miners' militias. Externally the government became increasingly dependent on US aid and internally came to rely more on the support of the government-sponsored peasant associations. However, the miners continued to exercise local power in their own areas and their leader, Juan Lechin, sought to organise the left of the MNR.[4]

Che's choice of Bolivia as a possible insurrectionary site in the mid-1960s was not as light-minded as it seemed to the more

---

4. James Dunkerley's *Rebellion in the Veins*, London and New York, 1984 is a brilliant reconstruction of twentieth-century Bolivian history and contains the most detailed account of the 1952 revolution. A footnote reference to myself is, alas, mostly inaccurate but of nil significance. Dunkerley concludes by predicting a new Bolivian Revolution. Given the historical turn of 1990 such a prediction could easily be mocked. However Morales' democratic triumph could have an impact on the country akin to that of 1952 and an update from James (rather than Professor) Dunkerley could be of value.

orthodox sections of the Latin American and global left at the time. The revolutionary traditions and historical memory of the country were strong, the objective conditions – a poverty-stricken peasantry suffering multiple oppressions and a politicised working class – favoured an upheaval. Even while Che's band of armed fighters was isolated in Nancahuaza, there were clashes between troops and miners. Both groups were defeated. Only a few guerrillas managed to escape Colonel Reque Teran's trap and leave the country, but the military failed to consolidate its successes. More importantly, the execution of Che Guevara in the presence of CIA agents, coupled with the brutality inflicted on the miners, precipitated a serious crisis within the Government and Army. Arguedas, the Minister of the Interior, resigned and despatched Che's diaries and other documents to Havana.[5]

The Bolivian state machine was divided between those who wanted to respond positively to the upheavals and a hardline faction which favoured smothering all dissent and, if necessary, shedding blood. The United States at the time also veered between repression and reforms in Latin America, much to the anger of the Cuban Lobby and the extreme right. The US

---

5. Antonio Arguedas (1929–2000) become Bolivia's minister of the interior during the 1964–69 military dictatorship of General René Barrientos; he was recruited by the US Central Intelligence Agency in 1965 and loyally aided the campaign to defeat Che's guerrilla band. The capture and execution of the revolutionary leader in 1967 had a deep impact on Arguedas and he began to regret his part in the affair. Hence his decision to smuggle copies of Che Guevara's diaries to Cuba; the subsequent publication of which (in Britain we joined forces with *Ramparts* magazine – co-edited at the time by one David Horowitz – in the United States and devoted a special issue of *The Black Dwarf* to publish the diaries in English for the first time much to the anger of Tom Maschler who had paid a large sum on behalf of Jonathan Cape. 'Pirates' is how he denounced us and pirates we were . . .) detailed the relentless pursuit of the guerrilla leader by Bolivian special forces, and was a big embarrassment for Barrientos. Arguedas sought exile first in Chile and subsequently in Cuba, where he spent most of the 1970s. On his return to Bolivia he was involved in fringe radical politics and according to some reports he died when a bomb he was carrying exploded.

favoured reforms that might help to keep the revolution at bay and isolate its partisans. Washington despatched a special team, headed by Nelson Rockefeller, to study prevailing conditions in Latin America. The Rockefeller Mission reported back to the State Department in 1969. It expressed its disenchantment with the traditional oligarchies whose privileges and mistakes provoked revolutions. Hence the document's insistence that revolutions could only be curtailed by serious reforms, including altering the traditional terms of trade and dependence:

> In the same way that other American republics depend on the United States for their capital goods needs, the US depends on them for a vast market for our manufactured products. And as these countries regard the US as a market for their raw materials, by selling which they can buy capital goods for their own development, the US regards these raw materials as necessary to our industries, on which the employment of so many of our citizens depends.
>
> But these forces of economic interdependence are changing and must change. A growing two-way flow of trade in industrial products must replace the present exchange of manufactured goods for raw materials.[6]

Like its opponents, the Rockefeller Mission sometimes over-estimated the depth of the social convulsions and assumed, far too simply, that a pre-revolutionary situation existed everywhere. But all agreed that the Cuban Revolution had opened a new chapter in continental history. That the situation had to be taken seriously was obvious in the following sober reflections of the Rockefeller Mission, some of which remain apposite today, but would be anathema to the partisans of the WC:

---

6. 'Quality of Life in the Americas', Text of the Rockefeller Mission Report, The Department of State Bulletin, 8 December 1969, Washington DC.

—The dynamics of industrialisation and modernisation have stretched the fabric of the social and political structures. The situation is dominated by political and social instability, by pressure which has built up in favour of a radical situation to problems, and an increased tendency towards national independence in relation to the United States.

—The ferment of nihilism and anarchism is spreading throughout the hemisphere.

—Most of the American republics have not yet mobilised the resources necessary for a broad industrialisation of their economies. In differing degrees they need: more and better education, a more effective system for channelling national savings into capital investment, laws which protect the public interest while encouraging the spirit of enterprise and expanding government services (i.e state intervention – TA) to support industrial growth.

—The dilemma of governments is the following: they know that the co-operation and participation of the United States can contribute greatly . . . but their feeling of political legitimacy may very well depend on the degree of independence they are able to maintain in relation to the United States.

—Although it is not yet widely recognised, the military and the Catholic Church are also among the forces today agitating for change in the other American republics. This is a new role for them.

—In many Central and South American countries, the army is the most important political grouping in society. The military are symbols of power, authority and sovereignty, as well as the focus of national pride. They have been traditionally considered the ultimate arbiters of the good of the nation.

—In brief, a new type of military is appearing, and often becoming a major force for constructive social change in the American republics. Motivated by a growing impatience with

corruption, inefficiency and a stagnating political order, the
new military are ready to adapt their authoritarian traditions to
the goals of economic and social progress.[7]

The report's findings were not popular within the intelligence and
military sectors of the US government, but the very fact that the
report had been published indicated a serious divide within the
elite. Military reformism was preferable to revolution. The impact
in Bolivia was almost immediate. In April 1969 the Bolivian
military leader René Barrientos had died unexpectedly in a plane
crash. His successor, General Alfredo Ovando, decided to change
course as suggested by the Rockefeller Mission.

   Under General Ovando the regime began to evolve in 1970
towards a Peruvian-style military nationalism. At the same time
leaders of the students' unions embarked on a short-lived guerrilla
campaign at Teoponte, a further example of the influence exerted
by Che Guevara. Despite its lack of success the Teoponte
guerrillas helped to accentuate further the crisis in the military
regime and led to rival attempts at a coup by different army
factions. In October the same year Ovando was toppled by the
conservative, pro-US General Rogelio Miranda, who insisted that
he spoke for the entire Armed Services, a statement that was
sensationally disproved when General Juan José Torres called for
resistance to the junta, and with the aid of the trade unions
defeated the right wing of the Army.[8]

   During these events a Commando Politico, including Juan
Lechin, the COB (trade union federation) and a combination of
left parties, helped Torres to defeat his opponents by mobilising
armed workers and students. The Commando Politico demanded

---

7. 'Quality of Life in the Americas', op. cit., pp. 502–5.
8. For an astute reading of these events see 'Bolivia: Military Nationalism and the
   Popular Assembly' by René Zavaleta, *New Left Review*, 73, May–June 1972.
   Zavaleta, a MNR Minister after the 1952 revolution, subsequently became one
   of the country's leading political analysts.

half the seats in the Cabinet, but although Torres appeared ready to concede this he could not persuade the Army to accept it. The Commando Politico then persuaded Torres to agree to the convocation of a Popular Assembly specifically designed to represent the workers and peasants. The Assembly met for the first time in June 1971, taking over the Legislative Palace in La Paz. Meanwhile the unions, the peasant confederation and different groups of the left seized control of a number of radio stations and newspapers so that all the events surrounding the Popular Assembly received great publicity. It was an amazing development, more reminiscent of the 1848 Frankfurt Assembly than the 1905 Soviets, the chosen analogy of the left groups who dominated its discussions.

The agreed composition of the Assembly was 132 workers delegates, (60 per cent of the total), 53 delegates for white-collar groups, 23 delegates for the Independent Peasants Confederation and 11 delegates for the left parties who had been most influential in the Commando Politico and the negotiations with Torres, but intra-left rivalries could not be cast aside and some left organisations were denied representation for purely factional reasons.

The meetings of the first session only lasted ten days but before dispersing the Assembly made arrangements for a second session in which more peasants would be represented. In the interim a number of permanent commissions were established and arrangements were made for setting up local Popular Assemblies in Bolivia's nine Departments. The latter, in fact, began to operate quite vigorously and to dispute the power of the Army's local commanders in a number of areas. The second session of the Assembly was to meet in September 1971, but well before this there were clear signs that the Army's right wing was preparing for a coup and was able to draw on substantial Brazilian help.

After months of coup rumours, and calls by Torres and the left for vigilance, the right moved decisively in mid-August 1971. One factor in their minds may have been the need to smash the regime before the reconvening of the Popular Assembly, scheduled for the first week of September. On 16 August the fiercely right-wing Bolivian Socialist Falange (FSB) called for a popular rising against the 'Communist danger', and the next day the Armed Forces, which had been in a state of alert from the beginning of the month, announced that they had caught a coup of conspirators at a secret meeting. On 19–20 August a full-scale rebellion broke out in Santa Cruz: the PSB and MNR mobilised demonstrators to demand the release of rightists imprisoned by the government, and the military there came out in open opposition to the regime in La Paz. Calling for a general uprising, the rightists in Santa Cruz proclaimed Colonel Hugo Banzer Suárez president. Other right-wing military groups rose in Oruro, a mining centre, and in Cochabamba. In La Paz Torres issued an appeal to the Armed Forces and the popular masses to defend the revolution. Miners from Siglo Veinte and Catavi were given arms and formed into a hastily set up popular militia.

The next day fighting switched to the capital, which then became the pivot of the struggle. Militia units composed of miners and students occupied strategic points in the city, and units of the pro-Torres Colorado Regiment, headed by Colonel Sanchez, besieged the Army HQ at Miraflores in the centre of town. The fiercest fighting took place on the Lakaicota ridge, which dominated the Miraflores district. Although the popular militia captured the ridge towards the end of the day, the Right launched a counter-attack after dusk: armoured cars of the Tarapacá Regiment were sent into the Miraflores district from hill positions outside the town, while units of the Lanzas Regiment, posted in the Guachi district outside La Paz, moved in as well, forming a pincer movement that drove the Colorados back into their barracks and relieved the pressure on Miraflores. With the rest of the country either in Banzer's hands, or passive, the Left and Torres were on the defensive. Surrounded, the Colorados were forced to surrender; armoured cars and infantry occupied the 14-storey student stronghold in the tower of San Andres university after planes had strafed student positions there. Torres fled to the Peruvian embassy, seeking asylum, and Banzer was proclaimed president. The only continuing resistance came from part of the university campus, where 300 students resisted for another twenty-four hours until bombed into submission.

The defeat of the guerrilla groups in Bolivia had shown the dangers of an armed force insufficiently embedded in the masses. The experience of the Popular Assembly illustrated the obverse problem. The Assembly was invested with an authentic mass character. It declared that socialist revolution was the order of the day and knew the masses would have to carry out this revolution themselves, rather than take the lead from any military clique. But moving from this understanding to the effective organisation of a popular uprising proved beyond the Assembly. Moreover, US and Brazilian involvement had played a significant part, with the Brazilians helping the rebels in Santa Cruz de la Sierra for nearly a month. At one point there had even been talk of Bolivia – or a chunk of it – becoming a Brazilian protectorate.

General Banzer held Bolivia in an iron grip, but after some years pressures began to mount and he was compelled to concede an election in 1978. Yet the instability remained and James Dunkerley effectively summarised the starkness of the situation:

Following the overthrow of Banzer, Bolivia plunged into political chaos. Between July 1978 and July 1980 two further general elections were staged, five presidents held office (none of them as a result of victory at the polls), and of the cluster of groups under almost constant preparation four were essayed in practice, one failing and three successful.[9]

9. Dunkerley, op. cit., Chapter 7, pp. 249–344.

There was a brief reprise of the old Left and the trade unions in 1982, but it led nowhere. In 1984, the American shock-therapist Jeffrey Sachs arrived in Bolivia and helped to inaugurate the great neo-liberal experiment. The country was raped by Capital:

> After seventeen years of financial orthodoxy, the neoliberal programme was increasingly seen as sheer plunder. Per capita income had not risen since 1986, and Bolivia had the second most unequal distribution of income in the continent – only Brazil was worse. The top 20 per cent of the population owned 30 times more than the bottom 20 per cent, and 60 per cent lived in poverty; in rural areas, the figure reached 90 per cent. The official unemployment rate had tripled, to 13.9 per cent, while the proportion of people working in the 'informal sector' had risen from 58 to 68 per cent in fifteen years. Infant mortality was 60 out of 1,000 births, and life expectancy was 63 years – compared to continent-wide averages of 28 per 1,000 and 70 years respectively. Infrastructure remained rudimentary in much of the countryside: over 70 per cent of roads were unpaved, and in rural areas only a quarter of households had electricity.[10]

And soon after the world turned upside down again. The United States won the Cold War. The Soviet Union and Eastern Europe fell. Capitalist-roaders triumphed in China and, utilising the state structures created by the revolution, embarked on a programme of capitalist modernisation that shook the world economy. Neo-liberalism/neo-conservatism backed by US military power became the new orthodoxy and Hayekian stalwarts of the Mont Pelerin society could justifiably celebrate the triumph of ideas they had first articulated in 1947, and which had been

---

10. Forrest Hylton and Sinclair Thomson, 'The Chequered Rainbow', *New Left Review*, 35, September–October 2005.

mocked (but clearly not to death) by Keynesians and ignored by socialists of every variety.[11]

All seemed lost. Trapped underneath the rubble of the New Order were the majority of Bolivians. They had always been poor, but in the past they could still hope. Now, it appeared, even that had been taken away. The de-industrialisation and privatisation of the continent – Brazil and Argentina were the worst affected – was pushed through with revolutionary speed throughout the Nineties. The old working-class parties and attached trade unions began to crumble. Either they pushed through neo-liberal programmes and accelerated their own decline or they simply gave up, with many left intellectuals, politicians and badly scarred proponents of the armed road making their peace with the New Order and, in many cases, displaying the ardour of converts in their defence of the WC and globalisation as the only way forward.

Even before he joined the hundred per cent pro-WC Fox government in Mexico as its Foreign Minister, Jorge Castañeda bluntly stated that 'the only thing left to fight for is a future that is simply the present, plus more of the same . . .' [12] A decade later it was obvious that a majority of South American citizens disagreed.

---

11. The Mont Pelerin Society was set up in April 1947 because, according to its founding document, 'the central values of civilization are in danger.' Its aims included:

    'The redefinition of the functions of the state so as to distinguish more clearly between the totalitarian and the liberal order. The possibility of establishing minimum standards by means not inimical to initiative and functioning of the market. Methods of combating the misuse of history for the furtherance of creeds hostile to liberty. The problem of the creation of an international order conducive to the safeguarding of peace and liberty and permitting the establishment of harmonious international economic relations.'

12. Jorge Castañeda's *Beyond Utopia: The State of the Left in Latin America*, 1994. Together with Roberto Unger and others, but well before Anthony (now Lord) Giddens, he began to search for a 'third way'.

The collapse of the traditional Left and nationalist currents in Bolivia that followed the fall of Communism was hardly a surprise. The MNR had deserted to the oligarchy a long time ago. The far left was fractured organisationally and ineffective ideologically. National politics had been reduced to determining which political party or oligarchic faction could best implement the policies of the Central Bank, the mechanism through which WC institutions controlled national economies. The same process was visible in most parts of the world; it spanned every continent. What could fill the vacuum? Who would take on the global corporations? Who would speak up against them?

Already in 1973, the Bolivian poet and novelist Jaime Saenz (1921–86), who spent his entire life in La Paz, had written of the helplessness that afflicted the city – and by extension the country:

> If you have nothing to eat but garbage, don't say a word.
> If the garbage makes you sick, don't say a word.
> If they cut off your feet, if they boil your hands, if your tongue rots, if your spine
> Splits in two, if your soul fines down to nothing, don't say a word.
> If they poison you, don't say a word, even if your bowels slide from your mouth
> And your hair stands straight up; even if your eyes well with blood, don't say a word.
> If you feel good, don't feel good. If you fall behind, don't fall behind. If you die,
> Don't die. If you're sad, don't be sad. Don't say a word . . .[13]

No single force was forthcoming, but gradually the interests of the deprived began to coalesce. They were going to speak many

---

13. Jaime Saenz, *Immanent Vistor: Selected Poems*, tr. Kent Johnson and Forrest Gander, Berkeley and Los Angeles, 2002.

words and if nobody listened they would do more. By the turn of
the millennium, the Andean struggles against privatisation (water
in Cochabamba, electricity in Cuzco) were far more advanced
than anywhere else in the world. La Guerra del Agua (the War
For Water) erupted after the killing of 17-year-old Victor Hugo
Daz, who was was shot dead by the Army in April 2000 for joining
a protest in Cochabamba against the increase in water rates. As his
body lay in the main square of the city, many wept as they saw the
bullet holes that had disfigured his face, but which could not hide
the nobility and innocence that lay underneath. Anguish turned to
anger. The government had declared martial law, but Cochabamba, suffering from chronic water shortages, would not be
silenced. A million people inhabited this old Andean town and
most of them appeared to be on the streets. The plaza where the
body of the slain youth lay was now occupied by demonstrators.
Their leaders had been arrested and taken to remote prisons in the
Amazon, but the movement carried on. A woman shouted: 'We
are the Amazon. They cannot stop our flow.' She was right. The
water warriors demanded the end of privatisation. The consor-
tium that controlled Bolivia's water was dominated by well-
known US companies, Bechtel and (prior to its demise) Enron.
They had made it illegal for the poor to collect rainwater, giving
the exclusive rights to do so to Bechtel's local proxy, Aguas del
Tunari. Now everyone – townspeople and farmers – was involved in this struggle; one of the most respected leaders was
Oscar Olivera, a cobbler. This was the democracy from below
that is feared by neo-liberal elites everywhere. Like the *Caracazo*
in Venezuela, the rebellion in Cochabamba marked the beginning
of the end for the political elite. Unlike the *Caracazo*, the people of
Cochabamba won a significant victory. Bechtel was run out of
town and the city government once again took charge of its water
supply, and a new water law prioritising the needs of the people
against the 'rights' of the corporations, a law 'written from below',
was passed. The armies of the people had defined their right to

water as a 'human right', lost their fear of authority and triumphed in the struggle against privatisation. Morales could not have won without the support of social movements of this type.

The political instincts and actions of the Bolivian and Peruvian rural and urban poor masses were decades ahead of the European or Japanese trade union movements, which had capitulated after defeats or often without waging a consistent struggle. The political mood in Bolivia was about to change. The Cochabamba effect and threats of more rebellions had stymied water and gas privatisations since the defeat of Bechtel. Now they would go one step further. They would aim for power. When I briefly met Evo Morales in Caracas in April 2003, he glowed with confidence. He explained calmly that the conditions in Bolivia were unacceptable to the majority of its citizens and predicted that something had to and would change. Since the people knew what they wanted it was the elite that would be forced to make massive concessions or be removed by a popular revolution. They would not do the former because the US embassy in La Paz, which more or less ran the whole show, had expressly forbidden any concessions. At this point Morales chuckled. His optimism was infectious.

In October 2003 the indigenous Aymara communities launched a mass movement, which soon enveloped the entire country. The cause of their anger was the decision by a WC favourite, President Gonzalo Sánchez de Lozada, to privatise the country's energy resources. Sánchez de Lozada responded to the mass protests in time-honoured WC fashion by unleashing a 'humanitarian war' against his own people just as Carlos Andrés Pérez had done in Caracas in 1989. Troops and tanks were deployed to defend Mont Pelerin values and crush the protests. Dozens of demonstrators were killed and hundreds injured.[14] It was a critical

---

14. According to Amnesty, the death toll stood at fifty-nine (http://web.amnesty.org/report2004/bol-summary-eng).

moment for both sides. The poor on the streets had wanted a
show of strength. Sánchez de Lozada (backed by the US embassy)
went for a test of strength. He won the skirmish, but lost the war.
The Opposition trebled in size and took to the streets. Once
again, fear was banished. Sánchez de Lozada fell. The noise was
heard all the way to Washington:

On October 17, dense crowds snaked their way through
downtown thoroughfares to take over the Plaza San Francisco
in the heart of La Paz, political capital of the Bolivian republic.
The marchers were members of popular neighborhood associations from El Alto, a city of more than 800,000 on the upper
rim of La Paz, of whom 74% claim indigenous Aymara
identity; members of the heavily Aymara hillside neighborhood associations of Munaypata, Villa Victoria, and Villa
Fátima; market-women belonging to urban guild associations;
students and unemployed youths; mine-workers from Huanu-
ni, an enclave south of the city of Oruro; coca growers and
peasant settlers from the subtropical Yungas valleys northeast
of La Paz; and members of Aymara peasant communities from
the high plateau, led by the insurgent district of Achacachi.
Their numbers ranged between 250,000 and 500,000, making
this Bolivia's largest demonstration since October 1982, when
opposition forces ended the long period of military dictatorship
(1964–1982), inaugurated the era of representative democracy,
and brought the Popular Democratic Unity (UDP), a centre-
left coalition government, to power.

This was unlike earlier crowds, however. In 1982, left
political parties and the still robust Bolivian Workers' Central
(COB) had organized the demonstrations expressing progressive 'national-popular' forces that united middle-class dissidents, including students, intellectuals, and professionals, as
well as workers from urban and mining centers, and peasants.
In 2003, neither the opposition parties nor the trade unions

headed the multitudinous assembly or provided comparable
political representation during the uprising that had led to it.
The turnout of progressive students, intellectuals, and professionals from the mestizo and creole middle classes was low,
while the ranks of urban and rural laborers of Aymara descent
swelled downtown streets.

The distinguishing features of the massive urban protest
on October 17 – the self-organization of those who took
over the capital and their largely indigenous profile –
reflected the overall insurrectionary dynamic that brought
about the downfall of President Sánchez de Lozada that same
day. In important respects, this was a leaderless Aymara
uprising rooted in a history of communal Indian struggle
dating back over two centuries to the time of the great
Andean revolution of 1780–81. Yet despite the differences
between 1982 and 2003, there were also important resem-
blances between the 'Days of October' and previous popular
uprisings and revolutionary processes in modern Bolivian
history . . . They shared a central agenda of sweeping away
an unrepresentative and repressive political regime, establishing sovereign control over national resources, and convok-
ing a constitutional assembly to restructure national political
and economic life.[15]

A week later, on 25 October, Evo Morales flew to Mexico City
to attend a conference of left intellectuals and activists and explain
what had taken place. He spoke of the failure of capitalism to meet
the needs of the poor, of imperial brutality which encouraged its
satraps to employ force to crush those opposed to its policies, and

---

15. Forrest Hylton and Sinclair Thomson, *Revolutionary Horizons: Past and Present
in Bolivian Politics*, London and New York, 2007. See also Forrest Hylton's
evocative account of the Morales triumph in 'The Landslide in Bolivia', *New
Left Review*, 37, January–February 2006, pp. 69–72.

he demanded new institutions that could represent and reflect the needs of the majority.[16]

Two years on, in the Bolivian general election of December 2005, Evo Morales and his comrade Álvaro Garcia Linera, a leading Marxist intellectual, were elected as President and Vice President of Bolivia respectively; their party, the Movement Toward Socialism (MAS) won a clear majority of seats in the Chamber of Deputies. Morales' first public act after his victory was to fly to Havana where he was awarded a hero's welcome, followed by a lengthy tutorial with Fidel Castro on power. On his way back he made another stopover: Caracas. Here, too, an overjoyed Hugo Chávez warmly received him. There were now three governments in the continent committed to the idea of a Bolivarian Federation.

During his first hundred days in office, Morales pledged that the new government would not betray its supporters and would take control of the country's energy resources to help fund its social development. Squeals of rage were heard in Washington and several EU capitals. The WC does not look kindly on such radicalism, and treats as pariah states movements that are foolish enough to promise serious social reforms to help the poor and then attempt to carry out their programme when elected. This is not what democracy is supposed to be about these days. 'Why can't Morales be more like Lula?' became a popular refrain in the transatlantic media. In the early years of the last century, unions created by the bosses became known as company unions. In the twenty-first century mainstream political parties have become increasingly corporatised and company journalism has become the norm. 'Evo Morales tilts towards Chavismo' was the worried headline in the *Financial Times* as it became obvious that Morales was determined to implement his programme.

16. For complete text of speech, see Appendix Five.

The Bolivian peasants and semi-employed urban dwellers have become, not for the first time, protagonists in the history of their country and their class. The convocation of an elected Constituent Assembly to decide on a new constitution offers them the possibility of retaining control of their own and their children's future. Their leaders know full well that the stakes are high, that brute force might be used against them; more importantly, they are aware that they are linked objectively to the rest of the continent and politically to the Bolivarians and the Cubans. This can only strengthen the project as a whole.

As in the case of Venezuela, what is being proposed in Bolivia is not a Cuban-style revolution, but a form of radical social democracy that is today unacceptable to the WC and its institutions; however, to succeed the reforms must be structural and built into the new system. What Castro, Chávez and Morales have understood is that strength lies in unity. That is why the talk of a Bolivarian Federation that can defend the common interests of Latin America is not rhetoric or bluster. It is an attempt to realise Bolívar's dream of a unified South America in today's conditions. Interestingly, it is the end of the Cold War and the establishment of a rigid and fundamentalist WC that has created the objective conditions for a regional unity to defend South American interests against the North. The victory in Bolivia has strengthened the anti-imperialist bloc. The WC won in neighbouring Peru, but even here the story is far from over. Structural changes in Bolivia will impact on the general consciousness on the other side of Lake Titicaca. All Andean paths that divert from the neo-liberal motorway will be worth exploring. There is a long way to go in Bolivia itself. Evo Morales and his comrades won the argument and the Presidency but the elite, unlike its Venezuelan cousins, does not yet feel demoralised and crushed. The Creoles in Santa Cruz dream of a US-backed counter-thrust and a possible 'independence'. Santa Cruz is the only Department that the MAS did not win — though even here they obtained 33 per cent of the vote against 42 per cent won by the right. It is vital that the elites are skilfully detached from their base by a set of inclusive measures that benefit the bulk of the population. Important political battles lie ahead.

Chapter 5

The Old Man and the Revolution: Notes From a Havana Diary

When I see and touch myself,
I, Juan with Nothing only yesterday,
and Juan with Everything today,
and today with everything,
I turn my eyes and look,
I see and touch myself,
and ask myself, how this could have been.

I have, let's see,
I have the pleasure of going about my country,
owner of all there is in it,
looking closely at what
I did not or could not have before.
I can say cane,
I can say mountain,
I can say city,
say army,
now forever mine and yours, ours,
and the vast splendor of
the sunbeam, star, flower.

I have, let's see,
I have the pleasure of going,
me, a farmer, a worker, a simple man,
I have the pleasure of going
(just an example)

to a bank and speak to the manager,
not in English,
not in 'Sir,' But in compañero as we say in Spanish.
I have, let's see,
that being Black
no one can stop me at the door of a dance hall or bar.
Or even on the rug of a hotel
scream at me that there are no rooms,
a small room and not a colossal one,
a tiny room where I can rest.

I have, let's see,
that there are no rural police
to seize me and lock me in a precinct jail,
or tear me from my land and cast me
in the middle of the highway.

I have that having the land I have the sea,
no country clubs,
no high life,
no tennis and no yachts,
but, from beach to beach and wave on wave,
gigantic blue open democratic:
in short, the sea.

I have, let's see,
that I have learned to read,
to count,
I have that I have learned to write,
and to think,
and to laugh.
I have . . . that now I have
a place to work
and earn
what I have to eat.
I have, let's see,
I have what I had to have.

Nicolás Guillén (1902–89), 'I Have' (1964)

25 November 2005

The first thing one notices on arriving in Havana from almost anywhere in the world today is the absence of ugly skyscrapers and giant billboards advertising global products. This is pleasing. Whatever happens in the future, I hope the Malecon isn't wrecked by the global coastal architecture that masquerades as modernity in so many parts of the world, not least South America. On the long flight from London, I had finished reading Richard Gott's stirring and educative new history of Cuba. It had revived many memories, but also raised some uncomfortable questions.[1] It is my first trip to the island, a fact that surprises many people, including myself.

Despite all the attempts by the US Empire and its newfound allies in Eastern Europe to suffocate Cuba, it is still here and that is also pleasing. Not because it is a perfect state or a paradise or anything remotely resembling that, but because despite everything it is better than what would replace it if Miami moved back to Havana. We know because we have been here before and even Hollywood issued a health warning: Francis Ford Coppola provided us with a few memories in *Godfather Two*: images of 1959 Havana as a Mafia-infested brothel and the Mafia bosses

---

1. Richard Gott, *Cuba: A New History*, New Haven and London, 2004.

fleeing the country with Fulgencio Batista as the revolution moves ever closer to the capital. Their heirs will be back if Cuba falls. And that would be a tragedy for most Cubans.

The legitimacy of the regime still derives from that Revolution, among the single most important events of the twentieth century for Latin Americans of every hue. It affected the politics of both Right and Left in North and South America. Questions are still asked about whether disaffected Cuban exiles might have been involved in Kennedy's assassination. After the Bay of Pigs disaster he had refused to authorise a full-scale assault. And every US President since has been careful to continue the blockade of the island, and staid histories of relations between the North American giant and its tiny opponent record every year that 'US-Cuban relations continued to deteriorate during . . .' One could fill in the blank with every year following 1959.

Cuba's revolution affected every left current in the continent, and thinking back one is reminded of the impact it had on Salvador Allende's socialism, the openness with which he spoke of it with one of his interlocutors: his meeting with Guevara was particularly poignant. How could they have known that soon, within years of each other, each of them would be executed by officers acting on imperial instructions, and mourned on more than one continent:

> *Debray:* Comrade President, you were one of the first politicians to arrive in Cuba after the victory?
> *Allende:* . . . Yes . . . I arrived, and there was Che . . . he was lying in the hammock, stripped to the waist and when I arrived he was having a violent attack of asthma. He was using an inhaler, and waiting for him to recover, I sat down on the bed and said to him: 'Commandante', but he broke me off, saying: 'Look, Allende, I know perfectly well who you are. I heard two of your speeches during the '52 presidential campaign; one very good, and the other very bad. So we can talk in complete confidence, because I have a very clear opinion of who you

are' . . . we had dinner, and then we went into a room with
Fidel to talk. There were peasants playing chess and cards,
lying on the floor, machine guns and all . . .

Debray: You were talking about Fidel. How did the two of you
become friends?

Allende: In fact, from the first moment. I was impressed by his
immense intelligence – an incredible phenomenon that sweeps all
before it like a sort of human cataract – and by his candour . . .

Debray: Differences of opinion?

Allende: Yes, fundamental and violent ones.

Debray: But always frank.

Allende: Always.

Debray: How did Fidel react when he heard of the victory of
Popular Unity in Chile?

Allende: He sent me a copy of *Granma*, the official organ of the
Cuban revolution, which had the news of our electoral victory
splashed across the front page. He had been at the offices of the
newspaper waiting for the news from Chile, and he sent his
congratulations on the front page proclaiming that ours was a
victory against imperialism, signed it and had it signed by
everyone around him. I keep it as a souvenir.[2]

Castro and Guevara had come after Zapata and Villa in
historical time and for that reason their impact was greater on
the continent as a whole though, through no fault of their own,
never reaching the epic grandeur of Bolívar and San Martín. Fidel
and Che had wanted to scale such heights and both men dreamed
continents (Castro still does), but the empire they fought in the
last century was on the rise, unlike decrepit old Spain.[3] The

---

2. Regis Debray, *Conversations with Allende*, New Left Books, 1971.
3. As Bolívar wrote in a letter to a Spanish Governor rejecting further negotiations: '. . . it is the height of nonsense and absurdity to suggest that Colombia
should submit to Spain, always the worst governed of all countries, and now the
laughing stock of Europe and the horror of America . . .'

twenty-first century might, however, be different. It has begun
well in South America. The change in Caracas has brought badly
needed relief and the Old Man is known to become irritable when
yet another visiting foreign journalist springs the cliché: 'After
Fidel, who?' Now he replies: 'After Fidel, Chávez and after
Chávez, Morales and after Morales, our continent will throw up
others who will take over the revolutionary baton.'

From the beginning of the Revolution, its leaders emphasised
the continental aspect of the struggle. There was a real charge
when one read the Second Declaration of Havana (1962), an
angry call to arms that still resonates:

> What is Cuba's history but that of Latin America? What is the
> history of Latin America but the history of Asia, Africa, and
> Oceania? And what is the history of all these peoples but the
> history of the cruelest exploitation of the world by imperialism?
>
> At the end of the last century and the beginning of the
> present, a handful of economically developed nations had
> divided the world among themselves, subjecting two thirds
> of humanity to their economic and political domination.
> Humanity was forced to work for the dominating classes of
> the group of nations which had a developed capitalist econ-
> omy.
>
> The historic circumstances which permitted certain Eur-
> opean countries and the United States of North America to
> attain a high industrial development level put them in a
> position which enabled them to subject and exploit the rest
> of the world.
>
> What motives lay behind this expansion of the industrial
> powers? Were they moral, 'civilizing' reasons, as they
> claimed? No. Their motives were economic.
>
> The discovery of America sent the European conquerors
> across the seas to occupy and to exploit the lands and peoples of
> other continents; the lust for riches was the basic motivation for

their conduct. America's discovery took place in the search for shorter ways to the Orient, whose products Europe valued highly. A new social class, the merchants and the producers of articles manufactured for commerce, arose from the feudal society of lords and serfs in the latter part of the Middle Ages.

The lust for gold promoted the efforts of the new class. The lust for profit was the incentive of their behavior throughout its history. As industry and trade developed, the social influence of the new class grew. The new productive forces maturing in the midst of the feudal society increasingly clashed with feudalism and its serfdom, its laws, its institutions, its philosophy, its morals, its art, and its political ideology . . .

Since the end of the Second World War, the Latin American nations are becoming pauperized constantly. The value of their capita income falls. The dreadful per centages of child mortality do not decrease, the number of illiterates grows higher, the peoples lack employment, land, adequate housing, schools, hospitals, communication systems and the means of subsistence. On the other hand, North America investments exceed 10 billion dollars. Latin America, moreover, supplies cheap raw materials and pays high prices for manufactured articles. Like the first Spanish conquerors, who exchanged mirrors and trinkets with the Indians for silver and gold, so the United States trades with Latin America. To hold on to this torrent of wealth, to take greater possession of America's resources and to exploit its long-suffering peoples: this is what is hidden behind the military pacts, the military missions and Washington's diplomatic lobbying . . .

Wherever roads are closed to the peoples, where repression of workers and peasants is fierce, where the domination of Yankee monopolies is strongest, the first and most important lesson is to understand that it is neither just nor correct to divert the peoples with the vain and fanciful illusion that the dominant classes can be uprooted by legal means which do not and will not exist. The ruling classes are entrenched in all positions of state power. They monopolize the teaching field. They dominate all means of mass communication. They have infinite financial resources. Theirs is a power which the monopolies and the ruling few will defend by blood and fire with the strength of their police and their armies . . .[4]

Slightly different from the blandness of 'another world is possible', a slogan that has become too much of a cliché and is especially irritating when mouthed by 'NGO' bureaucrats who desire to change very little, excepting their apartments.

The real question is 'After Fidel, what?' Or to put it another way: is the Bolivarian victory in Venezuela simply having a viagra-effect on an ageing Cuban Revolution or might it help repair and build on the existing foundations so that the voluntarist appeals can be transcended and new institutions developed to take the process forward? The more I travel and the more people I meet, the more strongly I feel that this Cuba must not be left to the tender mercies of the demolition squads waiting patiently in Miami. That would be a defeat for the entire continent. Miami may not be the same as it was a few decades ago, containing as it does many economic migrants from Cuba, but nests of Cuban fascists are still active. It is not a word I apply loosely, but how else to categorise the radio hosts who spread hatred? In 1994, a discussion on one of these shows elicited the following comments on the topic, 'What to do with the leftover Communists' after the triumph of the market. The replies from callers included remarks such as 'burn them alive' and 'open the incinerators and throw them all in – men, women and children.' The enlightened compere thanked them politely for their contributions.[5]

4. Fidel Castro, *The Second Declaration of Havana*, London and New York, 1994.
5. Ann Louise Bardach, *Cuba Confidential*, New York, 2002. Bardach is a critic of Fidel Castro, which gives her account of the old gangs in Miami a certain objectivity.

28 November 2005

My host is the Cuban Book Institute and, apart from a lecture in
the Great Hall of the University of Havana, I have been invited to
participate in a public tribute to Jean-Paul Sartre, who visited
Havana forty-five years ago. To commemorate the event, the
Institute has just reprinted *Nausea* and there is a moving exhibi-
tion of 1960 photographs of Sartre and Simone de Beauvoir during
their visit. They spent a month here and I have rarely seen that
couple looking so happy in photographs. They appear relaxed,
their faces soft and joyful. A few *mojitos* with Fidel Castro and
Che Guevara (who also seem very cheerful) appear to have
worked wonders. But it is a revolutionary excitement on Sartre's
face that shines through the photographs. Back in Paris, he writes:

> What surprises me here is that the troubles began so abruptly.
> Nothing announced them, not the slightest visible catastrophe.
> Four years earlier a coup d'état had brought Batista to power.
> Few people had protested – they were resigned to the dictator-
> ship by disgust with their prattling and corrupt assemblies.
>
> One day, all the same, July 26, 1953, a young lawyer, Fidel
> Castro, launched an attack on the Moncada barracks with a
> handful of comrades. But he was taken, imprisoned, con-
> demned. Public opinion did not give him much support.
> 'Who is this blusterer? There's an escapade for you! And
> which leads to nothing. If Batista were angry he would have
> taken it out on us!'
>
> The opposition parties were quick to blame this rash man
> who had failed. The Cuban Communist Party spoke of
> adventurism. The Authentic Party threw up their hands; the
> Orthodox Party was more severe. Castro was a member of it
> when he attempted his coup.
>
> 'We need a left wing,' said all these mature and reflective
> men. 'It carries the hopes of the country. On his side, by

demagoguery, in order to persuade America that there is freedom of opinion in Cuba, the President tolerates it on condition that it doesn't so much as raise a little finger. Very well! Let's do nothing except be here. Time is working for us! But we don't need an irresponsible kid to risk breaking this equilibrium by an escapade . . .'

The Cuban masters of the island, lazy and morose tyrants, were suspicious of knowledge because it led to subversion. The shabby state of higher education was premeditated. To protect the underdevelopment of the Cuban economy, they tried to produce in Cuba only underdeveloped men . . .[6]

Later in 1971, like García Márquez and others, he would get angry about the treatment accorded to a homosexual poet, Herberto Padilla, and signed an open letter, but the signatories would later divide further into those who remained supportive but critical, and those who were already on the move to staler pastures and used Padilla as 'the last straw'.[7] There were to be other 'last

---

6. Jean-Paul Sartre, *Sartre on Cuba*, London, 1961.
7. Alain Jouffroy, Alberto Moravia, Andre Pieyre de Mandiargues, Carlos Franqui, Carlos Fuentes, Claude Roy, Dionys Mascolo, Francisco Rosi, Gabriel García Márquez, Hans Magnus Enzensberger, Italo Calvino, Jean Daniel, Jean-Paul Sartre, Jorge Semprún, José Maria Castellet, Juan Goytisolo, Julio Cortázar, Luis Goytisolo, Marguerite Duras, Mario Vargas Llosa, Maurice Nadeau, Octavio Paz, Rossana Rossanda, Simone de Beauvoir, 'An Open Letter to Fidel Castro': 'Herberto Padilla, one of Cuba's leading poets, was arrested and imprisoned in Havana on March 20. No details have yet been made public of the charges against him. The following open letter to Fidel Castro from prominent European and Latin American writers was published in *Le Monde* on April 9 1971. The undersigned, supporters of the principles and objectives of the Cuban Revolution, address you in order to express their disquiet as a result of the imprisonment of the poet and writer Herberto Padilla and to ask you to re-examine the situation which this arrest has created.

Since the Cuban government up to the present time has yet to supply any information about this arrest, we fear the re-emergence of a sectarian tendency stronger and more dangerous than that which you denounced in March, 1962, and to which Major Che Guevara alluded on several occasions when he denounced the suppression of the right of criticism within the ranks of the revolution.

straws' in the years to come. As Stendhal recounts in his memoirs, in post-revolutionary France (but after the Restoration) some recanted by burning their copies of Rousseau and Voltaire (perhaps they never got as far as Holbach and Diderot). In Latin America, all that was required to impress Washington was a public denunciation of Cuba as an evil, authoritarian dictatorship. This was the first hurdle, after which tickets to a different future became freely available.

Some of us who were or are critical did not feel any urgent need to desert the Revolution. It is important to restate this in a 'human rights' dominated world – as if 'rights' were an anthropological rather than a juridicial norm – in which a majority of human needs are ignored.[8] One such 'human right' as stipulated by the US in its notorious ultimatum at Rambouillet (which paved the way for NATO's assault on Yugoslavia) was 'that Kosovo must have a market economy'. And when the West blithely disregards the rights of others because it is inconvenient – the US and Britain in Guantanamo, Abu Ghraib, Falluja, Basra, Haditha; Israel in its own country as well as occupied Palestine and

---

7. 'At this moment – when the installation of a socialist government in Chile and the new situation in Peru and Bolivia help make it possible to break the criminal blockade imposed on Cuba by North American imperialism – the use of repressive measures against intellectuals and writers who have exercised the right of criticism within the revolution can only have deeply negative repercussions among the anti-imperialist forces of the entire world, and most especially of Latin America, for which the Cuban Revolution is a symbol and a banner. In thanking you for the attention you may give to this request, we reaffirm our solidarity with the principles which guided the struggle in the Sierra Maestra and which the revolutionary government of Cuba has expressed so many times in the words and actions of its Prime Minister, of Major Che Guevara, and of so many other revolutionary leaders.' *New York Review of Books*, 6 May 1971.

8. And lest this is misinterpreted by the enemies of light, let me make it clear that the basic human needs – shelter, food, education, health – also include the human need of expressing an opinion in public. This is a relatively recent addition, a result of the Enlightenment and the French Revolution, but it is a need.

Lebanon; France in Haiti and its colonial possessions in Africa – the human rights industry is, naturally, sympathetic to their collective dilemma. The hastily appointed professors attached to US campuses in this new industry have a great deal to say in defence of 'humanitarian wars', but little about the horrendous violations of existing laws by those whose largesse led to their appointments in the first place.

30 November 2005

An informal meeting with Cuban writers and intellectuals at the Casas de las Américas. A few familiar faces are present, including Lisandro Otero – whose novel *The Situation* is an incredibly strong evocation of the torpor that gripped bourgeois society in pre-revolutionary Cuba. Lisandro has just returned from exile in Mexico City and Fernando Martínez, a gifted veteran of the Revolution and an old comrade who once edited *Pensamienta Crítico* ('Critical Thought') in the Sixties, probably the most intelligent political magazine in the Americas, which was 'discontinued' in the early Seventies for attempting to live up to its name. The result was a monochrome media, little different from its counterparts in Moscow or East Berlin: predictable, dull, dreary, dry and dead. This was one of the tragedies of this Revolution. Before we exchange memories I am asked by a sprightly white-haired woman to explain 'your attitude to our revolution'. I reply:

> It was our revolution, too. We grew up together. My generation fell in love with the Cuban Revolution. It was the lyrical element that appealed to us. The element that conditions the psychology and morals of any society. We read your books, those amazing posters you produced were up on our walls, we reprinted speeches of Fidel and Che in our magazines, we defended you against dogmatic Marxists who didn't believe you had made a revolution and against the liberals who believed you

had . . . and because we loved you we trusted you. Then you betrayed us by going to bed with a fat, ugly, bureaucrat named Brezhnev and you defended the Warsaw Pact invasion of Czechoslovakia and this turn affected your culture and the lyrical element almost disappeared and so we had to separate.

There were a few sad smiles and then silence, till my inter-locutor spoke again:

'And now?'

'Now,' I replied. 'We are both old. We need each other. It's love in the time of cholera.'

After this the discussion became animated. Questions were asked about the *New Left Review* and two women present who had known one of my colleagues when he had spent a year in Cuba in 1962 wanted a theoretical explanation as to why his hair had turned white when he was still a twenty-something. I have a number of theories on this, but resisted the temptation.

The colleague they were referring to was Robin Blackburn and it was appropriate in the circumstances. Political affinities are often the basis of long friendships. I had read Blackburn's seminal essay on Cuba in the *New Left Review* some weeks after arriving in Britain in 1963, and a few years before I met him for the first time. He had started off modestly:

Like other great revolutions, Cuba's is a proclamation that man can make his own history. But this history can only be made within certain material and social conditions. This essay will study these. At this stage, any attempt will inevitably suffer from many limitations and failings. But with this reservation, a historical and theoretical analysis is possible. This essay will, it is hoped, contribute towards one.[9]

9. Robin Blackburn, 'Prologue to the Cuban Revolution', *New Left Review*, 21, October 1963.

He then proceeded to explain the specific circumstances that had delayed the independence of Cuba in the nineteenth century, compared to Venezuela and Bolivia, and suggested that the reason the Creole elite was not too keen to get rid of the Spaniards was because of race more than class: 'The white population was outnumbered by the black: 291,021 to 339,959 by the census of 1817. By comparison, only 2 per cent of the population of mainland Spanish America was African in origin at this date; there were fewer negroes in all the mainland colonies of Spain put together than in Cuba.'

In the West, the dominant postmodernist trends virtually exiled history so that it became an unpopular academic discipline and needed constant revision to cater to present-day needs. Citizens who felt the urge could always watch a circus of television historians prancing round the globe and, in most cases, providing a simpleton's view of world history. Cuba overflows with history. Its own and that of the rest of South America. José Martí and Simón Bolívar are points of reference for everyone but the future of the island is uppermost in many people's minds. The worst may be over, but the 'special period in peacetime', a euphemism for the privations the Cubans had to endure after 1990, has left many traumatised. During a dinner with friends we discuss frankly the mistakes that have been made and the future.

If, three or four decades ago, I say to them, any voice had prophesied that by the turn of the next century, the USSR will have collapsed, capitalism will have taken China and Vietnam and you too, dear Cuban comrades, will have to re-examine the principles for which you fought and made your revolution, it would have been drowned in hoots of derisive laughter. On this we could agree and then we talked of bad times.

All were agreed that 'the special period in peacetime' that followed the restoration of capitalism in Russia was the worst period in Cuban history. Dependent on cheap oil from the Soviet Union, the economy collapsed when the Russians demanded payment in dollars and the Cubans responded: can't pay, won't pay. Despite everything there were no famines (as in North Korea) or mass unemployment (as in Eastern Germany), but there were some in leading positions who had become so used over the years to following the Moscow line that they were quite prepared to follow the Russian and Eastern European examples, become the new entrepreneurs by buying state assets they supervised and amassing private fortunes. For some, the logic was simple: Let's Miamise ourselves to keep Miami out. They even forgot capital's laws of motion, imagining they could deal with their Cuban-American cousins as equals. It was not to be. And it is hardly a secret in Havana that it was the Old Man who stood up and refused to surrender any of the basic gains of the Revolution, insisting that what had been achieved was incompatible with what was being demanded by global capitalism. He won. The 'international community' responded by continuing to punish the country.[10]

In 1993, the Cuba Lobby in the United States (otherwise the Cuban-American Foundation) believed that this was the time to tighten the noose and bring about regime change in Cuba. They went on the offensive, with the full backing of President Clinton, then in need of cash and support for his re-election campaign. Clinton obliged the hard-liners in the Cuban exile fraternity as the *Miami Herald* triumphantly explained:

10. The hypocrisy of the EU on 'human rights' is particularly instructive in this regard since the only torture in Cuba takes place in Guantanamo without anyone suggesting any sanctions whatsoever; and there are only a handful of political prisoners in the country, compared to Egypt, for example. EU member states are happy to comply with 'rendition' requests from Washington. And torture has been carried out in some US satellite states in Eastern Europe, where leading politicians, Vaclav Havel and Adam Michnik, totally supported the war in Iraq. 'Human rights' torture is acceptable as long as it is carried out to maim and punish those who abuse human rights, like the men and women in the prisons of Occupied Iraq and the citizens of Falluja and Haditha.

The decision to punish Castro directly – by cutting off the flow
of dollars brought in by families and by limiting the number of
charter flights, among other steps – came straight from
Clinton. Indeed the president all but discarded a set of milder
options prepared by his advisers in favour of a tougher plan
advocated by many exile hard-liners, including Jorge Más
Canosa. That decision was taken at a late-night White House
meeting attended by several Cuban-American leaders in Miami. When one remarked how impressed they were with
Clinton's understanding of the entire situation, he explained
he had been engaged in a personal, concerted study of Cuba
and the exile community since 1990. During visits to South
Florida, the Arkansas governor – guided by his Cuban-exile
sister-in-law – would walk the streets of Little Havana . . .
Clinton did more to squeeze the Cuban dictator in a few days
than either Republican [President] accomplished during the
1980s.[11]

1 December 2005

I have always been allergic to heritage culture and Potemkin
villages. So when I was shown a tiny garden in downtown
Havana dedicated to the late Princess Diana, I was taken aback
by the surreality of it all. I was also curious. Why in Havana?
Simply a desire to appear normal by infecting themselves with the
celebrity disease, or had the Princess turned on the Old Man? My
guide smiled, but did not venture an explanation. All he said was:
'So I suppose you don't want to see the statue the Church here
built to commemorate Mother Teresa?'. He was lucky I wasn't
driving. It was true that the Albanian nun had been a dear friend
of the Duvaliers, *père et fils*, in neighbouring Haiti, but even Baby

Doc, when in power, had honoured her with a medal, not graced her with a statue.

As a result I was slightly apprehensive when invited to visit a brand new showpiece university. Might this not be a Potemkin village? Here I was in a total minority. Everybody, including the cynical, insisted I had to go and see it for myself. I did. The site was about fifteen miles outside Havana on the road to Pinar del Rio, which I'd already visited, sampling the delights of Cuban eco-tourism. Driving out of the city again, it was difficult not to compare Cuba with its sister Caribbean islands and poor countries in other parts of the world. Despite all the problems, the progress made is visible and nowhere more so than in this remarkable IT university – designed as a modest leap forward to bridge 'the digital divide' between South and North.

We entered the long driveway and the sculptures came into view; later I saw the giant murals on the walls. The aim is to create an environment in which the appreciation of art in the real world encourages creativity in its virtual counterpart. Sighting some of the older buildings on the campus, I wondered aloud whether it might not have been possible to find a better architect. I was told with a smile that the eyesore was military in origin. The university had once been the location of the largest Soviet surveillance centre in the Americas. 'From here,' they said, 'the Russians could observe the US President travelling every-where in his own country and listen in to the conversations that took place between him and his entourage.' The facility had been kept on after the Soviet collapse, with the Cubans now insisting (as the Russians had done in relation to oil) on a high rent payable only in dollars. On a visit to the island in 2000, the Russian President had pledged a long lease on the base, but following 9/11, the US had pressured Moscow to close down the station and Putin had agreed, probably in return for some trade-offs in Chechnya and elsewhere. Whether he got what he was promised, the consequences for Cuba have certainly been beneficial.

The UCI (Universidad de las Ciencias Informáticas) – 7,000 students, half of whom are women, and a staff consisting of 250 Professors – is ringed by a multi gigabit fibre-optic spine that provides high-speed capacity to the entire campus. The aim is to create a layer of software innovators and facilities that could service the whole of Latin America. What they have achieved in medicine is about to be replicated in information technology. 'In connecting to the future we are ensuring the future of the Revolution'. I made this note in my diary, but without specifying whether someone had said this to me or if it was a slogan on a wall. In either case it's a nice thought. GNU/Linux is the favoured system, which reminds me of Richard Stallman, a free software guru, who I last met in Caracas several months ago. He was in Venezuela to help Linux the country and had spoken of doing the same in Cuba. 'And China?' I asked. 'Oh,' he said, 'they invited me to Beijing and I told them what we could do. They got quite excited but when I insisted that the GNU/Linux system was free and that they could not charge users, negotiations came to a rapid conclusion. They were just not interested.' All the computers at UCI, however, were free and had been gifted to the Cubans by China.

Survival had necessitated some important concessions and opening up the country to the global tourist industry had generated much needed foreign exchange, but with this an older trade had been revived: pimps and prostitutes appeared on the scene in large numbers for the first time since the Revolution. It had been much worse five years ago and conditions were definitely improving. Everyone said that, including the critics based in the United States.

By pure coincidence, some weeks prior to this trip, I had been in Pakistan when the massive earthquake had struck and the figures released after the first week (which later turned out to be an underestimate) had indicated the scale of the catastrophe: 50,000 dead, 74,000 injured and at least 3.3 million – far more than after the tsunami – left homeless, virtually all of them in the mountains, where snow begins to fall in November. In Islamabad a relief worker told me that 'there is a stench of rotting corpses everywhere. In their midst survivors are searching for food. Local people say that 50,000 have died in this town alone. And more will follow if medicines and food are not equitably distributed.'

The President of Pakistan had appeared on state television bemoaning the shortage of helicopters to carry food and supplies. In neighbouring Afghanistan, where there is a glut of helicopters, NATO has been reluctant to release too many from the war zone despite the advice of Robert Kaplan in the *International Herald Tribune*, who had this to say about benevolent US–NATO rescue missions:

> The distinctions between war and relief, between domestic and foreign deployments, are breaking down . . . hunting down Al Qaeda in its lair will be impossible without the goodwill of the local population. That attitude can be generated by relief work of the kind taking place in Kashmir. It's the classic counter-insurgency model: Winning without firing a shot.

But what about the doctors? By the time I had left Pakistan the Cubans had despatched over a thousand doctors, half of them women, which was more than all those despatched by the 'international community'. The Cubans came with their field hospitals and medicines. The women doctors were immediately permitted to treat the peasant women and conversations between the Cubans and the locals, conducted no doubt through interpreters working for the local intelligence agencies, could sometimes take on a surreal air.

> 'Where are you from?'
> 'Cuba.'
> 'Where is that?'

> The Cuban explained the location of the island.
> 'So you've come a long way. Who is your leader?'
> 'Fidel Castro.'
> 'Never heard of him.'
> 'Would you like to see a photograph?'
> It's shown and the beard is greatly admired.
> 'He could be from near here. They have beards like that in a village twenty miles from here.'

In Havana, I was told that some of the doctors had been shaken by the levels of poverty they had observed in the mountain regions of my country. The experience was educative for both sides. Peruvian and Bolivian peasants would have been more familiar with Pakistani conditions. The doctors have long since returned and whether the villagers who survived are still receiving medical care is an open question.

Cuban medicine is the envy of most continents now and the best advertisement for what can be achieved under different social conditions. There are 69,000 doctors in Cuba, tending a population of 12 million. The Latin American School of Medicine (ELAM) established in 1999 is situated in a stunning location on the sea, unsurprising since this was a former training facility for naval cadets. This medical university – there are twenty-one others on the island – is for foreign students only. It takes several thousand students from every Latin American country and from some countries in Africa and Asia. I asked for the actual figures and they were supplied. There are 12,000 students from 83 countries studying medicine in Cuba, including South America (5,500), Central America (3,244), Mexico (489), the United States (65) and Puerto Rico (2). The Caribbean, with 1,039 students, and sub-Saharan Africa (777) are also represented, while 42 students come from Northern Africa and the Middle East, 261 from Asia (200 East Timorese had registered in 2005) and two from Europe. And, as we have seen, Cuban medicine is a notable export: in

Venezuela, 17,000 medical students are trained by Cuban doctors, while some 2,000 Cuban doctors work throughout Africa.

I spoke with some students from the Dominican Republic, all of whom were from poor families just like their Afro-American and Hispanic peers from the United States. Earlier that year the first 1,600 doctors had graduated from a six-year course, including Cedric Edwards from New Orleans. I read an interview with him in which he spoke of how he 'loved the fact that regardless of a person's economic situation, he or she can see a doctor and get preventive care, free of charge', and how his studies, like those of his fellow students from Latin America and the Caribbean, were completely free; his modest room-and-board, textbooks and tuition were all paid for by the Cuban state. General Colin Powell, the former US Secretary of State, aware of the economic plight of Afro-American kids at home, had ensured that when the Bush administration intensified its anti-Cuba policies in 2004, an exception clause was written in to the economic blockade and travel ban. The 76 young people from the United States studying medicine at ELAM could continue to do so, as could future students. The Cubans refer to the university graduates of their country as 'human capital'. Out of a population of 12 million, between 800,000–1 million graduates are produced by Cuban universities every year. What would happen to all this if Miami returned?

'So this is your answer to the School of the Americas,' I muttered to a young Cuban functionary as we left the university. He smiled, but I wasn't totally confident that he had understood the reference. I explained. The School of the Americas was a torture school in Panama, later shifted to Fort Benning in Georgia. Here US instructors, some of them veterans from imperial wars in Korea and Vietnam, educated Latin American policemen and intelligence agents in the most effective forms of torture. And, one has to admit, the education they received was on a high level. The graduates went on to demonstrate their skills in Brazil, Argentina, Chile, Uruguay and Central America. Torture has always been an integral part of imperial rule, which is why the expression of liberal surprise at revelations of torture in Guantanamo or Abu Ghraib or Pulcharkhi (Kabul), is somewhat perplexing and I was pleased to read that others are equally mystified by the collective loss of liberal memory.[12]

In the realm of foreign policy, the Cubans usually tread their own path. I met a staggering number of veterans from the Angolan

---

12. In an angry column in *The Nation* on 8 December 2005, Naomi Klein spoke for a great many people in Latin America and Asia when she wrote:

> It's not only apologists for torture who ignore this history when they blame abuses on 'a few bad apples' – so too do many of torture's most prominent opponents. Apparently forgetting everything they once knew about US cold war misadventures, a startling number have begun to subscribe to an antihistorical narrative in which the idea of torturing prisoners first occurred to US officials on September 11, 2001, at which point the interrogation methods used in Guantánamo apparently emerged, fully formed, from the sadistic recesses of Dick Cheney's and Donald Rumsfeld's brains. Up until that moment, we are told, America fought its enemies while keeping its humanity intact . . . On November 8 Democratic Congressman Jim McDermott made the astonishing claim to the House of Representatives that 'America has never had a question about its moral integrity, until now.' Molly Ivins, expressing her shock that the United States is running a prison gulag, wrote that 'it's just this one administration . . . and even at that, it seems to be mostly Vice President Dick Cheney.' And in the November issue of Harper's, William Pfaff argues that what truly sets the Bush Administration apart from its predecessors is 'its installation of torture as integral to American military and clandestine operations.' Pfaff acknowledges that long before Abu Ghraib, there were those who claimed that the School of the Americas was a 'torture school,' but he says that he was 'inclined to doubt that it was really so.' Perhaps it's time for Pfaff to have a look at the SOA textbooks coaching illegal torture techniques, all readily available in both Spanish and English, as well as the hair-raising list of SOA grads . . .
>
> In Latin America the revelations of US torture in Iraq have not been met with shock and disbelief but with powerful *déjà vu* and reawakened fears. Hector Mondragon, a Colombian activist who was tortured in the 1970s by an officer trained at the School of the Americas,

war, the high point of Cuban internationalism, which helped to bring down the apartheid regime in South Africa. Fidel Castro decided that the South Africans had to be stopped from pushing through regime change in Luanda, which was their declared aim. The Cubans decided to act. In 1975 Castro declared in a powerful speech that in the past many slaves had been transported to Cuba from the Angolan coast and revolutionary Cuba had a debt to honour. It would not allow the Afrikaaners to enslave a newly independent Angola.

Contrary to reports at the time, the Russians were not at all pleased by this decision and refused to allow Soviet transport planes to be used. The first Cuban soldiers were flown to Angola on hired British transport planes. These flew out with Cuban soldiers and weaponry from Trinidad and Tobago, whose prime minister, Eric Williams, supported the decision to help Angola. Later, under US pressure, Williams reluctantly stopped the flights, but by that time other avenues had been found. The Carter administration sent an envoy with a mafia-style offer to the Cubans: If the Cubans withdrew their troops from Angola, the US would lift the embargo. Castro's response was characteristic:

---

12.   wrote: 'It was hard to see the photos of the torture in Iraq because I too was tortured. I saw myself naked with my feet fastened together and my hands tied behind my back. I saw my own head covered with a cloth bag. I remembered my feelings – the humiliation, pain.' Dianna Ortiz, an American nun who was brutally tortured in a Guatemalan jail, said, 'I could not even stand to look at those photographs . . . so many of the things in the photographs had also been done to me. I was tortured with a frightening dog and also rats. And they were always filming.'

Ortiz has testified that the men who raped her and burned her with cigarettes more than 100 times deferred to a man who spoke Spanish with an American accent whom they called 'Boss.' It is one of many stories told by prisoners in Latin America of mysterious English-speaking men walking in and out of their torture cells, proposing questions, offering tips. Several of these cases are documented in Jennifer Harbury's powerful new book, *Truth, Torture, and the American Way*, Boston, 2005.

There should be no mistake – we cannot be pressured, impressed, bribed or bought . . . Perhaps because the US is a great power, it feels it can do what it wants and what is good for it. It seems to be saying that there are two laws, two sets of rules and two kinds of logic, one for the US and one for other countries. Perhaps it is idealistic of me, but I never accepted the universal prerogatives of the US – I never accepted and never will accept the existence of a different law and different rules . . . I hope history will bear witness to the shame of the United States which for twenty years has not allowed sales of medicines needed to save lives.[13]

For over a decade, 50,000 Cubans played a decisive role in helping Angola to defeat the armies of the Apartheid State. On 23 March 1988, the South Africans launched their last major attack against Cuito and failed. Castro mocked them: 'One should ask the South Africans: "Why has your army of the superior race been unable to take Cuito, which is defended by blacks and mulattoes from Angola and the Caribbean?"' The Cuban presence accelerated the independence of Namibia as well and Nelson Mandela's first port of call after his release was an emotional visit to Havana in 1991 to pay homage to Cuban internationalism: 'We come here with a sense of the great debt that is owed the people of Cuba . . . What other country can point to a record of greater selflessness than Cuba has displayed in its relations to Africa.'

There were some unpleasant side-effects, which should not be ignored or downplayed. They included the public trial of General Ochoa and the de la Guardia brothers (from the elite unit of the Ministry of Interior). They were charged with corruption, drug-trafficking in league with the Colombian barons and endangering

---

13. Piero Gleijeses' *Conflicting Missions: Havana, Washington and Pretoria, 1959–1976*, Chapel Hill, 2005, is the most revealing and best-researched piece of scholarship on Cuba and Africa.

the security of Cuba. This was the first and, mercifully, the last time that the Cuban Revolution devoured its own. There was much talk that the de la Guardias had been turned by the US during their frequent visits to Miami. If so, the evidence should be made public. But Ochoa? A veteran of the revolutionary movement, he had fought with the Venezuelan guerrillas during the heyday of armed struggle in South America. He was extremely popular with his soldiers. In his public trial broadcast live on Cuban TV, he admitted that drug money had been used, but to fund the war against the South Africans rather than for personal gain, and he pleaded guilty. It was the executions that angered many inside Cuba and led to another set of defections abroad. When I raised the subject on this visit with a few veterans of the Angolan war, their eyes became sad. The US press had speculated that Ochoa's popularity (at a time of big changes in Russia) had led to his fall. He was perceived as a successor to Fidel. I did not get the impression that this had much to do with the case. Why then the executions? These remain a mystery. Whether or not one supports capital punishment (and I don't), in this case it definitely did not fit the crime.

And what of culture? The continent as a whole had a rich and vibrant tradition that stretched back to Bolívar whose prose had a strong literary ring and helped to create a tradition that was not easy to repress. There have always been strong links between art and politics – of both Right and Left – in South America. Mexico's muralists had decided on that particular form to de-privatise works of art. The giant murals they painted could not be bought and were freely visible to all. Rivera's mural depicting the history of Mexico on the walls of the Ministry of Education is one of the most remarkable. Cuba's struggle for independence against Spanish rule was led by a poet, José Martí. Domingo Faustino Sarmiento, author of *Facundo* and Rómulo Gallegos, who wrote *Doña Barbara* and *Canaima*, became the respective Presidents of

Argentina and Venezuela. More recently, the Peruvian novelist Mario Vargas Llosa unsuccessfully contested the presidential elections in his country on behalf of the respectable Right. Poets, too, have been politically engaged, usually on the Left (Pablo Neruda, Ernesto Cardenal, Nicolás Guillén, Aimé Césaire etc.). The Uruguayan essayist and critic Eduardo Galeano invented a form of non-fiction storytelling (*Memory of Fire*, *Open Veins of Latin America*) that took both the Americas by storm.

And even Bolivia, where literature was over-determined by politics, produced its poets and writers, less well-known than those elsewhere in South America, but important in the part they played in the political culture of the country.[14]

Brazil, separated from the rest of the continent by colonial history and language, was not exceptional in this regard. It produced a rich crop of writers, poets, critics and, later, film-makers. Linguistic unity (barring Brazil), provided Latin America

---

14. An important generation of writers arose in Bolivia at the start of the twentieth century, notably Alcides Arguedas (1878–1946) and Franz Tamayo (1879–1956), who began to take an interest in the country's majority indigenous population, realising that national culture and literature could not be confined to the white settler class in the principal cities.

Then, after the great upheavals caused by the Chaco War of the 1930s, came a fresh group of writers with a commitment to social improvement and political change. Prominent among them were Augusto Céspedes (born 1904) and Carlos Montenegro, author of *Nacionalismo y Coloniaje* (1953). Céspedes became Minister of Education after the MNR revolution of 1952, and his novel *Sangre de Mestizos* (1936) describes harrowing scenes from the Chaco War, interspersed with events in La Paz. Another important book, *Metal del Diablo* (1946), deals with conditions in the tin mines. Céspedes also invoked the history of those years in *El Dictador Suicida*, about General Germán Busch, and *El Presidente Colgado*, about President Gualberto Villarroel, the general strung up outside the Presidential Palace in La Paz. As the dreams of the MNR began to go sour, new political writers appeared, notably René Zavaleta (who died young) and Mariano Baptista Gumucio (who was killed in a military coup). The powerful Trotskyist tradition in Bolivia was given voice by Guillermo Lora, whose magnificent historical work on the origins of the Bolivian labour movement, *Historia del Movimento Obrero Boliviano* (1967), is one of the jewels of Latin American history writing.

with an intertwined yet diverse political culture that could not be
matched by Asia or Africa, and was far more alive than most of
what North America had to offer. There, history dominated
culture: the first century of the decolonised United States of
America was dominated by religious fundamentalism, genocide,
slavery and continuous imperial expansion, both internal and
external.

Cuba, the last Spanish colony in South America, got rid of its
old colonial rulers in 1898 and their US-backed replacements in
1959, but the oppositional function of culture had been in evidence
since the last decades of the nineteenth century. Even though the
country was largely illiterate, the slaves and free blacks developed
their own combination of religion and culture, creating a separate
world in which they felt free. That this was not simply escapist
was evidenced in the large proportion of black Cubans who led
rebellions and participated in the wars of independence, often
continuing to struggle after the Creole leaders had accepted a
compromise. A number of leading black musicians were executed
after black-led uprisings.[15]

The entry of printing presses into the colony in the early years
of the nineteenth century provided the basis for a culture
independent of the metropolis and the press (even under Spanish
rule), while censored, displayed a vibrancy that reflected the
wider culture of the island.

Some of the worst effects of Soviet literary life and norms during
the stagnant Brezhnev period were to be deeply felt in Cuba, more
in the realm of literature and sexuality than cinema, which fared
better. Under the prudent but creative leadership of Alfredo
Guevara, the ICAIC (Cuban Institute of Cinematographic Art

---

15. I have learnt a great deal from Antoni Kapcia's excellent study of the formation
of Cuban national identity, *Havana: The Making Of Cuban Culture*, London and
New York, 2005.

and Industry) provided a shelter in which a few dozen flowers could bloom. The presence of a cinematic giant like Tomás Gutiérrez Alea, flanked by colleagues of high calibre, Octavio Gómez and Humberto Solas, helped to defeat the cruder attempts at censorship, and all suggestions that implied rigid, formal, aesthetic criteria were openly defied. At the same time Santiago Álvarez was developing a documentary film art whose poetry impressed friend and foe. Alvarez utilised the scarcity enforced by the US blockade to great effect: his use of photographs, television clips and old newspapers gave a new life to collage as an art form. Chris Marker and Joris Ivens marvelled at 'Now', and 'Hasta La Victoria Siempre' and 'Hanoi Martes 13' (Hanoi, 13 March). Eisenstein, had he still been alive, would have been pleased and amazed, as was a stray visitor from Hollywood, Francis Ford Coppola, who saw Alvarez's work (this was the late Sixties) and commented: 'We do not have the advantages of their disadvantages.'

These days the ICAIC largely concentrates on organising the Havana Film Festival. I met with some film-makers and while it would be unfair to judge them on the basis of a rushed meeting, the impression I got was that Cuban film-makers were working under the constraints of the global market, searching for commercial projects that could get funding from outside and suffering from an over-obsession with producing soaps for the Latin American market. Perhaps there are a few auteurs hidden away somewhere and they will suddenly emerge like the old mole and surprise us all.

Many Cuban novelists, too, challenged the notion that imaginative literature was frivolous or superfluous. The dead weight of Russian bureaucratic and critical traditions could be felt behind some of the criticisms, though it never went as far as Karl Radek's philistine assault on James Joyce's *Ulysses* at a Soviet Writer's Congress in the early Thirties, symptomatic of the barrenness of 'socialist realism'.

But the cultural commissars were on permanent watch to weed out all 'anti-state' sentiments or any 'gloomy or filthy' poetry or fiction that portrayed homosexuality. The rationale was borrowed from Tsarist and Stalinist Russia and even though anti-gay prejudices were the global norm at the time, they were marginally worse in Latin America, where macho culture was especially strong and movements for sexual liberation had not accompanied the growth of the far-left or armed struggle groups. Homosexuality was tolerated in its most repressed and secret form, though the late Alejo Carpentier was known to suggest in private that homoeroticism was integral to the culture of the Revolutionary Armed Forces.[16]

Much of this has changed. The novelist Abel Prieto, currently the Minister of Culture, has publicly criticised the persecution of a few poets and novelists in the Seventies. He realises that the artificial world of culture is dominated by mediocrity and creativity is either submerged or heavily disguised. The novels of Cabrera Infante and Reinaldo Arenas are being published in Cuba and there is a real attempt to draw a line underneath a past that many regret. It would be beneficial to the country and its people if a similar attitude was extended to the print media and television. I have always been of the view that revolutions can enhance democracy in a way that is (especially in today's world) forbidden in the capitalist world. Public debate, criticism, the exchange of conflicting opinions will strengthen Cuba and

16. Robin Blackburn, 'Putting the Hammer Down on Cuba', *New Left Review*, 4, July–August 2000. This essay also contains a revealing account of the Miami banana republic and how it influences Washington, as well as a moving description of how Cuba survives in bad times. The situation has improved a great deal since then, but Blackburn's essay provided an important corrective to the constant Cuba-baiting by the 'human-rights' brigade in the US academy and media, including the *NYRB*: 'In a class by themselves for lachrymose posturing are the contributions of Alma Guillermoprieto to the *New York Review of Books*: see "A Visit to Havana", "Love and Misery in Cuba", "Fidel in the Evening", "Cuban Hit Parade"'.

empower and arm its citizens, already amongst the best educated in the world. This is now a political necessity and should not be indefinitely delayed.

Washington is waiting for the Old Man to die. Then a new offensive will begin. It will be an economic not a military assault, offering money in unlimited quantities to buy the loyalty of the island-people and promising them a consumer paradise for eternity. If they succeed it will be a tragedy for Cuba and Latin America. The choice in neo-liberal times is between the destruction through privatisation of the remarkable system of health, education and culture that has been constructed here, and the strengthening of the Revolution by preserving its gains by creating an effective internal mechanism that makes the leadership and politics accountable to the people. This will not happen overnight, but it is worth working for. Perhaps it wasn't a total coincidence that an unpublished manuscript and notes by Che Guevara on Political Economy was published in the summer of 2006. The economic dependence on the old Soviet Union was a necessity, given the US blockade. The educational dependence was a burden. Most Soviet textbooks in economics and political science were primitive and instrumental. They have been discontinued, but Samuelson's *Economics*, on its own, is not a perfect solution. Che noted that:

. . . we have the firm commitment not to hide a single opinion for tactical reasons; while at the same time drawing conclusions that because of their logical rigor and the high degree of vision, may help solve the problems and not just pose questions without solutions. We think the task is important because Marxist research in the field of economics is walking along dangerous paths. The intransigent dogmatism of Stalin's time has been followed by an inconsistent pragmatism. And what is tragic, this does not refer just to a given field of science, it is taking place in all aspects of the life of the socialist countries, creating already damaging disruptions whose final outcomes are incalculable.

This was written half a century ago and while the critical tone is admirable, the text is essentially voluntarist in character, in keeping with Che's other writings.

It should be debated seriously, since it includes prescient warnings of why the Soviet Union might collapse into capitalism. The interesting question not posed by Che is this: Will the Soviet masses mobilise to prevent a restoration? Did they feel they had a stake in the old system? These questions are not abstract and will become important after the death of Fidel Castro.

And what of the Old Man himself? In August 2006, he became an octagenarian and has now seen off five US Presidents, each of whom tried to topple him by virtually any means necessary and restore Cuba to its old status as a US dependency. His *bête noire* in Miami, Jorge Más Canosa, is also dead. Regularly insulted by the White House and referred to as an outdated relic, he remains steadfast. Travelling regularly in Latin America, it is difficult to avoid Fidel Castro's presence. He has become a continental icon in the tradition of Martí and Bolívar. History and location helped Cuba to avoid the fate of Eastern Europe.

Why did Fidel not retire like Nelson Mandela? Because he knew that the struggle was not yet over; that Havana was not Johannesburg; that no millionaires from Miami would help build his life-size statue to serve as a backdrop for photographing visiting delegations of cooing businessmen from the globalised world. And more importantly because, like Bolívar, he thinks continents, not bank-balances. He has a real sense of history, its zig-zags, its surprises and its originality. Twenty years ago, few would have thought that the aspirations expressed in the First Declaration of Havana would receive a tremendous impetus through democratic elections in Venezuela and Bolivia.

The Old Man is reported to have jumped up with joy like an adolescent at a baseball match when the results from La Paz were confirmed in December 2005. Banish adolescence and you banish dreams. He knows, better than most, the big difference between revolutions and electoral victories. Revolutions begin with excess and immoderation. They dance to the rhythm of a utopian drumbeat that others cannot hear, and their leaders are always looking upwards and wondering when the rain of stars will begin. It never does and then real life begins. Bolívar and Martí, Castro and Guevara, heard that sound. Che could never stop hearing it and went to Bolivia to carry on the dance. He was still dancing when they killed him.

The triumphs in Caracas and La Paz are of a different order, but in a world where wealth has become increasingly insolent, they mark the end of a phase of defeats and retreats and the beginning of a new forward march in difficult conditions. The Cuban Revolution once offered new hope to a continent affected by what Aimé Césaire referred to as the 'hideous leprosy of imitations', but was brutally quarantined. Bolivarianism has broken its isolation. One can only hope that this will help Cuba survive its leader.

Chapter 6

The Past as Epilogue:
The Lives Of Simón Bolívar

At that time . . . he (Bolívar) had the outlandish appearance of an exotic vagabond guerrilla. He wore the helmet of a Russian dragoon, a mule driver's espadrilles, a blue tunic with red trim and gold buttons, and he carried the black banner of a privateer hoisted on a plainsman's lance, the skull and crossbones superimposed on a motto in letters of blood: 'Liberty or Death.'

Gabriel García Márquez,
The General in His Labyrinth (1990)

So he, too, was an early pirate of the Caribbean. Born in 1783 – midway between the US Declaration of Independence and the outbreak of the French Revolution – Simón Bolívar's life and ideas were to be asymmetrically affected by both events. If the British could be driven out of the Americas by a people belonging to the same race and religion, why not the Spaniards in the South? Three hundred years of colonial rule – beginning with the fall of Mexico and ending with the conquest of Peru – was more than enough. And if the superior wisdom of the French Enlightenment had laid the foundations of the French Revolution, might it not serve the same purpose in Spanish America? Much of this would come later, when Bolívar travelled through Europe, comparing the decay and lethargy of the Madrid Court with the ferment of revolutionary Paris, albeit on the eve of Napoleon's coronation. Till the final defeat of Napoleon and the Restoration, Paris would remain qualitatively superior to Madrid and quantitatively ahead of Philadelphia. And, of course, there was always London. Sly, slippery, opportunist London, which could not be ignored. Despite the loss of its American colony, it remained the hub of a strong and growing Empire and, more importantly, one whose mastery of the seas was now unchallengeable. For that reason alone it had to be won over to the cause of South American independence and be reminded of its own imperial interests in the Americas.

Of all the revolutionary leaders that bestrode Europe and the Americas in the eighteenth and nineteenth centuries, Bolívar's political goal was the most audacious. He wanted nothing less than the liberation and unification of the entire Spanish-speaking continent. San Martín, O'Higgins and Sucre were undoubtedly brilliant generals, but Bolívar far excelled them in his capacity to think strategically. Experience taught him that if even a single Spanish base were allowed to exist on the continent it would always remain a focal point of counter-revolution. For fifteen years he led an epic resistance against the Spanish Empire, conducting a series of long marches across the Andes that have no equal in anti-colonial history, and in 1825 finally succeeded in expelling the Viceroys and Captain-Generals of the Spanish Army. But though the liberation movement now controlled a region that was five times larger than Europe, continental unity remained elusive. The idea and its originator had triumphed themselves to death. In 1830, as Bolívar lay dying from consumption in a remote farmhouse in Santa Marta, surrounded only by a few loyal friends and retainers and far away from the cities he had liberated, he compared his struggle to unite Spanish-America as 'ploughing the sea'. It was necessary, he stressed repeatedly, to start all over again.

Despite Bolívar's singular achievement, the orthodox Left in the Americas and elsewhere tended to avoid the subject of Bolívar and treated Marx's ignorant remarks on the subject as gospel, which – until recently – left the field wide open.[1] Yet the rise,

---

1. John Lynch's timely *Simón Bolívar: A Life* (New Haven and London, 2006) is the first new biography of the Liberator for over half a century, and the first by an Anglophone historian. A significant addition to our knowledge of Bolívar, it is particularly informative on the tormented question of race. Here, Lynch is ahead of the two most distinguished biographers of Bolívar whose works are available in English, Emil Ludwig and Gerhard Masur. Both were Germans who fled the Third Reich – the first to Switzerland, the second to Colombia – but continued to regard European civilization as innately superior to that of the colonised natives. Each successive biographer has felt obliged to

decline and fall of Bolívar is an epic of Schillerian dimensions: politics, passions, wars, triumphs and betrayals. Carlyle compared Bolívar to Ulysses who required a Homer to do him justice. Márquez is the closest we have got to that injunction. That is why the work of Bolívar's biographers, even taken collectively, has a magnificent rival in Gabriel García Márquez's mesmerising historical novel, *The General in his Labyrinth*. This work of fiction contains a wealth of factual details and rare psychological insights that should be the envy of any biographer.

The facts of Bolívar's life are well known. He was a prodigious correspondent and left behind volumes of letters, diaries and declarations. One of his adjutants, Daniel Florencio O'Leary, recorded a great deal every day and later produced a 34-volume account of Bolívar's life and campaigns, a navigational map which, despite contradictory passages, became essential reading for every biographer. A reconstruction of Bolívar's life from these alone would not be such a taxing enterprise. Each of his three biographers has stressed different aspects of his youth and there are varying interpretations of the circumstances that led to the radicalisation of a young man from a privileged family who could have lived out his life without a care for the world. Gerhard Masur's description of the empty lives led by the Creole aristocracy, unaffected for two hundred years by war or revolution, retains its force:

> Luxury, wastefulness, indolence and pleasure characterised the life of the white upper classes . . . they led the inglorious life of drones, surrounded by a host of slaves, cut off from contact with the rest of the world, in a climate where idleness was

---

1. mock his predecessor. Masur referred to Ludwig as 'neither authentic nor profound'; Lynch writes more politely of Masur's work 'showing its age'. Lynch's biography too reflects the spirit of its – more conformist – times. But all three accounts, if read in tandem, offer a captivating portrait of their subject, with the weaknesses of each highlighting the strengths of the others.

desirable. It is not these facts that are surprising, but rather that
these people did not degenerate more than they did . . .

How did young Bolívar, who belonged to one of the richest
slave-owning families in Venezuela, break loose from this atro-
phied and corrupting environment? Orphaned at an early age –
three when he lost his father and nine when his mother passed
away – with three older siblings, he was placed in the care of his
uncle, whom he loathed. He was often left to his own devices and
fantasies until his uncle and guardian decided that the boy needed
to be educated and despatched him to the Escuela Pública de
Caracas in 1793. Bolívar detested this too, and soon ran away to
the home of an older sister; it was eventually agreed that he would
live with his teacher, Simón Rodríguez. Rodríguez was a devotee
of the French Revolution, violently anti-clerical, a revolutionary
and a believer in free love, writing on one occasion to a friend to
'please send my wife back soon. I need her for the same purpose as
you.' He was to flee Venezuela after an insurrectionary conspiracy
was uncovered, change his name to Robinson (after the hero of
Defoe's novel) and wander like a vagabond through Europe.

While in France, the young Rodríguez had discovered the work
of Holbach and Rousseau and was to remain a steadfast believer
for the rest of his life.

In the open-minded and intelligent young Bolívar, Rodríguez
had found his Emile and he filled the young boy's head with a
mixture of French philosophy and heroic tales of resistance and
struggle. He spoke to Bolívar of Túpac Amaru's rebellion in Peru
only a few years ago, of how it had taken the Empire by surprise,
of how Túpac had been betrayed by his own side and the
punishments that had been meted out; the defeated Inca leader
had been publicly tortured and killed by the soldiers of the
Spanish King, while the Creole aristocracy had watched from
their carriages. All this left its mark on Bolívar. In time he, too,

became addicted to Rousseau and wrote to his old tutor: 'I have travelled the road you have shown me . . . You educated my heart to liberty, to justice, to greatness, to beauty.' Later, a British envoy to Bolívar, well attuned to the general's radar, brought with him a gift, a miniscule proportion of the post-Waterloo war booty: Napoleon's copy of the *Social Contract*. They certainly had no illusions as to where his real sympathies lay. Rodríguez had also instilled in the boy a lifelong atheism and distrust of religion.

When a 16-year-old Simón Bolívar, attired in the regulation outfit of a Creole aristocrat, first arrived in Madrid in 1799, he was welcomed by high society, dazzled by the court and entertained in style by his relations. He received a higher education from the Marquis de Ustariz, a cultivated Venezuelan-born Spanish official. But the young man soon understood, helped by an unpleasant encounter with some officers, that a Creole from the colonies, however pale his skin (unlike that of Bolívar), would never be treated as an equal in Spain. *Limpieza* (pure blood) had become an obsession in the Peninsula after the Reconquest. Nonetheless the idea of joining or fomenting a rebellion against Spanish rule in the Americas had not yet entered his head. Lurking in his subconscious were the lessons Rodríguez had taught him, but he had, for instance, no knowledge of the fact that in 1783, soon after the US Declaration of Independence and his own arrival in the world, a leading Spanish courtier, the Count of Aranda, had despatched an astonishingly prescient memorandum to his monarch (way ahead of the French *philosophes*, few of whom thought politically about colonies) warning against the folly of trying to hold on to the colonies by force, advocating Home Rule and predicting the rise of the United States:

> Great possessions cannot be held forever. The present situation is rendered more difficult by the enormous distances, which hampers the dispatch of help, by the slowness of the authorities and the selfishness of the government . . . That pygmy

republic (US), which today needs France and Spain to exist at all, will one day grow into a colossus, will forget all the benefits it has received at the hands of both powers and will dream only of might. The freedom of conscience, the growth of a huge population in that vast territory, the advantages of the new government, will draw workmen and peasants from all countries, for men pursue success, and the time will come when we shall painfully feel the tyranny of the giant. It will then attempt to get Florida and the Gulf of Mexico into its power, will hamper our trade with New Spain and endeavour to conquer it, since the two countries are strong and adjacent, while we shall hardly be able to defend it. These apprehensions, Sire, are only too well founded, unless their realisation is forestalled by other, yet graver changes in our parts of America. Everything will combine to urge our subjects to fight for their independence at the earliest opportunity.

We should therefore give up all our possessions, retaining only Cuba and Puerto Rico in the north and a small part of the south to provide us with ports for our trade. To realise this great idea in a way worthy of Spain, three Infantes should be made kings of Mexico, Peru and the Costa Ferma, Your Majesty receiving the title of Emperor. Trade should be built up on terms of perfect equality. The four nations must feel themselves bound by an alliance, offensive and defensive, for their common welfare. Since our industry is unable to provide America with all necessities, France must send them; England on the other hand must be rigorously excluded . . .[2]

Charles III dismissed Aranda as an inveterate pessimist. His successor, Charles IV, immersed in the pleasures of the hunt, and his Queen, who exercised effective power from her chamber with a train of notables in and out of her canopied bed, were equally

---

2. Quoted in Emil Ludwig, *Bolívar: The Life of an Idealist*, New York, 1942, p. 56.

uninterested in such ideas. By the time Bolívar arrived in the
mother country at the century's close the court and society had
become even more stagnant. He distracted himself from Spanish
realities by falling in love with María Teresa Rodríguez del Toro,
a young beauty from an upper-class Spanish-Venezuelan family
with estates in the Basque country. On a brief visit to France in
1802 he was impressed by a young general named Bonaparte and
fell in love again, but this time with post-revolutionary Paris. He
returned to Madrid, married María Teresa and returned to his
hacienda in Venezuela, determined to raise a family and improve
his estates. Six months later his wife had died of fever. A
distraught Bolívar was alone once again. He would never
remarry, relying in the years that followed on a large variety
of women for solace. Only one amongst them, the *quiteña*,
Manuela Sáenz (married to an Englishman, Dr Thorne), would
remain lover, confidante, soul-mate and political ally for the rest
of his life, though, at times, even she got on his nerves. Later,
after independence, when bad times returned, he entrusted her
with his archives, which she guarded till they could be safely
transferred to Daniel O'Leary in Jamaica, hard at work on his
history of the Liberator.

Bolívar left Venezuela after his wife's death, spending 1804–6
in France and Italy. On his return to Europe he was struck
another blow. While in Paris he saw the crowds celebrating
Napoleon's coronation. Bolívar felt a deep unease and bewilder-
ment. The Republic had been betrayed from within. The figure of
Napoleon haunted him for the rest of his life. Rodríguez was
scathing in his comments, but Bolívar continued to admire the
military genius of the Corsican and when, decades later, a
Bonaparte nephew arrived in South America to fight alongside
him, the Liberator was thrilled. It was in Paris, on this occasion,
that Bolívar met the explorer Alexander von Humboldt, freshly
returned from the Americas. He listened in wonderment as the
German described the beauty of South America and became

thoughtful when Humboldt wondered whether a Spanish minority could hold on indefinitely to its colonies, but he, too, like the
Enlightenment thinkers (Tom Paine was a solitary exception)
could not contemplate total independence for subject peoples. The
meeting with Humboldt left a strong impression on Bolívar and
compelled him to think seriously for the first time of independence. Once he did, Bolívar, unlike others from his class, was
never to compromise on this issue. He wanted full sovereignty. It
was too late now for Aranda's solution and as Humboldt himself
was to later realise it was foolish to believe that what one observed
was all that existed: 'During my time in America, I never
encountered discontent; I noticed that while there was no great
love for Spain, at least there was conformity with the established
regime. It was only later, once the struggle had begun, that I
realized that they had hidden the truth from me and that far from
love, there existed deep-seated hatred.'[3]

Bolívar played a leading role in these events. But he was not
the first to take up the cause of liberation: there was a precursor in
the shape of the remarkable if slightly eccentric figure of Francisco
de Miranda, also a Venezuelan. Relations between the two men

---

3. Quoted in Lynch, *Simón Bolívar*, p. 36. Spanish rule had created sharp divisions
   along lines of race and class, in documenting which John Lynch's biography
   represents an undoubted advance on his predecessors. He discusses the contradictions within the liberation movement on the race question and their legacy in
   post-colonial South America. At the end of the colonial era Venezuela was
   dominated by a tiny number of Spaniards and elite Creoles – less than half a per
   cent of the total population of 800,000, according to Lynch – who ran the
   colonial administration and owned the cattle-ranches and plantations of the
   interior. Around a quarter of Venezuelans were poorer Creoles, who worked as
   artisans and in small trade. Half the population were *pardos* – a category
   including free blacks, mulattos, *mestizos* and *zambos*, those of mixed black and
   indigenous descent – while a tenth were black slaves working in fields of cacao,
   tobacco, cotton and indigo. While the elite resented Madrid's taxes and colonial
   officers, they were wary of independence for fear that it might encourage the
   pardo majority to assert themselves. It took Napoleon's 1808 invasion of Spain,
   and the ensuing crisis in the Peninsula, to convince the Creoles to push for
   independence, which was eventually declared in 1811.

were never easy, for which both shared blame. This led ultimately
to the most shameful episode in Bolívar's life. The 1811 declaration of independence in Caracas prompted an armed backlash
from royalists in the province. Angered by Miranda's proposal of
a ceasefire in 1812, Bolívar and others arrested their commander-
in-chief and later handed him over to the enemy. Miranda would
spend the rest of his life rotting to death in a Cadiz prison. To his
younger arrival would accrue the prestige and much-desired glory
as the leader who finally drove the Spanish out of the continent
they had made their own.

Bolívar had become a military leader through political necessity. As Márquez noted: 'He did not have an academic education
even comparable to that of any of his officers, most of whom had
been educated at the best military schools in Spain, but he had the
ability to conceptualise an entire situation down to the smallest
details.'[4] This was no mean accomplishment when an entire
continent had to be freed. Add to this the difficult geography
he encountered, which he also enjoyed despite the hardships, as
evidenced in his lyrical address – a travelogue of political
liberation – to the citizens of Caracas in 1813 on the occasion
of their second attempt to throw off the Spanish dominion:

> Your liberators have arrived, from the banks of the swollen
> Magdalena to the flowering valleys of Aragua and the precincts
> of this great capital, victorious they have crossed the rivers of
> Zulia, of Tachira, of Bocono, of Masparro, Portugesa, Morador
> and Acarigua; they have traversed the bleak and icy plateaus of
> Mucuchies, Bocono and Niquitao; they have made their way
> over the deserts and mountains of Ocana, Merida and Trujillo;
> they have triumphed seven times in the battles of Cucuta, La
> Grita, Betijoque Carache, Niquitao, Marquisimeto and Tina-
> quillo, and have left beaten five armies, which to the number of

---

4. Gabriel García Márquez, *The General In His Labyrinth*, New York, 1990, p. 206.

10,000 men were devastating the fair provinces of Santa Marta, Pamplona, Merida, Trujillo, Barinas and Caracas.[5]

There would be much more of this in the years that followed, as the liberation struggle came to encompass the whole continent. Venezuela's Second Republic was, like its predecessor, crushed by royalist forces in 1814, and by the following year Spain was once more in control of New Granada, forcing Bolívar to flee to Jamaica and then to liberated Haiti, where Pétion provided him with rifles, ammunition, supplies and funds. He returned to South America in 1817, this time engaging the Spanish in the *llanos*, the vast plains of central Venezuela, where guerrilla war raged inconclusively. Making a tactical switch to the liberation of New Granada, Bolívar crossed the Andes in 1819 and defeated the Spanish at Boyacá. Colombia was founded at the end of that year, and Venezuela was liberated in 1821; Ecuador followed soon after, and the three states joined to form the republic of Gran Colombia, of which Bolívar was immediately appointed president. But he could not rest until the Spanish had been expelled from the continent altogether. Together with Sucre, he moved on Peru and took Lima in 1824, before inflicting a decisive defeat on Spain at Ayacucho. In 1825, Bolívar climbed up to Potosi in Upper Peru and saw with his own eyes the silver mines that had, for nearly three hundred years, acted as the de facto treasury of Spain. Within months, Upper Peru had been renamed Bolivia in his honour.

A new set of troubles came after independence had been achieved. Andean unity crumbled as local *caudillos* defended provincial vested interests; attempts to assassinate Bolívar in Bogotá narrowly failed in 1828, but opposition and fractiousness mounted. In 1830, Sucre was murdered and Gran Colombia broke into its constituent parts: Venezuela, Ecuador and New Granada

---

5. Quoted in Lynch, *Simón Bolívar*, p. 76.

(modern Colombia). During the Spanish war, Bolívar had been ruthless in dealing with disobedient officers. Two of them, Piar and Padilla, had been tried and executed. Both of them were mulattos and had raised racial issues that Bolívar considered divisive. General Santander, a Creole, was permitted exile despite his involvement in the Bogotá plot to kill Bolívar; another general, Páez, an illiterate *mestizo*, was foolishly left in control of Venezuela because Bolívar thought him an ally against Santander. Páez banned Bolívar's return to the country, which he treated as a fiefdom as he accumulated a vast personal fortune, including estates worked by slave labour – despite the formal abolition of slavery.[6]

The Haitian Revolution had frightened whites of every stripe and there was a great deal of nervousness especially amongst the Creoles, which partially explained the reluctance of many of them to fight with Bolívar's armies, whose ranks contained *pardos*, *zambos* and mulattos. At least a quarter of his soldiers were slaves or former slaves. Bolívar knew perfectly well how much he owed Haiti. They had helped him financially and militarily to return to Venezuela from his Jamaican exile. In return for Pétion's financial and military assistance he had pledged to abolish slavery, and duly issued a series of decrees. But as for Haiti itself, he preferred to salute it from afar. When he convened an ill-fated though well-intentioned Congress of the Americas in Panama in 1826, Haiti was not invited. What of the indigenous population? They were given the same rights as everyone else but, as Lynch writes, in practice this never worked: the rural communes of former slaves and Indians were dismantled by the Republican authorities, leaving behind resentments – the result of racial, social, economic and political discrimination – that exist to this day.

Bolívar's last days have been brilliantly reconstructed by

6. See Robin Blackburn, *The Overthrow of Colonial Slavery*, London and New York, 1988, pp. 331–79.

García Márquez. He died angry and embittered, but ready to fight once again for the unity of the continent. Till his last hours he was preparing fantastical plans to topple Páez and retake Bogotá, but the killing of Sucre had left him without an obvious political heir. A few days before his death, his doctor read reports just received from France. During the July Days of 1830, as barricades went up in Paris, the crowds were chanting a new song as they stormed the Hôtel de Ville and which included this verse:

> *America, to cheer us,*
> *Looks on us from afar.*
> *Her fire-ring of republics*
> *Was lit by Bolívar.*

Temporarily unpopular at home, his glory had crossed the seas. What of his friends? Santander expelled Manuela Sáenz from Bogotá; and she lived the next ten years in Paita, a small, miserable port in Peru, selling sweets, medicines and advice to lovers in the market-place. 'Three memorable visitors', wrote Márquez, 'consoled her abandonment: the tutor Simón Rodríguez, with whom she shared the ashes of glory, the Italian patriot Giuseppe Garibaldi, who was returning from the struggle against the dictatorship of Rosas in Argentina, and the novelist Herman Melville, who was wandering the oceans of the world gathering information for *Moby Dick*.'

Within a decade of his death, Bolívar's name, though not his spirit, was politically resuscitated and he was transformed into a cult by the various *caudillos* who presided over states that he had liberated.

And today? Bolívar's most recent biographer, John Lynch, allows his ideological prejudices to surface in a few concluding paragraphs:

In 1998 Venezuelans were astonished to learn that their country had been renamed 'the Bolivarian Republic of Venezuela' by decree of President Hugo Chávez, who called himself a 'revolutionary Bolivarian'. Authoritarian populists, or neo-caudillos, or Bolivarian militarists, whatever their designation, invoke Bolívar no less ardently than did previous rulers, though it is doubtful he would have responded to their calls . . .

This is what Lynch terms the 'new heresy', deeming Castro an even worse offender than Chávez. It is worth noting, though, that not all Venezuelans were surprised at the renaming of their Republic: Chávez had already proposed it in public on many occasions. More importantly, Chávez is an elected leader who has been given majority support by Venezuelans on five separate occasions. As to whether he should or should not be characterized as Bolivarian, it is a matter of opinion. In his desire for continental unity, in his opposition to the newest Empire – also foreseen by Bolívar – and its grip on Latin America (including support for three attempts to oust Chávez himself), in his direct appeals to all South Americans and his popularity in other parts of the world, there are undoubted analogies.

That Chávez is loathed by the Creole oligarchy in Venezuela is also something that Bolívar might have understood. In fact the failure of Bolívar to reach out to slaves and the indigenous population was, as Lynch explains, a tragic weakness. Chávez and Morales are trying to be far more inclusive, with some success, and it is this that makes them unpopular with the traditional elites. Lynch writes of Bolívar that 'he was not a slave to economic liberalism and was never doctrinaire. He envisaged a larger and more positive role for the state than classical liberalism allowed, and to this extent he showed his awareness of the particular problems of underdevelopment.'[7] In this light, Bolívar and Chávez would appear rather closer, as Chávez grapples with the same problems two centuries later. As even a fellow historian

---

7. Lynch, *Simón Bolívar*, p. 161.

noted recently while reviewing Lynch: 'Yet perhaps there is
something of Bolívar in Chávez. Alberto Garrido, a Venezuelan
political analyst, has described the Venezuelan president as
"tactically pragmatic, but strategically obsessive". It is a description that would just as well do for the Liberator himself.'[8]
Criticisms of Chávez along the surreal, pre-post-modern lines
adopted by William Burroughs in criticising Bolívar might at least
have led to mirth. The novelist was possibly high when he wrote
that given the power of language, Bolívar's ultimate failure in
liberating South America from oppression lay in his failure to
dump Spanish; Chinese, he suggested, would have freed the
masses psychologically.[9]

For the rest, the choices are clear. Either one pushes for the
Washington Consensus or one attempts to create an altogether
different programme which prioritises not market values but
human needs. John Lynch is, no doubt, basically quite happy
with the status quo. The majority of Venezuelans and Bolivians
are not. This does not automatically make the leaders they elect

8. 'The First Bolívarian Revolution', by J. H. Elliot, *NYRB*, 13 July, 2006.
9. In more serious mode, Burroughs was a pirate sympathiser, as he articulated in
Cities of the Red Night:

> . . . we have allies in all those who are enslaved and oppressed throughout
> the world . . . the whole Indian population of the American continent
> peonized and degraded by the Spanish into subhuman poverty and
> ignorance, exterminated by the Americans, infected with their vices
> and diseases . . . all these are potential allies . . .
>
> Imagine such a movement on a worldwide scale. Faced by the actual
> practice of freedom, the French and American revolutions would be forced
> to stand by their words . . . The principles of the French and American
> revolutions became windy lies in the mouths of politicians. The liberal
> revolutions of 1848 created the so-called republics of Central and South
> America, with a dreary history of dictatorship, oppression, graft, and
> bureaucracy . . . Your right to live where you want, with companions of
> your choosing, under laws to which you agree, died in the eighteenth
> century with Captain Mission. Only a mircale or a disaster could restore it.
>
> William S. Burroughs, *Cities of the Red Night*, New York, 1981, pp.
> xiii–xv.

'authoritarian' if they begin to implement the political programme on which they were elected. The reason for the sudden revival of interest in Bolívar is undoubtedly due to the emergence of Hugo Chávez on the world stage. Had it not been for that, would John Lynch have been commissioned to write a new biography?

The fact is that South America is on the march again, offering hope to a world either deep in neo-liberal torpor or suffering daily from the military and economic depredations of the New Order. The continent is full of echoes from past struggles and a new wave of leaders and activists are aware of their importance. History cannot be repeated, but nor should it be ignored. It has to be assimilated and understood.

Bolívar himself always counselled against despair or political capitulation. If necessary, he argued, wipe the slate clean and start all over again. That is what is beginning to happen again as the old tired smiles on the faces of weary veterans are replaced by the noise of a new laughter from below. Hope has been reborn and that is half the battle won.

Postscript:

Notes from a South American Diary
January–December 2007

Seid umschlungen, Millionen,
Diesen Kuss der ganzen Welt!
[Be embraced, you millions,
Here's a kiss for all the world]

Friedrich Schiller,
'Ode to Joy' (1789)

'It could not be denied that there was an increased turnover of thoughts
and experiences in this new age, and indeed it was inevitable, if only
as the natural consequence of shunning the time-consuming process of
assimilating them intellectually. He pictured the brain of the age
replaced by the mechanism of supply and demand, and the painstaking
thinker replaced by the businessman as regulating factor, and he could
not help enjoying the moving spectacle of a vast production of
experiences that would freely combine and dissolve again, a sort of
nervous blancmange quivering all over at the slightest jolt . . .'

Robert Musil, 'The Man without Qualities' (1942)

With each passing year it becomes obvious that capitalist politics today, deprived of a socialist enemy, is little more than a business operation, tending to the needs of the system rather than its victims. This has been true of the United States for a long time, but now applies equally to major political parties in Britain and Italy, India, Brazil and South Africa, with China as a *sui generis* case. Parties have become money-making machines. As I've argued in this book, the revolt against the sameness of the global political economy erupted in Latin America as early as 1989. Debating alternatives to neo-liberal capitalism is no longer an abstraction. The process is continuous but uneven, punctuated by victories and setbacks.

As 2006 drew to an end, the Venezuelan people re-elected Hugo Chávez with a huge majority. He received 61 per cent of the votes cast. Teodoro Petkoff did not stand against him, but instead became the campaign manager of the agreed opposition candidate, Manuel Rosales, who had openly backed the coup of 2002.

The Sandinista leader, Daniel Ortega, won the Presidency in his country. Blessed by the Church, flanked by a former Contra as his vice president and still loathed by the US ambassador, he may be a sickly shadow of his former self, but his victory undoubtedly reflects the desire of Nicaraguans for change. Will Managua follow the radically redistributive policies of anti-imperialist

Caracas or confine itself to rhetoric and remain a client of the International Monetary Fund?

There was much better news from Quito. The substantial electoral triumph of Rafael Correa, a dynamic, young, US-educated economist and former finance minister, who pledged in his election campaign to reverse Ecuador's participation in the US-backed free trade area for the Americas, to ask the US military to vacate its base at Manta, and to join OPEC and the growing Bolivarian movement that seeks to unite South America against imperialism. He is definitely a pirate.

Fidel Castro was still alive in Cuba, but the transition was proceeding smoothly. Caracas was making it difficult for Miami to move to Havana. After Venezuela, Bolivia and Ecuador there were reports that the ghost of Bolívar had been sighted in Paraguay. There can be no definitive postscript.

It takes nearly two hours to reach my hotel in Caracas from the Simón Bolívar airport. The old viaduct carrying the main airport road across a chasm had collapsed a year ago and its replacement is still a few months from completion. This compels a detour via small winding roads through the hills that encircle the city. Here is where the poor live. As the traffic comes to a standstill you can see up close the dishevelled slopes covered with houses. Building works everywhere. The dwellings are being improved and provided with modern amenities. Some of them must have spectacular views overlooking the sea, very different from the bowl-shaped Caracas where the water is hidden from view. This was true long before it was architecturally wrecked by a chaotic 'modernisation', which, apart from aesthetic considerations, makes the city virtually impossible to walk.

Glistening in the heat of the tropical sun, the Sixties skyscrapers seem uglier than usual. As we finally enter the city, the streets resound with the familiar if unwelcome noise of endless traffic. The upmarket hotel Gran Melia is not particularly appealing. The kitsch ceiling in the giant lobby is reminiscent of the Dubai School (why does oil wealth invariably disfigure the imagination?) and soon I'm missing the shabby, bare, miserable, but atmospheric Caracas Hilton, where I normally stay. This feeling is enhanced when I'm told that the WiFi charge is $12 an hour. In the Hilton lobby it's free.

I'm here to speak at a conference on information/global media networks and to attend a meeting of the Advisory Board of the bilingual (Spanish/Portuguese) cable news channel Telesur – a joint initiative of Venezuela, Argentina, Uruguay, Bolivia, Cuba and now Ecuador. Designed as an alternative to the CNN/BBC worldview, the new channel is a modest success, with 5–6 million regular viewers. It has yet to gain access to the Hispanic population in the United States. It stresses regional cohesion in South America: while the private media channels devote hours of coverage to the US Congressional results or the latest serial killing on a US campus, Telesur announces these events in a terse bulletin, devoting the rest of the news to live coverage from Nicaragua, where elections are also taking place, or from Ecuador, where a Bolivarian referendum to draft a new constitution has been won by the new government.

I had first raised the idea of a continental station to counter the Washington Consensus networks at a public assembly here in 2003. It was seized upon quickly, but the name I had suggested (al-Bolívar) was firmly rejected. It was inappropriate, I was told, since it would exclude the largest continental state, which had no links to the Liberator. As it happened Brazil excluded itself. 'Why won't you support Telesur?' Chávez asked Lula a few years ago. 'I don't know,' replied a slightly shame-faced Brazilian President. The reason was obvious: a staunch WC supporter, Lula had neither the desire nor the will to antagonise the Brazilian media or annoy Washington. But Telesur is trickling into the country nonetheless.

The conference centre is packed for the inaugural speech. When we are all seated, Hugo Chávez is whisked in and a few pleasantries exchanged. 'You must be really happy now that Blair is going', he tells me. I point out that my happiness is somewhat circumscribed by the succession. 'Long live the revolution', he says in English. Which revolution?

Then we all settle down for a three-hour address, which is being broadcast live. Occasions like this always make me regret not bringing a picnic basket. The speech is not atypical. A mélange of facts: the increase in oil revenues by charging more royalties alone is a few billion dollars; homespun philosophy; autobiography; the most recent conversation with Fidel together with a rough estimate of the hours the two men have spent in conversation (well over a thousand); how proud the Venezuelan government is to be funding Danny Glover's film on Toussaint L'Ouverture and the Haitian slave uprising; the horrors of occupied Iraq; a sharp attack on the Pope for suggesting during a recent visit to Brazil that the indigenous population had not been badly treated and had willingly embraced Christ. The Bavarian, much more hardline than his Polish predecessor, had to apologise yet again. Why does he bother? Obvious that he's a card-carrying neo-col (sympathetic to the current neo-colonial ideology).

Following the denunciation of the Pope, an impromptu song is sung. This normally indicates that the speech is nearing its end – but not today. There is a shortish (30-minute) historical detour, much of it to do with Bolívar and how he was let down by men in the pay of the local aristocracy/oligarchy: 'The history books at school never taught us about these betrayals.' And then a discussion on planetary survival ending with a slogan borrowed from Cuba in bad times: 'Socialism or Death'. It's a truly awful message and can sound threatening. When I point this out to one of his close aides, he explains that the President was in Rosa Luxemburg mode. What he really meant was 'Socialism or Barbarism'. I'm not convinced.

And then the day is over. It's past midnight when we return to the hotel. The kitchen is closed, despite the vaunted 24-hour room service. In the absence of food, I digest the speech. I thought Chávez was slightly subdued, and had the distinct sensation that the audience he had in mind was the army rank-and-file. The next day my instinct was confirmed when I heard stories of assassination plots.

The former vice president, José Vicente Rangel, tells us that the government had uncovered a joint US–Colombian operation to infiltrate Colombian paramilitaries, including some expert snipers, into Venezuela. This was 'a new phase in the dirty war against Venezuela'. The plot was designed to create a national emergency by assassinating both government and opposition leaders, so that each side would blame the other. Rangel insisted that the man in charge was John Negroponte (Reagan's overseer in Central America who had no problems whatsoever with the death squads), currently Condoleezza Rice's deputy in the State Department, and who, to the consternation of a few Democrats in Washington, had lately been spotted in Colombia, where high-level government collusion with death squads has recently been exposed. There is also talk of Venezuelan state security having uncovered a plot to assassinate Chávez involving three senior army officers, two of whom are now in prison. The third reportedly fled to Miami.

Chávez's military studies had taught him that the enemy must never be reduced to desperation, since this only increases its strength. Instead he offered bridges of silver as escape routes. Despite unconstitutional attempts to topple him, the Bolivarians were not vindictive. Which is why the Western media chorus portraying the regime as authoritarian has always been wide of the mark. The chorus was back in action while I was in Caracas, this time defending a privately owned TV station (RCTV) when the government refused to renew its 20-year license.

Why was this treated as a big surprise? RCTV, together with 80 per cent of the local media, had been involved in the 2002 coup against a democratically elected government. RCTV openly mobilised support for the coup, falsified footage to suggest that Chávez supporters were killing people, and when the coup failed did not show any images of Chávez's triumphant return to power amidst scenes of popular rejoicing. A year later they made daylong appeals exhorting citizens to topple the government during an opposition-engineered oil strike. They were not alone, but their appeals actively encouraged violence. They had done as they pleased for decades. They had made massive profits, defended the privileges of the oligarchy, ignored the needs of the poor, and defended the interests of Washington and its wars. Their time was now past and the Tartuffery of the Western media chains could no longer help them.

Asked by a *Guardian* pup in the UK whether I supported the RCTV decision, I said I did. He expressed shock. 'But now the opposition is without its TV'. He wasn't even aware of the double standards being evoked. I inquired whether the opposition in Britain or anywhere else in Euro-America, leave alone China, had 'its TV'? Which Western government would have tolerated any of this? Thatcher did not, when she refused to renew Thames TV's franchise – and that was for showing one critical documentary. Blair sacked Greg Dyke and neutered the BBC. Bush (except for comedy shows) has the luxury of a non-critical television with Fox TV as a specialist propaganda network.

So why single out Venezuela and refuse to accept the popular will? It has vast reserves of oil. It defies the WC by pushing forward a set of social-democratic reforms funded by oil wealth that challenge the misery and destitution both at home and in other parts of the continent. The Bolivarian project has revived hope. Despite the armed resistance in Iraq and elsewhere in the Middle East, it is South America that is now the weakest link in the imperial chain. The social vision here is something that can appeal to many citizens in the United States. For the old politicians of the oligarchy and their supporters, blinded with hatred, the electoral victories of Chávez appear to be unreal and, therefore, illogical. Something that can never be accepted. It is as if the grotesque reality of their own lives, distorted by race, wealth and privilege, had blotted out all other realities.

At the conference itself I warn against an unhealthy obsession with the power of the media. After all, was it not the case that Chávez had won six electoral victories in the face of a near-universal media opposition that was always vicious and occasionally racist? Had not Evo Morales in Bolivia and Rafael Correa in Ecuador won despite the unremitting opposition of the entire media in their respective countries? Nor was this process confined to South America. The French had voted against the European Constitution without the support of a single daily newspaper, TV station or media commentator.

And did not this apply even to the United States where a strong minority (now a majority) had always opposed the war in Iraq, despite a media used to broadcasting government handouts? And to go further back: had not state control of the media in the old Soviet Union and Eastern Europe accelerated the isolation of those regimes and failed to prevent their downfall instead of helping them? The preponderance of the pro-WC media should not become a substitute for analysing the real weaknesses of the Left in Latin America. And this was as true of Caracas as Cochabamba, where I am headed next.

The flight to the central Bolivian city of Cochabamba takes four and a half hours, a straight line downward over the Amazon and its rainforests, and into the Andes. The plane transporting us to Bolivia – to attend a conference 'defending humanity' and, more importantly, to express our solidarity with the first serious radical government since 1952 – is packed with South Americans, a few US professors, TV crews, some hangers-on as well as veteran Latin America hand Richard Gott and myself.

I was last in the city forty years ago as part of a four-man team (the others were Perry Anderson, Robin Blackburn and Ralph

Schoenman) sent by Bertrand Russell to attend the trial of Régis Debray in Camiri, not far from where a besieged Che Guevara was fighting to escape the Bolivian Army. Debray had been captured while attempting to leave the guerrilla encampment and head home. I had also been asked by the Cubans to photograph every Bolivian army officer in the region. This got me into trouble a few times. On one occasion a colonel, pistol drawn, walked up to me and asked for the film. I gave him a blank roll. 'If you take any more photographs of me,' he said, 'I'll shoot you.' I didn't. These photographs and others (including one of Robin Blackburn having a long shower) were dispatched to Havana, where they must still be held in some ageing archive.

Cochabamba was where the US Military Advisory Group, which was supervising the operation to capture and kill Guevara, established its HQ. And it was to Cochabamba that I fled from Camiri in 1967 after being briefly arrested, accused of being a Cuban guerrilla called Pombo, who was Che's bodyguard and one of those who escaped the encampment and returned safely to Cuba. I holed up in Cochabamba till I could get a flight to La Paz and a connection to Europe via Brazil. Hearing me reminisce with Richard Gott, who was also defending humanity, and who had been the *Guardian*'s chief Latin America correspondent in 1967, Patricia, a young Telesur journalist from Madrid says: 'God. It's just like listening to Spanish Civil War veterans returning to Spain.'

Bolivia's population has not risen dramatically. It was 2 million in 1900 and is slightly over 8 million today, with a GDP of $8 billion. The country has a large Indian population: 62 per cent of the people describe themselves as indigenous. Thirty-five per cent live on less than a dollar a day. Add to this a turbulent history: wars, coups, revolutions, the odd guerrilla *foco* and numerous uprisings. The armed trade wars with Chile in the last decades of the nineteenth century lost Bolivia its coastal strip on the Pacific and the port of Antofogasta. Between 1825 and 1982 there were

157 coups and 70 presidents, half of whom held office for less than a year. Neo-liberal slumber lasted throughout the 1990s, but as the twenty-first century dawned, Jeffrey Sachs's social engineering triggered a ferocious backlash. It is worth restressing that it was the unrest from below that created the basis for the triumph of Morales and the Movement for Socialism in the elections of 2005. Not only was Morales on the left, he was an Aymara Indian, and his victory ended a century and a half of Creole rule. The rich were furious. Within a few months, a campaign of destabilisation, centred in the Creole stronghold of Santa Cruz, had begun. 'They predicted economic chaos,' Rafael Puente, a former government minister and Jesuit priest, told us. 'They said Bolivia would become another Zimbabwe. They accused Evo of starting a civil war. They exchanged doctored photographs on their cell phones depicting their elected president bleeding from a gunshot wound in the head with the words "Viva Santa Cruz" painted above him in blood.' The government went ahead and carried out its election promises, nationalising energy resources and taking direct control of operations. The increase in state revenues was to be used to help poor families keep their children at school. The government aimed to reduce poverty by 10 per cent, a modest enough aim, but the Santa Cruz businessmen screamed 'Communism!' When economic conditions improved, the Opposition moved on to Morales' relationship with Chávez. The walls of Santa Cruz were plastered with posters reading 'Evo, Chola de Chávez' (chola meaning 'Indian whore'). When one looks at the newspapers in Santa Cruz it is hard to work out which man they hate more.

Richard Gott and I wander around Cochabamba. The Paris Café on the Plaza de 14 Septembre is still there, looking much less dilapidated. The Roxy cinema, where I watched Lee Marvin and Jane Fonda in *Cat Ballou*, has also survived, although it is now an evangelical church. Gott insists that we visit La Cancha. This is the indigenous market opposite the old railway station, reminiscent of an Arab bazaar with its narrow lanes and commodities transported by wheelbarrow; among other things it has to offer is the most ravishing assortment of multi-coloured potatoes anywhere in the world. Little has changed since 1967, though the quality seems to have declined a bit. I buy two cheap tin plates painted with flowers, which turn out to have been made in China.

Back at the hotel I am ambushed by a Spanish journalist from *El Mundo*: 'You've described Venezuela, Bolivia, Cuba and Ecuador as an axis of hope. What is your axis of evil in this continent?' I tell her that I avoid the terms good and evil because they are religious concepts, but that my axis of despair consists of Brazil, Chile and Mexico. 'Could you please add the Dominican Republic?' asked Sherazada 'Chiqui' Vicioso, a feminist poet. 'We're always being ignored.' I do so. Then I ask the reason for her name. Her father, a composer, adored *The Thousand and One Nights*. 'I got off lightly', she adds. 'My brother is called Rainer Maria Rilke.'

Sherazada's own impact on Dominican literature over the last thirty years has won her both fame and respect. And not just for her defence of women's rights. She has stressed the importance of the 'African element' in her own country and criticised Creole prejudices against a neighbour with a richer and more honourable history:

> *Haiti*
> *traveler who eagerly greets me*
> *interrupting the quiet of paths,*
> *softening stones, paving dust*
> *with your sweaty, bare feet*
> *Haiti who can give art a thousand shapes*
> *and who paints the stars with your hands*
> *I found out that love and hate*
> *share your name.*
>
> (Viaje desde el agua,
> tr. D.C. De Filippis)

Later the Bolivian Vice President, Alvaro García Linera, a leading Marxist intellectual (and *New Left Review* contributor) is describing the lineages of the Latin American intelligentsia, the dangers that lie ahead. Change has come through the ballot-box, but it's going to be a long slog. Many have accommodated to Washington's New Order, but the challenge is to maintain the old intellectual traditions of dissent. The 'false, germ-ridden ideology of the Vargas Llosa types' has a limited future in South America. Hope he's right.

Just as I'm getting politically acclimatised, it's time to leave again and this time on an early morning flight. An Indian, his back bent, a brush in each hand, is cleaning the streets. For how long, I wonder. Then we're on the plane and it begins to ascend in circles out of the Cochabamba valley, to avoid the mountains. The Andes are like a vision and the peaks appear like islands in a sea of clouds. In Cochabamba I'd shared the conference platform with Abel Prieto, the Cuban novelist and Minister for Culture, and someone I had not met before: a distinguished Afro-Ecuadorian poet, Antonio Preciado Bedoya, now his country's Minister for Culture. 'The only blacks on our TV are football stars. Now there's me. They must be wondering who I am.' Over dinner he talked of the changes taking place in his country. The pattern in Ecuador is roughly the same as elsewhere. It's the second largest South American supplier of crude oil to the United States. A US oil corporation, ARCO, in league with the local elite and especially the rural oligarchy, wrecked the ecology of the Amazon, and the indigenous population began a peaceful resistance against the multi-layered exploitation.[1] In April 1992

---

1. The entire process has been well described in Suzana Sawyer's excellent *Crude Chronicles: Indigenous Politics, Multinational Oil, and Neoliberalism in Ecuador* (Durham, 2004). Sawyer teaches Anthropology at UC, Davis, and her book is essential reading for anyone seriously interested in understanding some of the root causes that underlay Rafael Correa's electoral triumph.

thousands of indigenous people had celebrated 1492 as '500 years of Resistance' and marched over a hundred miles from Pastaza on the Amazon to the capital Quito in the Andes. Their demands were simple: land reforms and constitutional change. They wanted the rainforests to be designated communal property. Two years later one of their leaders, Hector Villamil, threw down the gauntlet: 'We must change the paternalistic and unequal relations that run through oil operations throughout the Oriente and we must stop the cultural and ecological chaos they produce.'

Fast forward fourteen years and a democratic revolution is in motion. In under a year, Rafael Correa's 'Alliance for Peace' has triumphed four times: the two rounds for the Presidency at the end of 2006; the referendum to elect a constituent assembly in the spring of 2007; and the election of a majority of members (80 out of 130 seats) to the same assembly in September 2007. This last victory gave the Alliance a popular mandate to draft and vote on a new constitution demanded by the powerless citizens back in 1992. A few days later Rafael Correa, emboldened by this support, demanded that the oil companies dish out a larger share of their profits to the state. The additional revenue of a billion dollars would be spent on social expenditure. For 2008, many activists are demanding that the new Ecuador repudiates all 'odious and illegitimate debts'. Whether it will remains to be seen. But Correa has promised that he would rather lose an arm than permit Washington to renew its lease on its only military base in Ecuador, in the city of Manta. The lease expires in 2009 and during a state visit to Italy (where local social movements are agitating against the US military base in Vicenza) Correa remarked: 'We'll renew the base on one condition: that they let us put a base in Miami, an Ecuadorian base. If there's no problem having foreign soldiers on a country's soil, surely they'll let us have a base in the United States.'

In his Presidential address Correa announced that 'it is a change of epoch, not an epoch of changes'. What does this mean, if anything? What he is saying is that this is no longer the epoch of 'wars and revolutions' as Lenin proclaimed the twentieth century to be, but one of social and cultural shifts pushed through in times of peace via democratic earthquakes.

There is, of course, no guarantee that these will succeed, but then nor did the other variety. The cultural revolution is already visible. The Creole oligarchs are livid that an Aymara is President of Bolivia, a 'zambo' occupies the Miraflores Palace in Caracas and a 'mestizo' has been elected in Ecuador, all three with the active support of previously disenfranchised sectors of the population. This is something new. Whether it works remains to be seen. The enemy is economically strong and its friends abroad are even stronger.

Bogged down in Iraq and Afghanistan, obsessed with Iran's rise as a regional power (a direct result of the wars in the aforementioned countries), the State Department has woken up to the fact that South America is in turmoil. Its last major intervention in the region was a crude attempt to topple the democratically elected government in Venezuela. This was in 2002, a year before the adventure in Iraq. Since then a wave of Bolivarian unity has swept the continent, successful in Bolivia and Ecuador, creating ripples in Peru and Paraguay and, above all, breaking the long isolation of Cuba. It is this that is causing the panic in Miami.

The fact that this tiny island has defied US intervention, bullying and blockade for almost half-a-century, remains an imperial obsession. Washington has been waiting for Fidel to die so that it could try and bribe senior military and police officials (and no doubt some well-chosen party apparatchiks) to defect. Bush's speech of 24 October 2007 is a sign of panic: so convinced was Washington that mega-bucks would do the trick that it had let its attention wander in recent years.

But, the US President inform us without any sense of irony, Raul Castro is unacceptable as a successor because he is Fidel's brother. This is not the transition that Washington had in mind. It's a bit rich coming from W, given his own family connections, not to mention the fact that if Mrs Clinton is nominated and wins, two families will have held power for over two decades. And dynastic politics is now so deep-grained in official culture that it is being happily mimicked in tiny circles of supporters (the editorial chair of the neo-con magazine *Commentary* having been smoothly handed over from father to son Podhoretz).

What worries the Bush brothers and their clientele in Florida is the fact that Raul Castro has inaugurated and encouraged among Cuba's people an open debate on the island's future. This is not popular with apparatchiks, but is undoubtedly having an impact. State censorship is not only deeply unpopular, but has crippled creative thought on the island. The new opening has brought all the old contradictions to the fore. Cuban film-makers are publicly challenging the bureaucrats. Pavel Giroud, a well-known director, explains how the censorship works:

> Censorship works here just like it does everywhere, except that because it's Cuba, it's closely scrutinized. It isn't a national monopoly. Every television network and publication in the world has its guidelines for broadcasting or editing, and whatever does not fit the requirements gets left out. HBO in the States refused to broadcast Oliver Stone's documentary about Fidel Castro, because it didn't take the focus that the network wanted. So they insisted on another interview with Fidel. In other words, what Stone wanted to say about his interviewee didn't matter – what mattered was what the network wanted to show.
>
> Personally, I prefer that a work of mine not be broadcast, rather than be told to change my shots or remove footage. Nor am I interested in hearing their explanations. The mere fact of being silenced is so serious that the reason why pales in comparison, because it will never be a good enough reason

for the person who is silenced . . . Banality and lack of creativity are favored everywhere. Turn on any music video channel in the world, and you'll see that for every artistically worthwhile video, you have to put up with several others. the same buttocks writhing around the *machista* reggaeton star, the same seductive gestures by the 'in' singers, the same slow-moving shots of love scenes at sunset, the same sheen on the biceps, the same sensual moves, the same phoney little smiles. I think we in Cuba are definitely not the principal producers of these.

The same happens in politics – there is opportunism on both sides, by the makers and by the broadcasters. The broadcasters know that a video full of praise for the system won't make any trouble for them, and the creators know perfectly well that they will get on television much faster if they write a song, produce a video or film, or paint a picture in praise of a political figure.

That the Cuban system needs to be reformed is widely accepted in the country. I have been told often that the decision 'forced on us by the embargo' to follow the old Soviet model was 'not beneficial'. The choice now is Washington or Caracas. And while a tiny layer of the Cuban elite will be tempted by the dollars, most Cubans would prefer a different model. They do not wish to see an end to their health and education systems, but they do want more economic and political diversity, even though the model of the Big Neighbour under whose shadow they live does not exactly offer that choice. And that model never changes. The highly respected Cuban leader Ricardo Alarcón reflects on

fifty years of the same US policy, which is, it has to be said, a failed one. Of course, now they are waiting for the next generation, based on the idea that this government is finished. Well, if that's the way it is, I guess I'm done with, too, because I'm a member of the outgoing generation. A half century in

France passed from the time of the monarchy of Louis XVI, the great revolution, the guillotine, all the counter-revolution that ensued, Bonapartism, the bourgeois republic of the thirties. All the twists and turns that France underwent took place in the same period of time that we have managed to keep the Cuban revolution in power. Not even Robespierre could say that; Napoleon couldn't say that. Hey, we've done a lot!

During the last week of the November–December 2007 referendum campaign in Venezuela, I was in Mexico attending the Guadalajara Book Fair. The day they were voting, a friend took me to a local cinema to see Luis Mandoki's documentary, *Fraude*, which is playing to packed houses when distributors permit. Millions of people worked together and shared hundreds of hours in filmed material to build this film, a powerful indictment of the Mexican elite that stole the elections from Andrés Manuel López Obrador (AMLO). Obrador would now be Mexico's president if votes had not been fraudulently tallied in the 2006 elections. Yet Western media and numerous other apologists turned a blind eye to the fraud because Felipe Calderón, the conservative PAN candidate, was Washington's friend and therefore the EU's friend as well. Whereas everything in Venezuela is inspected with a microscope, in the case of Mexico fraud is ignored.

Compare and contrast this attitude with the fact that in the six-month period leading up to the Venezuelan referendum, the *Washington Post*, *New York Times* and the *Los Angeles Times* devoted 11,000 words in 14 op-eds and editorials to questioning the Bolivarian electoral system. The *Miami Herald*, located where market and social geography combine, published 16 op-eds and editorials on its own. On 30 November 2007 the White House organ-grinders took centre position, with the President's Press Secretary, Dana Perino, querying the Venezuelan electoral system's democratic credentials. They were obviously expecting a blow. They were proved wrong.

Hugo Chávez's narrow defeat (50.3 per cent to 49.3 per cent) on 2 December 2007 was the result of large-scale abstentions by his supporters. Forty-four per cent of the electorate stayed at home. Why? First, because they did not either understand or accept that this was a necessary referendum. Second, because food shortages, engineered or accidental, had created a mini-crisis. There were sixty-nine proposed reforms. The measures related to the working week, along with other important and admirable social measures, could be easily legislated by the existing parliament. The key issues were the removal of restrictions on the election of the head of government (as currently exist in most of Europe) and moves towards 'a socialist state'. On the latter there was simply not enough debate and discussion on a grassroots level.

As Edgardo Lander, a friendly critic, pointed out:

Before voting in favour of a constitutional reform which will define the State, the economy, and the democracy as socialist, we citizens have the right to participate in these definitions. What is understood by the term socialist state? What is understood by the term socialist economy? What is understood by the term socialist democracy? In what way are these different to the states, economies, and democracies that accompanied socialism of the 20th century? Here, we are not talking about entering into a debate on semantics, rather on basic decisions about the future of the country.

And this was further amplified by Greg Wilpert, a sympathetic journalist whose website, venezuelaanalysis.com, is the best source of information on the country:

By rushing the reform process Chávez presented the opposition with a nearly unprecedented opportunity to deal him a serious blow. Also, the rush in which the process was pushed forward opened him to criticism that the process was fundamentally flawed, which has become one of the main criticisms of the more moderate critics of the reform.

Another error was the insistence on voting for all the proposals en bloc, on a take-it-or-leave-it basis. It's perfectly possible that a number of the proposals might have got through if a vote on each had been allowed. This would have compelled the Bolivarians to campaign more effectively at grassroots level through organised discussions and debates (as the French Left did to win the argument and defeat the EU Constitution). It is always a mistake to underestimate the electorate – and Chávez knows this better than most.

What is to be done now? The President is in office till 2013 and whatever else Chávez may be, the label of 'lame duck' will never fit him. He is a fighter, and will be thinking of how to strengthen the process. If properly handled the defeat could be a blessing in disguise. It has, after all, punctured the arguments of the Western pundits who had been claiming for the last eight years that democracy in Venezuela had died at the hands of authoritarianism.

Anyone who saw Chávez's speech accepting defeat last night (as I did here in Guadalajara with Mexican friends) will not be in any doubt regarding his commitment to a democratically embedded social process. That much is clear. One of the weaknesses of the movement in Venezuela has been its over-dependence on one person. It is a dangerous situation for that person (one bullet can be enough), and it is unhealthy for the Bolivarian process. There will be a great deal of soul-searching taking place in Caracas, but the key now is an open debate analysing the causes of the setback, and a move towards a collective leadership to decide on the next Presidential candidate. It's a long time ahead but the discussions should start now. Deepening popular participation and encouraging social inclusion (as envisaged in the defeated constitutional changes) should be done anyway.

The referendum defeat will undoubtedly boost the Venezuelan opposition and the Right in Latin America, but they would be foolish to imagine that this victory will automatically win them the Presidency. Some of them have begun to understand this reality. 'This is not a 100-metre sprint, but a marathon', said Teodoro Petkoff, burnt no doubt by his support for the 2002 coup and deafened by the noise created by his own counter-revolutionary polemics. If the real lessons of the defeat are understood it is the Bolivarians who will win. But that means an open and public debate on the way forward, and resisting the temptation to denounce friendly critics as 'traitors', or voters who stayed at home as lazy scumbags. The stakes are high, the alternatives worse on every count. The anxious eyes of the poor all over South America are watching Venezuela.

Appendix One

Teodoro Petkoff: A Man for All Seasons

Gain and loss are twins and all profits, wrote Montaigne, are made at the expense of others:

> The merchant only thrives on the extravagance of youth; the farmer on the high price of grain; the architect on the collapse of houses; the officers of the law on men's suits and contentions; even the honour and practice of ministers of religion depend on our death and vices. No physician takes pleasure in the health even of his friends, says the ancient Greek writer of comedies [Philemon]. And what is worse, let anyone search his heart and he will find that our inward wishes are for the most part born and nourished at the expense of others.

Add to this the socialist turned neo-liberal, who now has a vested interest in the success of the market economy and will accept any ministerial post to further his cause. Were he to be offered the position of minister in charge of watching boiling cauldrons in hell, he would accept as long as the commodity was not being boiled in violation of IMF rules. Alas, poor Teodoro. He really did believe that history was over and all the old baggage could now be safely dumped and, as I have demonstrated elsewhere in this book, he was not alone. Today he edits the daily *Tal Cual* (As It Is), which is a necessary (and sometimes the only) port-of-call for Western journalists in a hurry to do a quickfire number on Chávez and return home.

The old messianic passion is still there but its object has changed. The narcissism remains and fuels his anger. He, not the upstart Chávez, should be President of the Republic. This side of him was remarked on by a prescient Régis Debray, who drew on the less heroic sides of Petkoff for the portrayal of Joaquim, a leader of the armed struggle, in *L'Indesirable*, his novel set in Venezuela during guerrilla times in the Sixties:

> A perfect Secretary General for the change of key that's coming, thought Frank, as he looked at Joaquim. A solid man with no cheap swagger about him, despite the Young Turk image. And well-educated too: the keenest brain in the political bureau, so everyone said. All this and heaven too. Oh yes, the peace would be in excellent hands. But can a man win the peace who is quite so easily reconciled to losing the war?[1]

As I write, Petkoff is the only publicly declared presidential candidate representing the anti-Chávez opposition, which is entirely to his credit, especially as the latest opinion polls (July 2006) suggest he is on 3 per cent. Personally, I hope he does not withdraw his candidature under pressure from the oligarchy and vigorously defends the Opposition case against the Bolivarians, which is necessary for the health of Venezuelan democracy.

Who is Teodoro Petkoff and whatever happened to him? He was born in Maracaibo, Zulia state in January 1932, to a Bulgarian emigrant father and a Jewish-Polish mother. His father was the Communist son of two founding members of the Bulgarian Communist Party and a friend of Georgi Dimitrov. He fled Bulgaria after the failure of the 1923 insurrection led to massive repression (30,000 deaths) and moved to Brno in Czechoslovakia,

---

1. Régis Debray, *Undesirable Alien*, London, 1978, pp. 158–9.

where he met his future wife. He became a chemical engineer, she a doctor. They had thought of moving to the Soviet Union, but there were some technical problems which might have meant separation for a while, so they were advised by Bulgarian friends in Caracas to migrate to Venezuela, which they did in 1927.

In the 1950s, Teodoro was a student leader who participated in demonstrations against the regime of Marcos Pérez Jiménez. Later, his apolitical brother Mirko was shot dead by a policeman and the tragedy stunned his parents:

> It seems that around the time my brother Mirko was killed by a policeman, in 1957, my father lost much of his vital spirit. As I said, my parents never displayed much emotion, even in terms of affection. I remember, when I decided to formally enroll in the Communist Youth, I told papa who simply said: 'Very good. I think that's very good.'
>
> That was a big step for me because the Peréz Jiménez dictatorship [1948–58] was just beginning then, and it was no joke to be in the Communist Youth at that time. Ever since I was 13 or 14 years old, I had read a great deal, especially history. That was one characteristic that distinguished me from my younger brothers and the other boys. I was very moved by such books as Gorky's *Mother* and *Soviet Power* by Hewlett Johnson, the Red Dean of Canterbury. At the time I was an adolescent, it was very strange to find a boy of 15 involved in politics. The politicization of youth in Venezuela is a very recent phenomenon.

During the early 1960s, inspired by the Cuban Revolution, he joined the guerrilla *foco* under the leadership of the Venezuelan anti-imperialist Douglas Bravo. He was imprisoned a few times and escaped prison at least twice, most famously in 1967 when he succeeded in breaking out of the Cuartel San Carlos with his comrades Pompeyo Márquez (currently a prominent, pompous and ageing member of the current opposition to Chávez) and Guillermo García Ponce (the seventy-something editor of the pro-Chávez daily *VEA*). It is these episodes that form the subject matter of Debray's novel referred to above.

Petkoff and other Communist militants backed the 1969 'pacification' policy of the Rafael Caldera government, which offered a general amnesty to all those who had been involved in the guerrillas (Douglas Bravo was among those who refused to lay down his arms).

Soon after the Soviet invasion of Czechoslovakia, Petkoff and other dissidents in the Venezuelan Communist Party rejected its pro-Soviet line and founded the Movement Towards Socialism (Movimiento Al Socialismo – MAS), which quickly became a hit in left-wing intellectual circles (Gabriel García Márquez , awarded the Romulo Gallegos literary award in 1972, donated the $25,000 to MAS). Even though MAS found it difficult to acquire a real grassroots base, few questioned Teodoro's impeccable socialist credentials. He was still committed to socialism and democracy as is obvious from a speech delivered in 1976 and later published under the title, 'To no nation do we attribute the right to guide the destiny of the Venezuelan motherland', which was a reference to Washington, not Havana:

Yes, gentlemen, we assert the absolute, indispensable and unavoidable need for a socialist government that sets the social body in motion, that eliminates the power of small but powerful economic groups that have controlled all the country's life and have traced the fundamental orientations of all of the governments that Venezuela has had . . . The calamities of our society are based in the fact that the country is dominated by a few dozen economic groups that the rest of the population works for, and that build their fortune and political power in the work, the exploitation and the political manipulation of the immense majority. We advocate the need to place the control of Venezuelan life, not just economic life, but the totality of our social life, in the hands of the entire population . . .

We understand socialism to be the full recovery of national sovereignty and not as the substitution of one form of dependence for another . . .

Finally, gentlemen, we understand socialism as a world from which the word 'exploitation' will have been eliminated, even from dictionaries.

If he still believed this, *Tal Cual* could have been critical of the Bolivarian Revolution from the Left. But Petkoff was clearly becoming irritated with the failure of MAS to become a hegemonic force on the Left. In fact, throughout the 1980s it was generally regarded as an elitist and ineffective vehicle for Petkoff's personal ambitions, rarely obtaining more than 5 per cent of the vote in elections. Former friends of his told me that this became an increasingly sore point, and that he would erupt in anger at private gatherings when MAS was discussed. Petkoff ran for President twice in the 1980s: in 1983, despite receiving a passionate public endorsement from Gabriel García Márquez, he obtained only 4 per cent of the vote. Would he have received a higher vote if Vargas Llosa or Carlos Fuentes had thrown in their support as well? It's possible that he might have gained 4.5 per cent.

By 1988 he was becoming increasingly frustrated. He thought that the problem lay not in him (how could that possibly be the case?) but in the political agenda he had espoused. Shifting to a different gear, Petkoff projected a more centrist (but not yet a Hayekian) agenda, and received slightly over 10 per cent of the vote – a record for MAS and a tragedy for its *jefe maximo*. Petkoff was now convinced that the future lay elsewhere. By the early 1990s, MAS had given up on everything. The Soviet Union had collapsed and Petkoff thought it was time to move on. This time he wouldn't make any more mistakes. He then decided to publicly

support the candidacy of the Christian Democrat (COPEI) leader
Rafael Caldera in the 1992 presidential elections. Campaigning on
an anti-WC ticket, Caldera won. A financial crisis was orche-
strated by the local oligarchs and Caldera quickly capitulated,
introducing a new neo-liberal package of reforms (the third in the
country's history) known as the Venezuela Agenda.

And Petkoff? He was in heaven. He was named 'Planning
Minister' in 1995 and was the key official in charge of implementing neo-liberal reforms, which the government attempted to make
slightly sexier by linking them to very modest, largely symbolic,
social programmes. The planning Petkoff implemented was a
process of gradual privatisations and deregulation. The economy
was further liberalised, state spending was tightly reined in, public
administrations were streamlined, state-owned companies were
auctioned off and the Bolívar was devalued. International financial markets cheered, the Venezuelan poor and lower middle class
agonised, and by the end of his term Caldera was almost
universally despised in Venezuela, just as Pérez and others before
him had been. Petkoff's own web page biography is uncharacter-
istically modest:

> In 1995, in the midst of one of the country's most critical
> moments, he [Petkoff] became the Minister of Planning and,
> despite the barrel of oil being at seven dollars, saved the
> economy from imminent collapse and contributed (. . .) to
> avoiding an economic and social disaster by rationalizing
> public expenditures and fortifying social programs.

It's worth noting that the Venezuela Agenda included a set of
energy policies which further deepened the 'Oil Opening' (Aper-
tura Petrolera) policies initiated in the early 1980s, which set
Venezuela's state-owned petroleum company PDVSA on a path
towards ever greater autonomy and, eventually, privatisation.
Influenced directly by the PDVSA Executive Board, the Caldera

government called for the global market, rather than OPEC, to control oil prices, and backed a significant increase in PDVSA's oil production, far beyond the OPEC quota level, which contributed to lowering the price of oil to $7 a barrel and diminishing Venezuela's revenues.

In 1998, a desperate MAS, discredited by Petkoff's performance in the Caldera government, threw its feeble weight behind Chávez's candidacy (Petkoff had taught them to back winners and they were good students). There was much surprise when the great leader promptly withdrew from the party and, in his new capacity as the editor-in-chief of the news daily *El Mundo*, mounted an aggressive campaign against Chávez. Within a year, apparently because the *El Mundo* publishers wanted to make peace with Chávez, he was fired. He immediately put together a new daily paper, *Tal Cual*, which has, for the last six and a half years featured Petkoff's anti-Chávez editorials on its front page. Though he's now busy with his presidential campaigns he still finds the time to write weekly editorials, whose entertainment value is acknowledged by all. Petkoff has a sharp mind and a vitriolic pen, but amnesia is creeping in.

Over the last few years he has been quite effective at selling himself in the international press as a left-wing icon (ex-guerrilla, etc.) rather than an ex-Planning Minister who presided over the implementation of an orthodox neo-liberal programme. He is also usually represented as someone who is as critical of the rest of the Opposition as of Chávez. This is a rather distorted picture of his views, as any regular reader of *Tal Cual* knows only too well. While he attacks and ridicules Chávez in every issue of his paper he rarely takes a swipe at the Opposition; his salvoes are rare and seemingly only fired when he wishes to distance himself from a particularly outrageous move (for instance in the days *following* the April 2002 coup). *Tal Cual* is a striking demonstration of the fact that there is total freedom of speech in Venezuela.

As explained earlier in this book, the State Department's house journal *Foreign Affairs* and its siblings elsewhere have been promoting a stale notion of 'good' and 'bad' Latin Americans. Lula is good because he supports the Washington Consensus. Incapable now of independent thought, Petkoff jumped on this weak bandwagon in the company of Castañeda and Vargas Llosa with ill-concealed delight. He absolutely adores Lula. In 2005 he published a book called the *Two Lefts* in which he rambles at length about the virtues of the Latin American 'modern', pro-globalisation, left that Lula incarnates, and then derides the antiquated 'populist', 'authoritarian' version of the left that Chávez (and Castro) keeps alive.

Petkoff is also often portrayed by his fan club (Western journalists in Caracas and their friends in Mexico and São Paulo) as an honest, law-abiding, fair-playing freethinker. It's a myth – as evidenced by his reaction to the April 2002 coup, which challenged democracy and the constitution.

His editorial in the 12 April, 2002 issue of *Tal Cual*, beneath a giant banner headline 'CIAO HUGO', was exultant. A man he had made his enemy had fallen:

> With much pain, brought upon dozens of Venezuelan homes [a reference to the 19 people killed around Miraflores palace on 11 April] and without glory, Hugo Chávez's regime came to an end. The arrogant Hugo Chávez, who enjoyed announcing that he would retire in 2021, has been overthrown barely three years after his spectacular ascent to power . . . This is the hour of justice, not of vengeance. Those responsible for the assassinations yesterday should be found and brought to justice, starting with Chávez himself. The thieves that accumulated obscene fortunes, that pillaged the national treasury, cannot remain unpunished . . . Here there is no way to bring an institutional solution to the political change that's occurred. Vice President, President of the National Assembly, President

of the Supreme Court, don't outlive Chávez's collapse. This line of institutional command died with the regime.

On the back cover of the same issue is a large picture of a crowd of Opposition protesters on a wide avenue next to Miraflores, confronting a few national guard troops. In the middle of the picture is a young protester, brandishing a big Venezuelan flag. The caption reads:

> Intrepid and solitary, the young man who holds the flag symbolizes a new era for Venezuela. It is time for the reconstruction of a country that refused to sacrifice its freedoms and thus took to the streets so as to rescue its threatened dignity. In the midst of the scuffling and the flying bullets, yesterday's extraordinary popular demonstration, with record amounts of participants and happiness, a path was cleared and the goal of throwing Hugo Chávez out of Miraflores was achieved.

By the time the next issue of *Tal Cual* was published, on 14 April, the coup had been reversed by a popular uprising and soldiers' and officers' mutinies. What would our intrepid editor do? Embarrassed, but not ashamed, Petkoff now chose to criticise the unconstitutional behaviour of the Opposition. This was a common theme of the liberals caught celebrating the coup, who then had to face up to reality a few days later. If only, ran this editorial, there had been a better regime change replacement than Carmona (perhaps even Petkoff himself?), who could have united the Opposition and shared the ministerial spoils, then people would not have rallied behind Chávez. Day-dreaming of this sort is common in the more salubrious sections of Caracas.

But back to the fight for the Presidency. What does the 74-year-old Petkoff offer the electorate? As is usually the case with Venezuelan Opposition candidates, his political programme is deliberately vague. The only concrete measure proposed to date is the oil *cesta ticket* (monthly coupon books provided by employers that are used for food purchases). The idea is to do away with the current policy of using oil revenues to fund social programmes and, instead, provide Venezuelan households with an equal share of regular PDVSA dividends so that each may choose to spend the oil money at their discretion on health, education (and booze, casinos, drugs and brothels?). It's similar in concept to the new voucher school systems appearing everywhere in the US. Private medicine, private education, etc., will thus be subsidised while state-run institutions will have to learn either to compete with the private sector or die. It's doubtful whether this appeal will strike a chord with the majority of Venezuelans. Communism had led Petkoff to the armed struggle and then to socialism with a human face. From here he had pole-vaulted to the Washington Consensus and there he remains, a sad and marginal figure in a country he once wanted to change. Chávez's opponents constantly talk of 'authoritarianism', but the frank and free 2003 exchange between Petkoff and Maximilien Arvelaiz, a member of Chávez's political staff, indicates the exact opposite. Petkoff's puerile bombast and Arvelaiz' restrained response was part of a longer exchange, but it will give readers a flavour of the political scene in East Caracas:

'Teodoro Petkoff'
To: 'maximilien arvelaiz'
Date: Wed, 23 Jul 2003 18:49:26 -0400

I see you continue to be as irritating as usual. We interview everyone in this daily, any number of chavistas have been interviewed too. What is more, if you want we can interview you, to get you out of the closet. And you are right, what Maria Sol said (by the way, I have spoken to her no more than twice) was stupid. [Ignacio] Ramonet seems to me to be an idiot and a mercenary but he is not, of course, a nobody in France.

Now, I don't know if your little brain can cope with the idea
that the interviewer is not responsible for what interviewees
say. In this newspaper we don't do things like you do at the
Miraflores, where you don't even fart without Chávez's
permission, and nor do my journalists go around like you
do, licking Chávez's balls. I don't even know in advance who
the interviewees are because those decisions are made by the
journalists. The champagne you want to drink will be the
oldest in the world: your intellectual policeman's soul has
shown through. From what I can see (oh, [something about]
Freud!), every day you ask if *Tal Cual* has come out and it
frustrates you to see that we haven't folded.

What a pitiful devil you have turned out to be. How about
you give me permission to publish your letter?

Teodoro

Maximilen Arvelaiz to Teodoro Petkoff,
24 July 2003

It's always entertaining when you give us lessons in the ethics
of journalism. You and your court – and don't talk to me about
vainas, you too have your ball-tuggers. Yes, yes, every time I
have any doubts about what not to do, I read your editorial
from 12 April. Do you remember, Teodoro, what you wrote a
few hours after Venezuelan democracy had been overthrown?
'To the end, [Chávez] lived in the delirium which killed him
and his last act in power was truly criminal. That broadcast
from yesterday evening, grotesque, really Kafkaesque, was
deliberately carried out to cover up news of the massacre that
Bernal's killer snipers were perpetrating.' Over a year later we
are still waiting for the slightest proof of these extremely
serious accusations, but I think that, like the good guard-dog of

the media system that you are, you thought that the images transmitted by the TV stations on that sad day are sufficient. I also really miss your economics lessons, from those fine days when you 'ran' the Venezuelan economy. I imagine you dreamt of a fate like that of Fernando Henrique Cardoso, of the intellectual who becomes president. Poor Teodoro, you ended up being eastern Caracas's favourite editorial-writer. What's most fascinating about you is your continuing ability to make a few poor foreign journalists believe that you are from the 'Left'. I don't know if it's your moustache, but *chapeau*! Sometimes I come across these journalists from France, Brazil, from all over the world completely hypnotised after listening to your wise words. Damn it, what a magician's talent you have! By the way, have you seen *Le Monde*, another neoliberal evening paper which has gone bankrupt, from a fortnight ago? An amazing headline: '*TAL CUAL*, anti-Chávez paper of the Left'. What a laugh!

I'm surprised you ask my permission to publish my letters. You'd need much more than that for anyone to believe you are a balanced communicator, especially if they've ever read your rag. You'll see if you publish it. I would only suggest that, so no one thinks badly of you, you publish the full sequences of messages we have sent each other. Many of them are answers to things we've said to each other through this channel.

In any case, you can publish them. I don't give a shit. That way you can guarantee yourself the power to carry on presenting yourself as a moderate, open man, hiding the small, angry Stalinist you never stopped being.

When friends suggested to Arvelaiz that some of the material in *Tal Cual* was actionable, he replied: 'If a donkey shits on you, would you sue him?'

The real tragedy is that as Venezuela is being slowly transformed, and for the better, it needs good advice and help from those who played an important part in its radical past and suffered imprisonment and worse. Teodoro Petkoff, alas, decided to jump ship and even though he could have played an important and useful role in the Bolivarian process he found it difficult to row back. So he decided to become part of the problem, his witty monologues in *Tal Cual* finding receptive readers in the salons of the politically-disposed oligarchs. R.I.P.

Appendix Two

Le Monde Is Not The Worst, But . . .

Henri Maler

The 18 August 2004 editorial in *Le Monde* on the referendum result and soberly entitled 'Chávez's Victory', coming after many months during which the 'paper of record' published very selective information, often drowned in extremely biased commentaries, does not confine itself to freely commenting, as it should, on the results: instead, it dispenses prescriptions to all comers.

More precisely, *Le Monde* – being both a daily newspaper and a universal cure for all ills, manages to propose its prescriptions to both sides at the same time – both to the Opposition and to the Venezuelan government. This double prescription rests, no doubt, on a rigorous diagnosis.

Moderato

The medicinal editorial of *Le Monde* opens with two paragraphs where, nestling among factual information on the results, are inaccuracies which illuminate the past and evaluations which prepare the future.

> But this referendum, demanded by the opposition, will not end the crisis which has been dividing the nation for over two years. Having promised that it would respect the verdict of the electors, the heteroclite coalition of parties – united only by

their detestation of the populist leader of Caracas – denounced the 'massive fraud'. At the current time, it is refusing to comply with the democratic process, supported in this posture by the Bush administration, which has demanded an enquiry on the supposed fraud that no independent observer has raised.

This is a retrospective inaccuracy. It is wrong to say that the opposition had 'promised to respect the verdict of the electors'. On the contrary. The opposition had 'promised' that it would respect the results only if the elections were fraud-free, but it had announced in advance that if it lost the elections, this loss would necessarily be due to fraud. In other words, it had promised to respect the verdict of the electors . . . but only on condition that the opposition won.[1]

The prospective evaluation is as follows: the Opposition, we read in *Le Monde* is a 'motley coalition of parties only united by their detestation of the populist leader of Caracas'. So, Chávez is a 'populist' leader. The anonymous editorialist of *Le Monde* didn't have to search very far to form this diagnosis: the press releases of Agence France Presse (which *Le Monde* constantly reproduces and processes) deafeningly hammer this home. And we will see further that if this piece of 'information' opens the editorial, it is because our editorialist has absorbed it particularly well . . .

But so far all of this is still *moderato*.

Forte

'The ballot boxes have spoken in Venezuela and president Chávez has saved his office, in the face of an opposition which was demanding his downfall', notes our editorialist from the outset. 'Whether we like it or not, Hugo Chávez remains, until the 2007 elections, the

---

1. It should be added that the Opposition also stipulated that the result should be validated by international observers – now, it is reversing this condition.

legitimate president of his country', he first confirms – before engaging in a to-and-fro between 'the one hand' and 'the other':

> Democracy needs the opposition – which comprises almost half of all Venezuelans – to use this period constructively in order to find itself a leader (currently, it has far too many of them) – and the programme that it lacks at present. For his part, Mr Chávez should remember that he is not the elected representative of one fraction of his compatriots, but the president of the whole country.

On the one hand, then, 'Democracy needs'; on the other hand 'Mr Chávez should'. On the one hand, *Le Monde* wants . . . what democracy wants. On the other, *Le Monde* prescribes what Mr Chávez *should do*: i.e. 'remember' . . . the very things that he himself said the on the day his electoral victory was announced.

Exasperated by seeing the country reach a 'provisional compromise', the anonymous editorialist notes in passing that Venezuela is 'a country which was once prosperous and which for ages has lurched from political crisis to economic crisis': it's worth noting here the precision of 'once' and 'for ages', before seeing *Le Monde* perform a lurch of its own.

This starts with a Platonic wish: 'Until then, the best that one can hope is that no one will pour oil on the fire, either in Venezuela or abroad, in Washington or Havana.'

This is immediately followed by an injunction directed to the 'region': 'One must keep one's head in this terribly volatile region [but who says that this is a 'volatile' region?] and particularly in a country which is the fifth biggest exporter of oil.'

Fortissimo

'On the one hand' and 'on the other' are back. Let us first look at 'on the one hand':

It is not because this former putschist officer, now become a kind of tribune of a tropical national-populism resting on the support of the barracks, is defying Washington that he should be considered a responsible politician, or someone capable of pulling his country out of the mire into which others before him had thrown it.

'On the one hand', Chávez is irresponsible. He is a 'former putschist officer, now become a kind of tribune of a tropical national-populism resting on the support of the barracks'.

Words have meanings. And everyone knows that the mediator of *Le Monde* watches jealously over their use. 'National-populism' has resonances with 'national-socialism': no doubt a deplorable blunder on *Le Monde*'s part . . . Moreover, this 'populism' is 'tropical': an adjective surely stripped of its ethnocentrism and is strictly in character . . . And this 'national-populism' rests on the support of 'the barracks'.[2] And what about the majority of the people? *Le Monde* doesn't know: the absence of such a detail is thus not a regrettable omission . . .

It now remains to follow a little detour via 'the other hand':

But it is not because the Bush administration compares him without any nuances to the Cuban dictator and supports his adversaries – including during the abortive coup of 2002 – that one should consider Hugo Chávez a new Castro, a spokesperson for the disinherited.

'On the other hand', Chávez is not a new Castro. OK . . . But we don't know what role this expression, juxtaposed with 'the spokesperson of the disinherited' is supposed to play here.

---

2. In the absence of any precise commmment on the role of the military, the expression carries with it a strong whiff of dictatorship – but this is surely an involuntary allusion.

Perhaps we should refrain from 'considering' this as well? But, as *Le Monde* says, 'whether we like it or not', it is impossible to deny that Chávez is the 'spokesperson of the disinherited' and to claim that the 'national-populist tribune' draws his support only from the barracks. The 'On the one hand' and 'on the other' analysis is beginning to limp somewhat.

Why? Because the US administration is the touchstone for this squirming – an effect of *Le Monde*'s obsession, developed since its 'We are all Americans' pronouncement of 9/11: it is not because Chávez is opposed to Bush that he has become someone one cannot associate with. It is not because Bush compares him to Fidel Castro that 'one should consider Chávez as a new Castro'. After this extract from the 'geopolitics of thought' comes the explanation . . .

Allegretto

We had got this far: we should not consider 'Hugo Chávez as a new Castro, the spokesperson of the disinherited.' Why? 'Because it is above all thanks to the increase in oil prices that Hugo Chávez owes his political survival.'

Before coming back to this miraculous explanation, we should try to resolve an enigma: does this sentence explain why Chávez is not 'a new Castro' or why Chávez is not 'the spokesperson of the disinherited'? The mystery is total. We can try to proceed by elimination: it is not because his political survival is due to the rise in oil prices that Chávez is not a new Castro . . . But in what way would this stop him from being a 'spokesperson of the disinherited'? We have to keep our heads and untangle all this.

Let's start again: '. . . it is *above all* thanks to the increase in oil prices that Hugo Chávez owes his political survival' [my emphasis]. It follows that Chávez 'survives' (with, nonetheless, 58 per cent of the vote and with nearly 2 million votes polled). And that without the rise in oil prices, he would not have survived. This demands an explanation . . .

Here it is:

> Without this [rise in the oil prices], he would never have found the billion dollars he has spent these last months on social programmes whose electoralist character it would be difficult to deny.

Well informed as he is, the anonymous editorialist of *Le Monde* has certainly read – on the financial pages – articles regarding the rise in oil prices. He therefore knows that the stabilisation in oil prices and the subsequent first wave of rises were due notably to the role of the Chávez government in relaunching OPEC. He also knows that the profits that the government has redistributed were achieved despite the lockout imposed by the bosses' strike last year. Finally, he knows that these profits could have further served to enrich the wealthy, and thus that it was a political choice to devote them to 'social programmes'.

But *Le Monde*'s editorialist prefers to ignore all this: he 'knows' from now on that Chávez (on his own?) has spent billions of dollars 'on social programmes whose electoralist character it would be difficult to deny'. In other words, when the government[3] is more able than ever to honour the commitments that allowed it to gain the trust of the people, it is by . . . electoralism. And when we said he was a 'populist' . . .

Finale

And so the editorialist finishes his *pas de deux*:

---

3. Who, it should be said in passing, had for a good while adopted 'social measures' (as the saying goes), about which *Le Monde* hasn't been very specific.

He has two years to demonstrate *his sense of responsibility*, to stop managing his country in such a disorganised manner and, above all, to strictly respect the law and human rights. But this, in return, assumes that the opposition unreservedly accepts the verdict of the ballot box and *also shows itself also to be responsible* by letting Hugo Chávez finish his mandate.

This clarion call (in which vague allusions and accusations of hidden agendas resonate)[4] is more or less empty, saying nothing else than – how important *Le Monde* considers itself to be.

Reprise

What should we draw from all this? First that *Le Monde* has the perfect right to write whatever it wants. It even has the right to prescribe what it wants to the whole world: who would dream of stopping the party of *Le Monde* from being partisan?

Let us simply remark that the party of *Le Monde* functions and expresses itself in a curious manner. It has as its spokesperson an anonymous editorialist who speaks in the name of the whole of the editorial staff: not, we have no doubt, because it is applying 'democratic centralism', but by virtue of a pretty opaque variety of autocratic centralism. But let this pass . . .

Does the party of *Le Monde*, at least, distribute a newspaper that informs its readers? This is a problem to which we will return at some length, because of the 500 articles of all lengths that *Le Monde* has devoted, more or less directly, to Venezuela since 1999, *not one* gives details of the Bolivarian constitution, *not one* gives details of the decree laws adopted in 2001, *not one* gives details of the 'missions' encouraged by the government. Even in order to

---

4. Where are the assaults on human rights that are here denounced – before they have even happened?

evaluate them. Scarcely a few random paragraphs framed in 'analysis' or 'commentary' articles. Nonetheless, for *Le Monde* there is no doubt: the Chávez government is a form of 'tropical national-populism' . . .

Appendix Three

We Have Learned Our Lesson:
Whatever Doesn't Kill You
Makes You Stronger

Luis Reyes Reyes, Governor of Lara State
interviewed by Rosa Elizalde and Luis Baez

Barinas, Games and Friendship

I came to Barinas when I was two and, shortly after, my parents, my ten brothers and I moved to a neighbourhood near to where the Chávez family moved. There were only two options in terms of secondary education in Barinas: the industrial and technical school and the regular secondary school. The upper class sent its children to a private school.

During that time, Chávez and I studied in the same secondary school, the O'Leary, but we actually met in the waste grounds where we'd play baseball. We didn't have much to do with each other back then, because he played in one team and I in another. I have to admit his team was better organized than mine.

Which base did you play?

I was catcher and fielder, and he, well, he was always on first base. I pitched a number of times there in Barinas, but, most of the time, I was catcher when he was on first.

You enlisted in the Air Force . . .

When we finished secondary school, I chose to go to the Air Force Academy in Maracay instead of the Military Academy in Caracas. We went our separate ways. At the end of the first year, we met at the games between the two academies. Then, there weren't many of us from Barinas who went to military academies, there weren't more than ten of us.

I remember that, in that first game, they put me in as pitcher when the Academy was beating us. I kept them in check, but Hugo hit a grounder and made it to first base, though I've never let him get away with saying it was a good single; I've always thought what saved him was the fact first base was really close. We played against one another again in the second games, but, by then, we had a closer relationship. We became closer in third year, because, as a brigadier,[1] one has more independence and more chance for friendship. In fourth year, they sent me to the United States, to a flight unit that trained pilots, in Columbus, Mississippi . . . There, I became a pilot officer and graduated.

Did you have any contact with Chávez during this time?

No, we didn't have much contact that year. Chávez was closer to Hugo Ramírez, a fine young man from Barinas, and to another fellow from Barinas, who had been his classmate during the four years at the Academy. Being outside the country taking the course, I didn't even have a lot of contact with the people from my year, with now Chief Army Commander Jorge García Carneiro, for instance.

How long were you in the United States for?

I was there for a year and a half. I graduated as a pilot. When I got back here, they assigned me to another place, I transferred and left for Barquisimeto in 1975. One of my brothers graduated from the army's School of Communications around that time. They sent him to Barinas, where Chávez was serving as a second lieutenant. In January of 1976, during the first break I had to go see my family, we met and had a conversation at the Fort there . . .

---

1. In Venezuela's Military Academy, the students with the highest academic marks are given honorary ranks (e.g. 'brigadier primero', 'brigadier' and 'distingui-do').

When was it that you flew over the Cedeño Batallion with your plane and caused a huge stir?

In 1976, in October, that was during the Pilar fair, in Barinas. We had to simulate an attack on the Cedeño Batallion. The Fort was the last target. I looked to my right as we were entering the town and saw a rehearsal for the fair's parade. I went off course and the people on parade started waving at my plane. I kept in radio contact with the other three planes, who were flying behind me, 'Going in, target in sight, coming out'. I flew near the control tower, which reported my presence. The officer in charge of the manoeuvre said, 'No, it can't be, the planes are southeast of there'.

When I got out of the plane, the brigade commander approached me and said, 'Reyes, were you plane number four in that formation? What were you doing flying over the city?' 'I wanted to practice for the parade' – I answered. Our planes were going to the parade the next day. That man's face was telling me I ought to have been arrested, at the very least . . .

Chávez amuses himself remembering that story . . .

He always says they arrested me, but something worse happened: they didn't let me participate in the parade the following day. That was more painful, because the townspeople were there and one's always dreaming of doing one's manoeuvres and having people say, 'Look, there goes so and so's son'. The fact I had done a show anyway was a consolation. It was a one-man show, but I did it.

The First Conspiracies

Hugo and I saw each other a lot in the officer's mess the army had in Barinas. All officers met there, had a few drinks – he's never been much of a drinker – and played baseball. During those first few years, he built up a close relationship with my brother Anibal. In May 1977, the Cazadores Cedeño Batallion was transferred to Cumaná. By that time, Hugo was already with Nancy, the mother of his three older children, and my brother was engaged to his current wife. They got away together to go see them, because the women were neighbours.

We were promoted from second lieutenants to lieutenants in 1978. On December 17 of that year, we met near some palm trees in front of my house. I told him about something that had happened to me and he started to tell me about the way the generals behaved. When one is a lieutenant, one doesn't know what happens in the high command. I remember he criticized the loss of military doctrine and how the military conspired with the corrupt politicians of the time.

In 1979, already a lieutenant, I was sent to another course at the Air Force's Higher Academy in Caracas. There, I ran into then Squadron Leader William Izarra Caldera, who is today an air chief marshall, who shared with me a number of thoughts about military ethics which impressed me. I told him this and he replied, surprised to hear a lieutenant speaking like that, 'What do you think we should do?' 'We have to change the military from within'. Bear in mind we were thinking about the military, we weren't yet conscious of the need to change the country's political system. It was like being trapped inside of a bottle. I didn't know William Izarra Caldera was part of a subversive movement.

He had just returned from the United States. He had studied Education at Harvard and he invited me to take a look at some documents. For some reason, we didn't meet then. I returned to Barquisimeto – I had already married Milagros and, in 1980, Izarra was transferred here, to Lara State. 'We accidentally meet again', he said. 'No, it's no accident. Don't forget I wanted to hear your arguments'. I knew things had become difficult for him and that's why they had transferred him from Caracas to Barquisimeto. He looked and spoke like a subversive. Shortly after, in his apartment, he showed me the documents and outlined a whole political project.

Did it have anything to do with what later become the Bolivarian Movement?

No, it was known as the Revolutionary Action of Active Soldiers (Acción Revolucionaria de Militares Activos, ARMA). I offered to put him in touch with my friends – I was exaggerating, because I only had one friend who shared these ideas: Hugo Chávez. Some time later, the three of us met in Palo Grande, a rich neighbourhood in Caracas. What this gentleman outlined for us then was a broad civic and military movement.

What did it consist in?

It was like a left-over from the subversive movements of the sixties which had been very violently repressed. Squadron leader William Izarra may have had some involvement in these when he was a pilot officer. Hugo Trejo, Pausides González and others from the Marines had been in those groups, which had been the strongest subversive current in the sixties. After that meeting, we were promoted to captain in 1982, the year we took the Oath at Samán de Güere. We had already agreed that he would organize his friends in the army, and I would organize mine in the Air Force.

Did you see each other often?

We talked a lot. He was at the Military Academy and I was an instructor at the Air Force Academy. I probably had a closer relationship with the cadets than he did, because of the nature of the Air Force. We were forced to live on top of each other and to act as a group. Each of our lives depended on it.

Did your group have a name?

For our own safety, we didn't give anything a name. They did, though I never found out what the Movement was called until we were put in jail ten years later.

We continued to meet with some regularity. In 1983, we met in Maracay. He was already there with the paratroopers and lived near the city, in San Joaquín, at the border between Aragua and Carabobo.

We were crawling out of the bottle. That is, we had left the closed circle of the military and we were looking outside for the causes behind the problems of the Armed Forces and the distortion of military doctrine. We knew that corruption stemmed from the influence of politics.

During the elections, the Air Force transported the ballot boxes. I remember that, as lieutenant, they gave me the job of picking up a ballot box in a mountain town. As I was about to leave, the colonel told me not to go, because, in any event, such and such a party had already won the election. 'But, what about those voters?' He answered contemptuously, 'Pick up the ballot boxes and throw them off the plane'. That was corruption. When the ballot boxes got to the National Electoral Committee, the same thing happened: they would throw them out or change them. These were crimes that the Armed Forces participated in every day, not to mention the overt affluence the officers who served that political system flaunted.

Did you have troops under your command?

Yes. As captains, we began to recruit more and more officers and we became a large group. We would meet in Valencia, in Carabobo State, but we'd take a lot of measures to go undetected.

Did Chávez participate in the meetings?

He chaired the meetings and invited me. I would go with some Air Force officers like Wilmar Castro Soteldo, the current minister of production and trade. I would also go with a captain of Italian origin, who had a very impressive physique and was very impetuous and aggressive – he would even talk of shooting people; later, he beat it.

We started making contact with civilians in political groups, with Radical Cause (R Cause) particularly; this was a left-wing party that sold out to neoliberalism and is one of the worst. For the most part, we worked with members of R Cause in Guayana. They had set up a good work team there with iron and steel workers' unions and published a good newspaper. All of that was of use to us too.

Did you not feel persecuted?

Chávez did. As a matter of fact, they started transferring him from one unit to another. I remember that, from Maracay, they sent him to Elorza, in Apure State.

Had they already promoted you to major?

Yes, in 1986. Around then, we met with a lieutenant colonel, a man of strong ideological convictions, General Francisco Visconti Osorio, who was part of the ARMA group, and, thanks to some stool pigeons, the repression began. One of the officers linked to the group was gunned down in Los Teques. This was the situation when Hugo called me and asked to go visit him in Elorza. I remember we went on horseback around a sown piece of land he had in the unit, at the town's entrance, and that we went to a party in the evening. He had been named president of the Fair's Committee. Among other things, we spoke at length about the possibilities of a military movement, of a large-scale military action.

Do you remember the date, approximately?

Of course, it was the day of the Elorza festivities, the 19 March 1986. They were already after Hugo, suspecting a conspiracy.

But, as it turns out, they weren't able to destroy the movement.

Do you know what worked to our advantage at the time? There was a huge internal power struggle in the Armed Forces. That distracted them. They were fighting among themselves to decide who would command the army, who was such and such a party's favourite, who was going to win the elections and how each of them would then stand . . . that sort of thing. They probably thought that the young and restless officers would forget all about it when they were promoted.

Preparations for the Rebellion

After that meeting in Elorza, we met in the parking lot of the army's Higher Institute in Caracas. Some university professors started to attend the meetings. You could smell a military rebellion, but there were also tensions and run-ins.

Was Chávez using the pseudonym of José Antonio?

He used it in his group, but not with us. Communication between the two of us was very safe. I didn't use a pseudonym either. We were obsessive about security. What's more, their world was different from ours: we pilots lived as a group. No one raised an eyebrow if he saw four or five pilots together, talking. In the army, a captain and a lieutenant were very different; that wasn't the case with us, because the flying officer would fly with me, we risked our lives together. If the flying officer crashed, you crashed too.

Still, our precautions were not enough. I recall an anecdote Chávez tells all the time. Already as majors of the Armed Forces, we met at an inter-service softball championship on Aviation Day and got into game positions. A fellow who had a big mouth yelled out, 'There come the *comacates* head on!'. 'Comacates' was the name they had given the subversives – a word formed using the initial syllables of commanders, majors, captains and lieutenants. Chávez' face was red. Just like that, that man was recklessly giving us away in front of everyone. Chávez was my friend and I had invited him to that game. There had been a slight breach of security, but, luckily, it didn't have any consequences.

You returned to the United States.

At the end of 1987. I was assigned to the Venezuelan embassy in Washington, as an assistant to the Military Attaché. Ronald Blanco La Cruz, the current governor of Táchira State, was there. He sent me a note telling me he was taking a course in the southern United States and that he'd come and visit us. For some reason, that didn't happen, but, on one of my trips to Venezuela –

I would come and go every so often – I ran into Ronald, who was an officer in a fort, and got to know him . . . Of course, he expressed his concerns and I mine.

What had happened with the groups at the time?

We were a bit scattered. Many of us – Felipe Acosta Carlez was one – were sent to Central America, to El Salvador, as part of a joint military action by the Venezuelan and American governments. They returned and then came the *Caracazo*, in November 1989.

Did you fight against the insurgents at this time?

No, no, the Army and the National Guard were called in for those types of actions. They didn't use the Air Force, which is very specialized.

Once, I remember, we took some planes to Costa Rica, as part of a plan against Somoza, during Carlos Andrés Pérez's first term.

When did you return from the United States?

By mid-1991, and had a conversation with Major Chávez. He confirmed that the movement was still standing, that many things had got worse, including the repression against the group and against him in particular. I told him that, in Washington, one of the assistants to the minister of defence there, a major, had given me a secret list with the names of those who were being followed for subversive activities. My name was at the bottom of the list, but Hugo's was one of the first.

Did Chávez invite you to participate in the uprising?

Yes, we met at the beginning of November . . . I asked for some time to re-organize the Air Force, as I had just got back to Venezuela. Many of the people who had originally supported the movement were no longer in the Air Force, and the spirit of rebellion had dissipated a bit.

On around the 20th of the month, Major Chávez informed me that the military action would take place on 10 December, on Air Force Day, when President Carlos Andrés Pérez attended the public ceremony for that day. But the army officers were quite restless.

We saw each other in the first week of December. The rebel officers in the army were insisting we had to act quickly. I spoke with General Visconti, who had been my new superior ever since returning from the United States and he agreed with me that the Air Force was in no condition to join the uprising just then.

There was an age difference between the commanding officers in the Air Force and Army. We didn't have command of operative units. They wanted to assign me to an operative unit in Barquisimeto, and I delayed my transfer there to continue coordinating actions with Major Chávez. That was a mistake, I should have accepted the transfer, for I would have been able to back the whole operation from Maracay. Ultimately, the uprising didn't take place in December; on 10 January, after returning from vacation, we started to meet again, and more regularly, because of pressure from young officers . . .

In a letter your wife Milagros gave us, Chávez writes to you in code about a 'manager' that supported you in a place called Los Colorados. Who was he referring to?

To General Visconti. Los Colorados was a restaurant on Maracay road, near Los Teques. We would meet there, and those meetings became more and more regular after 15 January.

The majors were the highest ranking officers loyal to us. The army generals had changed sides. After being promoted, they lost the revolutionary impetus and didn't want to have anything to do with the young subversives. The system sucked them in.

Were you looking for someone higher up in the military?

Yes, and we knew Visconti was a progressive general. There was also William Izarra, who, even though he had left the Air Force, was a progressive thinker, who knew how to make a tough decision and how to listen.

The month of January hadn't ended and that major who had given me the list of suspected officers warned me there was a lot of tension, that people were saying the youngest officers would rebel anyway, if that major's fellow officers didn't act. Chávez asked me to meet with him on 2 February in that restaurant in Los Teques. That day, I left from Barinas, called General Visconti and told him I had to see him that same Sunday evening, in Los Colorados. Hugo and I got there at around nine thirty at night, the time we had agreed to meet. It was raining. The general was late and, at around eleven, we decided to leave. As we were leaving, Visconti arrived with a retired air chief marshall from the Air Force, Maximiliano Hernández. We've never wanted to reveal his identity.

Why did you not want to name him?

Because he's someone who helped us at the time and never again had anything to do with us. We're grateful to him. Now, he has ties to counterrevolutionary groups and detracts and lies left, right and centre.

Chávez told us the uprising would take place in a few hours. We were there, planning, until two in the morning. When we said goodbye, we knew the military action would begin that 3 February at nine forty five at night.

General Maximiliano agreed to send a major that morning who would offer backup at the periphery of the base, where I was, in Maracay.

General Visconti told Major Chávez that there were very few chances of securing air backup. He advised us to concentrate on avoiding an air attack on the ground forces that would capture Miraflores.

I remember Chávez asking Visconti at two in the morning, 'Why don't you come with us to Caracas?' He answered, 'I have to safeguard the Air Force's high command from the naval base'. He was referring to the Air Force's largest base, the one in Maracay.

He made the right decision. Visconti was stationed at that base, but he was not the commander of those troops; it was another general, repugnantly right-wing, whose father had been a minister in the Democratic Action party. Preventing an air attack on the rebel forces was vital.

Who was the commander of those troops?

General Juan Antonio Paredes Niño. His father, Paredes Bello, had been minister of defence, one of the those who did most harm to the Air Force. General Visconti had decided he would go to Miraflores once the Palace had been taken by Major Chávez. The other general, General Maximiliano, promised he would go to Caracas to take part in the uprising. Hugo and I left for Maracay. We went in my car, a Malibu. I left it at around four in the morning – after making a stop along the way – in front of the Páez barracks, where the battalion Chávez commanded was. I saw him walk toward the small sentry post they have there. A soldier verified his identity and I started the car.

3 February 1992

I lived in the air base, but, before getting to the battalion, I stopped at the home of Major Luis Sabatino, the famous Rambo who fled. I said, 'Listen, tomorrow's the day'. 'What day?', and his face went white. I was going to wait for him at eight in the morning in Maracay. He never showed up. He flew in the F-16 squadron and I wanted him to help me contact officers in that squadron and convince them to back the army, even though he had only been instructed to neutralize the Air Force.

At four in the afternoon, Major Chávez had to attend a briefing for the mission assigned to his unit by the army. Hardly anyone knows that, in fact, we used routine army manoeuvres, scheduled for 4 February, as cover for our uprising.

On that day, the troops were going to advance to El Pao (Cojedes) in the south. Of course, that division was backed by the Air Force and its paratroopers. Instead of heading for El Pao, Chávez set out for Caracas.

At three in the afternoon, I had a conversation with General Visconti in one of the Maracay parking lots and we agreed to take the base during the night. We would routinely go over the operations at four in the afternoon. All of the officers who were attending the final coordination meeting for the 4 February operation, which was the date of the El Pao manoeuvre, were arriving. All of the majors for paratrooper groups were to attend this briefing.

There, in Maracay?

In Maracay, at the base. I saw all of the officers save Major Chávez go in. A few moments later, he arrived in a rush. He was late. He went in to the meeting and came out a while later. I asked a soldier to go up to Chávez, telling him Chávez had a box of books for me. The soldier accompanied him to his car. He opened the trunk, took out a box and handed it to him. Inside it was the radio we were going to use to communicate with each other during the uprising. 'Hey, these books really weigh a lot' – the young soldier said to me. 'It's just some old books, put them there'. Inside were the codes that were going to be used over the radio.

At six in the evening, General Visconti, two other officers – majors who were commissioned at the same time as us – and I met. 'Did you tell these two anything?', the general asked me. I replied, 'No, I haven't told them anything, but I can', because I thought they were to be trusted and that, that late in the game, a leak would change nothing.

There'd already been one . . .

Yes, it had . . . Our meeting ended at nine and General Visconti went to his house, to 'put on his battledress and bring his gun'. The other two officers, supposedly, also left to change clothes. They never returned.

Clashes in Maracay

At quarter to ten at night, the first gunshots around the base were heard. The rebels went in through a sentry post near one of the garrison houses. General Visconti saw Major Torres, who was in charge of surrounding the base, arrive. He also brought a tank. They tried to surprise the soldiers, but they reacted. Shots were exchanged and one of Major Torres' men was killed.

General Visconti gave me the order to act. The group captains in command of the airborne troops – none to be trusted – showed up and the general suggested I try and maintain as normal an atmosphere as possible, to see what the colonels did. He ordered me to deal with the troop guarding the base from inside. No one knew what was happening. I prevented a lieutenant from taking a group of soldiers to the fence. I went out through the main sentry post and proceeded to the peripheral post, where Major Torres was . . . When I walked toward him, a burst of machine gun fire cut between the two of us.

DISIP forces had parked their car on the other side of the road and were firing from there. I ran toward the post, where there was another major, a pilot, who wore a Bolivarian bracelet. 'Major, I'm also involved in this'.

Torres did not know our objective was to neutralize the base, prevent the planes from taking off. I went back to where Visconti was, and he said, 'We're going to wait'. We had very clear instructions to wait until Miraflores was taken. Then, we would arrest the officers and back the insurrectionists in the army. General Visconti would address the officers and tell them, 'The country lacks a leader, therefore, we're taking over'.

But, to our surprise – it must have been at quarter to one in the morning, maybe a bit later – Carlos Andrés Pérez appeared on television. Obviously, we hadn't accomplished one of our objectives. If the president had been taken prisoner, we would have woken up on 4 February backed by the people and with some control of the streets, thanks to the groundwork with R Cause and other left-wing political parties, including the extremists from Red Flag, for we had met with them a number of times.

The hours passed and we had no news of our comrades in Caracas. We never had a chance to communicate by radio. The colonels started to suspect General Visconti. Carmelo Lauría, one of the leaders of Democratic Action, called the base and, when he asked to speak to the general, the latter replied he had nothing to say to him. They started to get suspicious and went to another unit to have a meeting. That young man, Torres, started to get desperate. The sun was already coming up.

Were you able to contact anyone else?

No. The tanks had managed to penetrate Miraflores Palace, but, without air backup, it was very hard for those forces to efficiently withstand an attack like that. Nevertheless, the operation was well conceived in as far as it left the Air Force out. Though we could have mobilized planes – something impossible, because we had no real command over those troops – we weren't going to take any action over the city. We would have had to prepare for an attack at night and illuminate the targets. None of that was done. The only thing we were able to do was put a mark on the top of the tanks used by the insurgents.

And Visconti?

At five in the morning of 4 February, the minister of defence ordered him to fly over the Military Museum where Chávez was and launch an attack. The general called that Italian major and told to him to take off with four planes but to attack no one, to not even take any weapons. That's what he did.

The colonels were watching the general closely, whom they still suspected, even more so at that point.

Why was General Visconti giving orders? Where was the base commander?

The commander had been arrested at the entrance of the base and Visconti had taken over. Afterwards, we found out that at six in the afternoon on 3 February, they already knew the uprising would take place and had warned all troop commanders. But the military elite was not able to warn the commander. He loved the good life and was out partying with his wife – the rebels arrested her with him and later released her. The colonels of the airborne troops were obliged to follow Visconti's orders, since he was the highest ranking officer in the commander's absence.

At sunrise, Torres was still extremely anxious. At nine or ten in the morning, I don't recall who I spoke to, but I realized that everything was lost. I told Torres the action in Caracas had failed. He insisted on taking the base. A few minutes after that conversation, Chávez appeared on television. I went out and informed Major Torres. I asked him to withdraw the men and to take the tanks to his unit. It wasn't easy to convince him, let alone the young officers.

What did you feel when you saw Chávez on television?

Grief and nostalgia. I would have liked to have been there, in spite of everything. I and many other officers heard his message in the logistics unit. A major came up to me, 'Did you hear him? He said that, for now, the operation has failed.' I answered him, 'One does not always win', and I left to look for Torres. I had interpreted that 'for now' as a 'there's more to come'.

There's More to Come

On the way to the sentry post I was thinking of what to do next. I thought we had to re-organize ourselves but, before that, survive the repression that was going to start immediately. I knew they would arrest me, and I didn't care if it was in Maracay or Barquisimeto, where they had transferred me well before 3 August. Milagros came to pick me up at the base at around five in the afternoon. The following day, they sent a plane to Barquisimeto and took me back to Maracay. They interrogated me and made me take a lie detector test. Well, I beat the machine. 'Did you know of the military operation?' 'No, I didn't know about the military operation.'

How did it turn out?

Well, I don't know. They put me in a helicopter and took me to Caracas. We got to the Air Force's General Command at around eight at night. To my surprise, the Air Force squadron leader told me he didn't want to besmirch the Air Force's image. 'Let the army go it alone. When are you expecting a promotion?' It was customary for those blokes to buy people with promotions. (Of course, I didn't accept anything: I was promoted in due course, in July 1994.) They took me to the DIM to interrogate me. They were up to their ears. They had set up additional tables in the corridors and, even then, they didn't have enough to deal with all of the arrested officers. A kind fellow got a policeman to attend to me. When I went across that basement, I heard Major Chávez singing.

What was he singing?

I think it was 'Palmares de Calabozo', a song by Elías Perdomo. My heart started racing. I tried to figure out why he was singing, and I suspected it was to warn his fellow men. If he went quiet, it meant something was happening to him.

I went down long corridors. The cells were packed, but one had to go through a passageway and go beneath the basement. Before I knew it, I was out in the street. I left without anyone interrogating me or noticing I had escaped. I took an empty car and returned to command headquarters.

I went in and went to the room where I was being held. I got into bed and slept for a few hours. The following day, the Air Force's intelligence director called me again. 'How did it go?' 'Well'. He told me I had to go back to the DIM the following day. There, I was attended to by someone who was quite scatterbrained. He told me they had arrested a lot of people who had nothing to do with what happened; he apologized and asked me to return to headquarters.

And he didn't ask you anything?

It wasn't a formal interrogation, he only wrote down the things I told him: that I was from Barinas, that I knew Chávez, that he had christened my son. They had seen me in his house the day before, and I told him that yes, that I had taken his wife a present.

All in all, they held me for forty five days in that room in the Command.

They offered me the directorship of the Force's nursing school. I didn't accept and they put me to work in command headquarters, a desk job. Visconti was also charged and they put him in the Air Force's Inspector's Office in the ministry of defence. We were both in Caracas. I sent him a note telling him we were organizing ourselves, that the movement had grown, to be patient.

The Road to 27 November

The war inside the Armed Forces started up again as though nothing had occurred. The month of July, a time of promotions and new assignments, was nearing. We went back to our conspiratorial work, right under their noses, in command headquarters and in the Ministry, inside Fort Tiuna. We used to go to a bakery near the Fort with Visconti and others. The conversations were brief, because we knew we were being watched. The movement started to grow again, but, this time, in the Air Force.

Were you in touch with Chávez in prison?

Not at first, no. They kept close watch over that and, of course, we weren't allowed to go see him. Milagros did manage to see Hugo and one of his brothers came to Barquisimeto and spoke with us. We didn't set a date. On 25 November 1992, General Visconti informed me, 'We're going into action on the 27th'. 'Why the 27th?' Later, I realized why. Rehearsals for the fly-past that was held every Air Force Day, 10 December, were starting then. All planes were concentrated at the Libertador base. On the morning of 26 November, I went to Maracay.

Did you make contact with army officers?

Differences arose. We contacted a number of retired generals, but they refused to take orders from Visconti, because he was an air chief marshall and, besides, the retired generals outranked him. Ultimately, we stopped meeting with them.

On the other hand, many army officers had been arrested and those who remained in the army were closely watched. We thought it better to contact the navy. On the night of the 26th, Visconti told me, 'We're starting the activity at four thirty in the morning'. We were at the Maracay base.

The captain in charge informed me we were ready to go into action. An F-16 commander also arrived. 'Are you also involved in this?' I replied, 'We have no option, brother.'

General Visconti was waiting with the other officers. We went into action as planned at dawn. By the afternoon, at around two or three, we had already lost, again, because the other forces had failed. In the early hours of the 27th, someone had given us away and our action was neutralized.

You are remembered in that action, among other things, for being the first person to break the sound barrier over Caracas.

I flew over Caracas three times. During the first flight, I ordered the captain to set the plane at maximum speed, to go into Caracas at a high speed. And, yes, we flew in very low and broke the sound barrier.

You shouldn't do that at under 10,000 feet, because it can cause the pilot a lot of problems, and we flew in at around 3,000 feet. It was the only way of going into the valley of Caracas, and it sounded like a bomb. This was when the first clashes were taking place in the city. A group of soldiers spontaneously joined our officers to attack Miraflores. They had attacked the Palace, even after we learnt the navy would not join us. But there was no going back at that point.

You can imagine what an effect the noise the plane made had on the city. Glass broke everywhere. And we went out the same way we came in. We did it not only to create a commotion that would help to take Miraflores, but also to get away from one of the planes which was following us, which was more up to date than ours.

Had you also planned to take the television station?

Someone played us a dirty trick. We had a tape ready. We had carefully planned the taking of the state channel, Canal 8, and we did it early in the day. Three generals were involved: Visconti and two admirals. Visconti, from Maracay, with a whole air fleet, and they, from the commandos unit in the navy, and I think they were at the museum too. One of the admirals was to take care of television.

But the tape we sent was changed for one of Chávez. They say the other didn't arrive in time. We still don't know exactly what happened, but it caused a lot of confusion. Some radical groups didn't stick to the plan we had agreed to and, unfortunately, those who took the television station were left on their own and were massacred.

Prison

When the uprising failed, they jailed us in the Páez barracks in Fort Tiuna. They released some eight or ten lieutenants and second lieutenants who had been in prison since 4 February and put us in. There were about 60 of us.

Did you have contact with the prisoners at Yare?

With Chávez, the whole time. Arias Cárdenas' wife also started visiting us to tell us about the conflict between Major Chávez and Major Arias. I didn't know that officer, because he never attended our meetings.

Cárdenas' wife didn't like the fact Chávez had earned so much affection as commander of the uprising and couldn't bear to see her husband subordinated to Chávez, who had less seniority than Arias in the Armed Forces. Hugo and I graduated from the Academy a year after he did.

So, his wife would come tell us that Chávez was lying, that this, that and the other . . .

How did you organize yourselves?

Being the senior officer, they put me in charge of the other inmates. It was a difficult task. There were many young people who didn't adapt to prison life, we didn't have psychologists or psychiatrists or anything like that there, so we had to do a bit of everything. I remember the case of Eliécer Otaiza, a very courageous young man, who gave us a lot of work, because he simply could not adapt.

They put him in prison when he hadn't yet recovered from the serious wounds he suffered – in the stomach and back – during the military action of 4 February. He was very thin and he still had his catheters. Basically, they sent him to us to die. He was very depressed. He gave us a lot of work. Three months later, Otaiza was already a different person. He recovered and started to overcome his situation.

Chávez has said that, during this time, he felt much more bitter than he ever had before, because they were blaming him for the failure of the 27 November uprising.

He had nothing to do with that failure. The navy, which didn't respond, is to blame. What went wrong during the first uprising? Air support, which would have facilitated many things. I remember – we have to remember certain things, even if they're unpleasant – that when we flew over La Carlota, there was a tank trying to knock down the fence to attack those who had already broken into the President's residence. We had to fire a missile at the tank. That prevented a terrible slaughter. Had we had air backup for our troops and tanks on 4 February, history would have been different.

How long a sentence were you given?

Seven years and nine months.

When did you get out of prison?

Two months before Chávez did. I was released due to special circumstances having to do with my son Augusto. He had cancer and his condition had worsened. I came to Barquisimeto and, shortly after, when we took the child to the hospital in

Caracas, I went to visit him at Yare. Chávez was in the Military Hospital recovering from an eye operation. Milagros would visit him all the time, even before I was released from Fort Tiuna.

Did you write to each other?

Yes, but they were more like very discreet letters to everyone. We were very closely watched.

The Campaign

In 1994, after everyone had been released, did you join Chávez's campaign?

No. After Augusto died a few months later, I decided to work with street children. I moved to Barinas and set up a centre for abandoned children in a small farm we had.

Chávez had already begun his tour around the country. I remember he stopped by the house before we took our kid to the United States to undergo radiation therapy. He brought a present for Augusto and invited me to a meeting of the Revolutionary Bolivarian Movement. There was all sorts of wheeling and dealing to try and have him removed as leader. Finally, we managed to get the situation under control.

Another time he came to Barinas and came to see me at the farm. I was doing work around the farm: I was wearing a pair of shorts and rubber boots. He hugged me and said. 'Let's go into battle.' I replied, 'I'm fighting a different battle now.' 'We have to join forces again, friend. We're going to have a meeting to decide on our future as a movement.' He convinced me. 'Okay, I'm going back to Barquisimeto, I'll start working for the movement again.' He returned to Maracay, to Los Teques, that same night. Two days later, I left Barinas for Barquisimeto and, from there, went on to Caracas.

Officially, I re-joined the movement on 19 April 1997. It was hard for me to digest so many political speeches and discussions, but I began work immediately. That day, the MBR–200[2] became the 5th Republic Movement. Shortly after that, we set up the first office in Barquisimeto, we put together a work group and began our political campaign. We had a lot of popular support, a lot of enthusiasm and determination, but we lacked organizational experience. I would accompany Major Chávez every time he travelled to our area and, little by little, things started to fall into place.

Did he talk to you about how he saw the future?
He's always been very optimistic.

Triumph of the 5th Republic

On the very day of the presidential elections, he called me at home and asked me to come to La Viñeta immediately. I arrived with Milagros on a Sunday, if I remember correctly. He proposed I become minister of transportation and communications. I wanted to continue with my social work. 'Look, brother, I don't know a thing about transportation, and less about communication. Planes are the only thing I know anything about.' And he replied, 'You'll be minister of urban development, we're going to merge the ministries.' He kept insisting and I kept saying no. One of the party leaders called me and said, 'Think it over, we have to help the Major.' Two or three hours later, we saw each other at dinner and I said, 'Alright.' That's how I got to the ministry.

How long were you there for?
Five months; I spent more time in Miraflores than at the ministry, because we'd meet every night, until one day he called to tell me about the Constituent Assembly. He said, 'I'm going to

2. On 19 April 1997, the Revolutionary Bolivarian Movement 200 (MBR–200), which could not became an official party because it contained the word 'Bolivarian' in its name, became the 5th Republic Movement (MVR), a name chosen to preserve the sound of MBR. The organization put candidates forward for the elections in Valencia.

put my best men in the Assembly. I'll have to sacrifice some.' I handed the ministry over to Julio Montes.

After I joined the Constituent Assembly, there came the elections for governor. The one in Lara, who had been Chavista, turned out to be a rotten turncoat. I put myself forward in the elections, and here I am as governor.

The Coup Didn't Surprise Us Much

Chávez's personality revealed itself more vividly during these years. He's an excellent strategist, intelligent, passionate, moderate in his decisions, a person that knows how to listen. Many criticize him and he's always listening, he consults with people before making a decision. If he's demonstrated anything, it is his courage and his profound faith in what we are doing. He's demonstrated it always, but especially in those days of the coup and those that followed.

What conclusions did you reach after the events of April?

We had been talking about the situation in the Armed Forces. I think we were very slack when we selected our key officers in the Armed Forces. We were overly trusting. We didn't properly gauge the damage the oligarchy could do.

We knew some things, for instance, about the feeble political convictions of some officers who liked the good life, affluence. We've learned a great lesson from all of this.

Where were you on the day of the coup?

We were following what was happening that 11 April with great concern. At around nine at night or a bit later, Chávez called me and told me the top army officer had defected and that he had doubts about Manuel Rosendo. 'Who do you think we can trust to lead the army now?' 'The most trustworthy officer at the moment is Luis Acevedo Quintero.' I called General Acevedo myself. At around eleven at night, I got another call from Chávez. 'Look, I'm sending Marisabel over to you (that was his wife at the time).

She's leaving now. Look after her. I'm staying behind and fighting this out.' I say. 'You have to fight, there's no option.' 'Agreed.' A few moments later, Adán Chávez calls me. 'Things here are looking far from good . . .' Diosdado called me at twelve, 'They could put the president in jail any time now.'

4 February came to mind again. Thoughts were racing inside my head. 'Should we go up into the mountains? What's going to happen tomorrow when the sun rises?' We didn't have to wait for sunrise. In the early hours of that same morning, the three generals in command of the troops in Lara showed up: the army, the National Guard and the air chief marshalls. I didn't know they had already changed sides.

At around two in the morning, one of the generals behind the coup who I didn't know calls me. 'Look, General Camacho Kairuz wants to speak to you' – the fellow from the National Guard told me. 'I don't speak to traitors. Did you hear? I don't speak to traitors.' But he insisted, 'Look, it would be good if you spoke with them.' 'No, I don't speak to traitors and I have nothing to say to you. I'm a state governor and I'll go when the people vote me out. Do what you have to do and tell the other traitors to do the same. The people will come down from the hills, sooner or later, they'll come down from the hills.' And the guy said, 'Look, they don't want your people to rebel . . .' 'You do your job, I'll do mine', and I ended the conversation.

I think that they had already planned to arrest me, probably in cahoots with those in Caracas. At four in the morning on 12 April, I was certain of what was going to happen: the general from the National Guard would come and arrest me and take the governor's palace. I acted as though I suspected nothing. I never once mentioned that I was planning to mobilize the people in defence of our positions. Meanwhile, the general was surrounding himself with more and more soldiers.

12 April: They Couldn't Arrest Me

At seven in the morning, he came again to try and get me to talk with that general in Caracas on the phone. I refused again and he transferred the call to the mayor of Barquisimeto. At eight thirty in the morning, I called a press conference and asked the three generals to go with me. They made a strange face – I didn't know they had just come from a press conference they had convened. They said, 'You go, governor, we'll wait here.'

Cameramen from all the different stations came in, but I noticed none of the cameras had the on lights on. Only the one from the local station. First, I asked for calm and added, 'We're going to analyze what's happened in Caracas, but I assure you the Bolivarian process will not be stopped.'

The National Guard major was thinking of setting a trap for me. He knew his men outnumbered mine. My security forces were divided: part of them were in the residence and the other in the Palace, with me. But he decided not to arrest me.

Let me give you an idea of how the media behaved. At one point, one of the journalists said, 'Listen, the people are going to kick you out of here.' I answered, 'Open the window to listen to those people you claim are coming to kick me out. The people *are* outside and they're supporting me. We've had to calm people down, because they're willing to do absolutely anything.' Thanks to that support, I was in the Palace the whole day. What those traitor generals wouldn't have given to arrest me! In the meantime, I was finding out about the situation, as I was constantly receiving calls from my comrades in Caracas.

Did they call you to try and have you switch sides?

Ah, yes. Even people who had been on our side called me. There was someone who proposed I become part of a transition government, whose president would be Teodoro Petkoff. I replied, 'Without Chávez, nothing is possible.'

Who proposed this to you?

The governor of Bolívar State. At first, I didn't think he'd propose I serve the people behind the coup. 'We have to accept reality' – he told me. 'What reality? What reality do we have to accept?' At that moment, I didn't imagine he was changing sides. 'Well, brother, that Chávez has fallen.' I said to him, 'If Chávez falls, the revolution falls with him.' About an hour and a half or two hours later, he called me again. 'Look, they called me from Caracas.' 'Aha! Who called you?' 'President Carmona' – he said – 'he's inviting me to a meeting.' 'You're going to sit down with traitors?' – I asked him. 'I'm only going to hear what they have to say.' It was then I realized he was on the other side. 'Well, let your conscience dictate what you have to do,' and I hung up.

That Friday, I also spoke with Ronald Blanco. We quickly went over some possibilities, including resigning to take up other forms of struggle. This was Ronald's advice: 'No, by no means. We cannot resign. We were elected by the people. I haven't seen Chávez's signed resignation anywhere.'

How did Chávez's children get to Barquisimeto?

María called me on Friday and told me she was near the Tuy valleys. 'María, come here' – I told her. She arrived that evening, with her brother Huguito and Gabi, her daughter, and we spoke late at night, when I returned from the Palace. Then came Rosa, Chávez's older daughter.

Did you speak with President Fidel Castro?

On Friday the 11th, at around six in the evening. And again at around nine at night. During our first conversation, he asked me if I knew where Chávez was. He seemed very worried. 'President, I don't know, but they've taken him somewhere, and they must be moving him to a different place now. I'm not sure where and I might say something that's not true.' I had spoken with Gerardo Espinosa some time before; he was in Maracay and had seen strange plane movements. 'I think a plane took off for Turiamo.'

Fidel suggested, 'Try and speak to CNN, try and make declarations . . . break the information siege . . .'

I saw the attacks on the Cuban embassy on television and tried to contact the generals behind the coup. A newly commissioned general answered, 'You're going to make the people wipe the floor with you . . . if you don't prevent those attacks on the embassy, no one's going to forgive you tomorrow.' I also called the National Guard general. 'Look, since you're in touch with your traitor friends, call Méndez Casanova and tell him that if anything happens to the Cuban embassy, you won't be able to control the people's anger.' The guy answered, 'Yes, I'll call him', but I don't know if he did or not.

When I spoke to Fidel in the evening, I told him the people were mobilizing and asking for Chávez's return. 'Who?' 'The Bolivarians in Caracas have started to come down from the hills' – I answered.

13 April: All Hell Broke Loose

On Saturday morning, I began to see the first signs that the coup was defeated. I thought, 'This nonsense is only going to last till midday, it's already falling to bits.' A man came with a message from Fernando Bermúdez, asking me to resign. I sent back an insult, a few nasty words. I went to the Palace at around ten in the morning. I started calling the generals in Lara, but I couldn't get a hold of them anywhere.

I spoke with General Baduel and with General García Montoya, in Maracay, and I warned them that the generals here supported the coup, and this when I still didn't know what they had said in their press conference on Friday. (Just think! I saw that video fifteen days later.) I still thought that at least the air chief marshals and army generals were indecisive but not turncoats. I knew the National Guard general was a traitor, because he was in contact with the pro-coup faction and he seemed more arrogant. When I spoke about the matter with García Montoya he was surprised, because he had spoken with the air chief marshall in Lara and that man had obeyed his orders.

At midday on Saturday, I called the generals again. A police colonel informed me they were at a meeting in the brigade headquarters with some opposition leaders. I had great difficulties getting the general from the National Guard to answer the phone. 'So, you're in a meeting with those people? Well, you put them all under arrest right now.' 'Well, things don't exactly work that way.' 'I'm giving you an order.' 'Well . . . I was thinking of having a word with you.' 'No, no, you arrest them first.'

A bit earlier, at around eleven in the morning, an army major called me and told me he was going to Miraflores with a group to help take back the Palace. He asked me to inform William Lara, so he could go to the Palace. William replied, 'Do you think that's advisable?' 'Yes, come on, you're the right man to receive the president.' With our people already in the Presidential Palace, making a huge, joyous racket in the background, I was given the excellent news: Miraflores was ours again.

Did you know then that Chávez was on La Orchila?

No. Later on, they called me to tell me that the people who staged the coup had taken him from Turiamo to La Orchila. I was told helicopters had gone to get him. 'We're going to Bolívar square in Barquisimeto' – I decided. Our people were gathered there. This called for a celebration. It was around eight at night.

What about the traitor generals in Lara?

Nowhere to be found. After four in the afternoon, they had gone out of circulation, they didn't turn up anywhere. After the President was rescued, I left for the square and gave the news: Chávez would be arriving in Miraflores around midnight.

When did you see Chávez?

The President sent for me Monday afternoon. It was his granddaughter Gabi's birthday. I told him the general who called me in the early morning of 12 April appeared next to him in the television coverage of his arrival at the Palace. 'Mr. President, what was that general doing there? He called a number of times on 11 April and told me we had to join the pro-coup generals.' He allayed my fears and I don't recall all of the things we talked about afterwards.

Later, he convened a meeting of governors . . . There was the governor of Carabobo State, who had also called me on Friday to ask me to change sides. 'Do you remember calling me on Friday?' – I asked him. He turned pale and I decided not to torment him further. The governor of Bolívar was also there. 'And why did you want to meet with the traitors?' It wasn't easy seeing those bastards there.

Can anything like this happen in the Armed Forces again?

We can't discount the possibility of seeing a small platoon rebel, for propaganda purposes. Four or five platoons, even, in different parts of the country, to destabilize things. 'A chain of military uprisings in the military garrisons . . .' It is not only a possibility. They've planned it on more than one occasion. But I don't think they'll attempt a coup of that scope again. We've learnt a lot.

But all of the people who were behind the coup who are not in jail are potential conspirators.

That's the down side of having to defend a system with the enemy within, conspiring with all of its economic power and enjoying the support of the transnational power. It's difficult, but we'll have to move forward in these conditions and strengthen ourselves. I'm always coming across the people who staged the coup here. General González González walks past me here in Barquisimeto, trying to make me think he matters. I act as though I don't see him.

With your experience as conspirators, how could this plot take you by surprise?

We made serious mistakes and had serious weaknesses which have been corrected today. Major Chávez did not have direct and immediate contact with the heads of operative units. When he tried to contact them, he couldn't get hold of anyone. The generals took the lead and no one even remembered the majors.

Support from battalion commanders should have been sought when things in Miraflores started to heat up and the first betrayals became evident. Chávez did not have, as he does now, a direct line of contact with the different command units. Those were, ultimately, generals who had no command or any direct authority over the troops. But, above all, we let those fascists confuse people.

We've learned some important lessons from this coup. Like the saying goes: whatever doesn't kill you makes you stronger. The generals who staged the coup, with very few exceptions, were very greedy for power and contacts. At one point, this created a vacuum in the Armed Forces. No generals with a revolutionary record were appointed. Of course, the President had, at that time, troops loyal to him that he could have mobilized, but the element of surprise was decisive. They had planned the coup meticulously, and on 11 April, in the afternoon, we still didn't know exactly what was happening.

I remember Chávez saying to me, at around eight at night, 'Why don't you go to Libertador?' I would have to go by car, that is, it would take me three hours to get there. The Libertador base is in Maracay, and there were already troop movements there. I would have been giving them a chance to neutralize me very easily. There was no time for anything.

Was Chávez in any real danger of being assassinated?

They didn't assassinate him in those days out of fear of the people. Perhaps they thought it was easier to control the people with a live Chávez than a dead one. They've always had the option of killing him anyway, even before 1999. I have the impression it's an option they're more likely to consider seriously after 15 August.

Nevertheless, little by little the people learnt where the truth lies and who the enemy is. The same thing as happened to us, the metaphor of the bottle: when we were in the barracks – the bottle – we would only look inwards. The people have stopped looking inwards, they see and understand that much hostility comes from without, they have started to organize to cut the strings that manipulate the enemy within.

Meanwhile, Comandante Chávez continues to oversee our strategies. Every step taken in the social field is also a strategic political move. For instance, the significance of teaching people to read and write transcends the mere universalisation of that right: we mustn't forget that elitist education was the instrument used by the oligarchy to perpetuate the population's intellectual and cultural impoverishment. It is very difficult to familiarise people with a revolutionary ideology when they can't even read the basic tenets of that ideology. So, providing education to the people is vital in this struggle.

The people of Venezuela are no longer the same. Ten years ago, we could not have withstood an oil stoppage with all of its shortages. Only a country inspired by a process like this one is capable of withstanding something like that. That means there has been a change in people's behaviour and convictions. But neither the opposition, nor their superiors in the United States, want to understand this. Dirty deals and treason will continue, as they always have.

How does your friendship with the President stand after so many things? Is it still the same as at the beginning . . .?

Our friendship becomes easier and stronger as the years go by. But we never abuse each other's trust. When we talk, I always call him 'Mr. President'.

But he still calls you Wicho.

Yes, but I continue to call him 'Mr. President', perhaps because of my military background, where the boss is the boss, regardless of the personal relationship one may have with him. I think it may also have to do with our topics of conversation in this new stage in our lives, which have to do with government issues, some military matters and the epic undertaking of the revolution.

If you had to live your life over, what would you do differently?
Nothing. I would live this life a thousand times over. Getting here has made the journey worthwhile, because, for the first time, we have a government concerned about the whole of Venezuela and not a tiny part of it. This does not mean I agree one hundred per cent with everything I've experienced and am experiencing now.

What do you reproach Chávez for?
What importance does that have now?

LETTER FROM HUGO CHÁVEZ TO LUIS REYES REYES FROM THE YARE PRISON

Yare, 12 July 1992
Dear Mota and Argimiro:

Your letter makes me very happy, as I had been informed, through a different channel, that you were being released. In any event, I want you to know that our friendship runs deeper than any passing circumstances. Send all my love to your better half and children. I have received and keep a photo that is a source of inspiration for me. I hope your son, and everyone, is doing well. Send my regards to your relatives in the town.

Mota, you're part of the original project. Your presence guarantees the strategic course we've always set for ourselves. To pull out now – and this goes for Armigiro as well – would be very detrimental to us. Everything could go down a different road. Please, get closer to Dr. Silva and *El Recio*, as well as Fidel. Yesterday, I received some not so uplifting news from your bunch. It seems many things have fallen apart. Get in touch with (1), who's in a very good place. What happened with (2) and (3)? My people want to be more involved. What about (4)? Now is when we need him. And (5)? Brother, please realize that these are the people we know share our political convictions. The rest are coming on board, but what we need to secure is the right direction. We need people to assume leadership positions. Please, so as not to repeat myself, meet with Argimiro and discuss this. You must work very closely with (6) and (7) aiming at a convergence of X and Y.

Nancy knows how to contact Silva and *El Recio*. They'll inform you about the device and the plans. Another very good contact for us is Juancho.

In addition to this, you can start political work with the civil front. Which is to say, brother: we need you. I would trust my life to you and Argimiro. I know you will be there. What we need to do is knock down some barriers. Argimiro was at a meeting with Dr. Silva and some comrades from the T. They tell me that Y demoralized people because he said that you didn't have anything. Evaluate this situation and act accordingly.

I am absolutely confident that we will triumph.

Argimiro: send regards to your better half and the kids. And to the rest of the family as well.
In love and brotherhood,
Sincerely,
Hugo

Code[3]

(1) Pedro Soto
(2) Cordero

---

3. The code was sent out before the letters, to avoid having the government of Carlos Andrés Pérez discover who Hugo Chávez's collaborators outside the prison were.

(3) Dalmiro
(4) Visconti
(5) Maximiliano
(6) Pablo Medina
(7) Roger
X Military uprising
Y General strike
Silva: Rojas Mujica
El Recio: Pérez Issa

Appendix Four

My Story Has Only Just Begun

Chief of Defence Staff
Jorge Luis García Carneiro
interviewed by Rosa Elizalde and Luis Baez

Childhood

What did your parents do?

My mum was a midwife who would also embalm and dress the dead. When someone in the neighbourhood died, they would call her and she would take a briefcase with needles, formaldehyde, white curtains and black ribbons to decorate the room where the wake would be held. People used to have wakes at home, not in funeral parlours like now. She didn't get money for it, it was a kind of charity work she did for the poor. She would also do the house work.

My dad was a businessman. He still lives and has always been with us. We had a very strict upbringing, mostly by my mother. Dad was always a very permissive and calm person. I don't even remember him ever reproaching any of my brothers for anything. Mum, on the other hand, was tough, she had a very strong character.

How many of you are there in the family?

There's seven of us: four girls and three boys. I'm the sixth.

Did you all finish secondary school?

The seven of us graduated through great sacrifices. I'm very much aware of where I come from. I know how much work my parents went through to support the seven of us. We all studied at the Gran Colombia school and graduated from the sixth grade there. Some of my sisters got technical and business secondary school degrees, others graduated from teacher's training college, I graduated from the Pedro Emilio Coll secondary school. Later, I took the entrance exam for the Pedagogic Institute of Caracas to study history and geography; I wanted to teach those subjects.

I took my last entrance exam on 25 July and, nevertheless, I started at the Military Academy on 8 August 1971. Which means, I scarcely had ten days of vacation. When I was already at the Academy, I would reproach myself, 'Shit, if only I'd started at the Pedagogic Institute . . .' But my doubts soon faded away. I finally decided to pursue a military career.

Do you remember when you met Hugo Chávez for the first time?

I met him on that morning of 8 August 1971, at the lecture hall in the Military Academy of Venezuela, when they were giving us words of welcome. One gets to know people so well after four years of studying with them that I can say I knew he was someone very talented from that first day, a very smart guy, he was always first in everything and was an exceptionally good speaker – I discovered this one day when he hosted a beauty queen contest.

We were in the same paratroopers course, something which brings officers very close to one another. We graduated on 5 July 1975, Chávez in Communications and I in Infantry. Later, as a lieutenant, Hugo took further weapons training and joined the armoured division. I stayed in Infantry.

Perhaps being in different divisions didn't allow us to get to know each other better, but we always kept in touch and met every now and then. Something that one shouldn't overlook, is that many of Chávez's followers, and he himself, were in our year, the Simón Bolívar year.

When did you meet Chávez again after that?

After graduating from the Academy, we would see each other all the time. We would run into each other during leave, in Caracas, or on courses, and also while on duty. Afterwards, when we went to the general staff school in the army, I went ahead of him and did the course before he did.

Why do you say you went first?

When I was commanding a battalion, he entered the higher institute as a student. We should have enrolled together, we were from the same year. But high officials were doing everything in their power to prevent him from commanding troops, from going up the ladder. There were rumours he was involved in a possible coup attempt, and they not only tried to prevent his promotion, they started to put pressure on him to try and make him fail his exams. They would take marks away for anything, even commas. But it was hard to flunk Chávez Frías, because, truly, I think he is one of the most brilliant professional officers I have met in my career. He always graduated among the top in his class, even when they tried so hard to prevent it.

The Uprising

Where were you during the Caracazo?

In San Juan de los Morros, in the Cavalry division. I was General Morales' aide. Chávez was on leave due to complications resulting from dengue fever.

Chicken pox.

Something like that, and Felipe Acosta Carlez, who was at the Academy, was ordered to look into a supposed outbreak of violence: they killed him there. It was on 27 February 1989, the same day 'they came down from the hills'.

Did you know Felipe?

Yes, he was our friend. And he was a very close friend of mine, because he was an infantryman as well; we served together in different units in the General Daniel Florencio O'Leary Battalion.

Did you have ties to the Bolivarian Movement?

No. Chávez and his group had been working with the Movement. They were very discreet about it because of the serious consequences that could result from being discovered. I was based at the border, maybe that's why they never established contact with me. Communication was difficult. You had to use the radio and they couldn't tell me anything through that channel.

I'm honest. I don't know what answer I would have given, I would have had to be there. What I can tell you is that, when the February 1992 uprising took place and I saw Chávez on television, bravely assuming responsibility for what had occurred, I was filled with pride. I felt that, at the very least, I had a friend with the integrity to assume great responsibility.

The uprising took me by surprise; I was the commanding officer of the Carabobo Infantry Battalion on the Colombian border, where theatre of operations number 1 was based. Because of sporadic actions by the Colombian guerrillas at the time, I was based there for virtually all the three years I served as lieutenant colonel. I remember that, after 4 February, we were gathered at the officers' mess and a deputy yelled out, 'Death to the pro-coup faction!' That was all it took for the people to make him pay for that remark in the elections and he was never elected deputy again.

April 2002

The coup took you by surprise?

Though we had been informed about a possible coup, and there was even talk of supposed and generalized discontents, I have to admit it took me by surprise. On 10 April, the then Minister of Defense José Vicente Rangel; General Lucas Rincón, inspector general of the Armed Forces; General Manuel Rosendo, commander of the National Armed Force's Unified Command (CU-FAN) and Efraín Vázquez Velasco, Vice Chief of the Defence Staff, met with me in this very office. The chairman of the joint chiefs of staff, Vice Admiral Bernabé Carrero Cubero and Vice Admiral Jorge Sierraalta Zavarce from the navy, were also present. I remember we spoke about the opposition's march, which was going to go from the east park to Chuao. Supposedly, there were still no signs of anything and, all of a sudden, we get General Néstor González González, an ex-major from the army schools, declaring that he will not recognize the President of the Republic as his commander in chief.

At that moment, in front of the television, I started to perceive strange attitudes in people and to suspect that not only González González but also Manuel Rosendo and Vázquez Velasco were involved in something very dangerous.

You had not been commanding the troops in Caracas for very long at the time . . .

I was major general and had officially been commander of the Caracas garrison for a month, with jurisdiction in greater Caracas. Before that, I had been in Mérida for eighteen months; from there, I had been transferred to the San Cristóbal division. While serving in this last division, the President called me to come and serve as head of his household troops. I spent six months there. In January, he decided to give me the Caracas garrison.

When was the decision to implement the Ávila Plan made?

It was decided on after they announced on television that the march in Chuao had changed course toward Miraflores.

You were at the Ministry of Defence at that moment?

Yes, and I heard Dr. José Vicente Rangel call Marcel Granier, director of *Radio Caracas*, and ask him what all this madness was about and how was it possible that the march was going to be detoured to Miraflores. Given the huge numbers of people there at the time, a head-on clash between the two blocks would have been unavoidable, and that was extremely dangerous.

I was able to overhear Marcel Granier assuring Rangel that he would do everything in his power to discourage the march from changing direction. The minister also called Dr. Alberto Federico Ravell, president of *Globovisión*, and told him the same thing, using the same words. He also committed himself to do something to stop the march. Both, however, were having Rangel on. They did absolutely nothing. They were involved in everything, and were acting according to plan. I think they had even foreseen those kinds of conversations.

Then, they decided to put together a statement for television. There were some cameras in the basement. José Vicente asked Lucas Rincón, as inspector general for the army, to address the country and make a call for calm. He was the highest ranking officer of the Armed Forces. When we all went down to hear him speak, Vázquez Velasco disappeared. He had hidden inside a bathroom and was nowhere to be found. Rosendo arrived, but Vázquez didn't.

Faced with this difficult situation, I proceeded immediately to the Third Division, where my command was. I remember asking General Wilfredo Ramón Silva to come out of a meeting where all generals were gathered, because we had doubts about Vázquez Velasco. After he'd disappeared into the bathroom, this general had called all army generals in Caracas to an urgent meeting on the fifth floor of army command headquarters and had sat them in front of a television for them to see what was happening.

At that meeting, they tried to convince a group of officers that the President no longer had control over the government, that he had virtually lost his authority and his legality. That is, they invited them to join the ranks of the pro-coup faction. All of this was explained to me by General Wilfredo Silva when I asked him to come out of the meeting. He excused himself and left for the Third Division. That is when I said, 'We're going to implement the Ávila Plan. We're going to proceed as established once and for all.' It was a matter of taking key locations in the area, particularly around Miraflores. We warned all units and gathered them in the courtyard of the Bolívar Battalion. We proceeded to the Ayala Battalion, took out the tanks and armed them. We prepared all vehicles that managed to get their motors running for battle. Of 45 tanks, only around 9 were left there. The rest were brought here.

The Intelligence Services Failed

Was Chávez aware of everything happening in Fort Tiuna at the time?

No. He didn't know what we were doing. I wasn't able to inform him. It was impossible.

And the intelligence services had not detected anything?

I've spoken with various intelligence officers and they've told me that they had given the President a number of warnings. 'Look, so and so is plotting against you, so and so is going to meetings,' but, actually, they hadn't put much stock on that intelligence and most of the time the information wasn't even verified. That, unfortunately, became more and more complicated, and it got to the point where the group of conspirators was fairly large, much larger than had been suspected.

On 11 April, I myself thought that there were two or three traitors, and it turns out that more than 100 high ranking officers were involved, nearly all of them without command. Among the generals, the only who had command of troops were the commanding officer of the army and his second in command, José Félix Ruiz Guzmán.

But you spoke with Chávez that day.

By a stroke of luck. While at the Bolívar Battalion, I overheard the President's attempts at communicating with General Rosendo, who was already up to his neck in the coup. He was calling Rosendo over the radio, using his codename. The general was Shark 3, I was Shark 6. I heard his voice, 'Shark 3 here', 'Shark three, Shark 1 here.' Rosendo wasn't responding. On noting the President's insistence, I replied.

What did you say?

'Look – I told him – I can hear you, I'm heading for the Palace. I've got my people ready and willing to implement the Ávila Plan. I only need you to tell me when to mobilize them.' He asked me how many troops I had under my command. 'All that are envisaged by the Plan, plus the tanks.' 'Look' – he answered

— 'let's do this, send me 20 tanks to protect the Palace and stay there with the troops.'

At that moment, I asked General Wilfredo Silva to leave immediately for Miraflores with the tanks and to go down Alcabala 3, through the tunnels that lead to Sucre Avenue, which was the quickest way there, and where we thought there were few chances of running into civilians.

What did you do?

They called me from the ministry and ordered me to appear immediately before General Lucas Rincón. When I arrived, they informed me we were leaving on helicopter for Miraflores, because the President was going to make a statement. General Rosendo, Admiral Sierraalta Zavarce and General Francisco Belisario Landis, National Guard commander, were also in the helicopter. I heard them say they would tell the President nothing could be done, that everything was already lost, that the National Guard wasn't recognizing the authority of its commander, that the commander of the army had also risen up and would be making a statement, that they didn't know what was happening with the navy in several garrisons. They were basically going to ask Chávez to resign. Dr. Rangel did not agree with that proposal.

He was also with you?

Yes. 'We're not going to tell him everything is lost, the situation isn't like that either' – he was saying. When we arrived at the Palace, it was around six thirty in the evening, almost nightfall. We went in and, while waiting for the President to see us, I told General Lucas Rincón I had no business there, that I wasn't part of the high command. 'I think I should be with my troops. I'm worried about leaving them all by themselves in Fort Tiuna, and I want to be there.' General Lucas Rincón gave me permission. I borrowed a car from Minister Nelson Merentes and left the Palace through the back entrance, heading directly for the Fort.

What were you thinking about during the drive?

That they were going to arrest me. There was a strange atmosphere about, but the plot was becoming more and more clear to me. I passed the sentry post without any problems. I was prepared to do whatever I had to to go in. I was really surprised that I was able to go through without problems. That gives you an idea of the craziness and the confusion all around us.

I proceeded directly to the Logistics Battalion. I was worried. Before getting on the helicopter, I had ordered the arrest of a number of officers who had risen up and had managed to capture sentry posts 1 and 3, the one at the National Armed Forces' National Experimental Polytechnic University (Universidad Nacional Experimental Politécnica de la Fuerza Armada Nacional, UNEFA). They had virtually taken control of the Fort's main points of entry. They were following orders from General Martínez Hidalgo, to obstruct traffic inside Tiuna and block the access route toward the west (Maracay, Valencia); they managed to bring every vehicle they came across around the regional highway into the Fort. They brought in articulated lorries, lorries, buses . . . They wanted to jam the Fort and use these vehicles to prevent tanks from leaving.

When did this happen?

Before I spoke with the President. When he asked me to send the tanks, we had already retaken sentry post 3. I had ordered the removal of all civilian vehicles from the Fort.

How were the posts retaken?

We had to arrest three captains who were commanding the posts. So, when I returned from Miraflores, I went directly to speak with those arrested. I was in there until eight thirty or nine at night. At that time, they wanted to arrest me.

Why were the tanks not in Miraflores, as the President had asked?

When the tanks arrived at the Palace, the Tank Battalion commander, who was also pro-coup, received a call from Vázquez Velásco and ordered the withdrawal of the tanks. It was decisive. When the armoured division went out, the threats against the

President began; they were saying there was going to be a bloodbath if he didn't resign, that they were going to bomb Miraflores.

Uncertainty

Who ordered your arrest?

General Luis Castillo Castro, who sent a colonel and a group of soldiers. They showed up at the Quartermaster Corps. I took out my pistol right there and then and told the general, 'If you try and arrest me, you know how far I'm willing to go.' I wasn't going to let them take me. And I went on, gun in hand. 'So, go ahead if you want to, because I'm going to blow your brains out.' First he hesitated, then desisted. I turned quickly to Colonel José Gregorio Montilla Pantoja and asked him, 'Is that your car?' 'Yes'. We both got into the car and I said, 'Let's go to Miraflores.'

At El Paraíso, the tunnel was blocked. One of the pro-coup mayors and the municipal police had blocked the road. They had taken the keys of all the cars at the front, such that the ones behind could not move.

We had been immobilized near the tunnel's exit. But we turned around there, went in the opposite direction, switching beams, zig-zagging among the cars coming at us, until we came out at the cemetery.

There, we cut towards the DISIP building on Victoria Avenue. The pro-coup faction had already taken it and had arrested the director, Captain Carlos Aguilera. When we arrived, I almost got arrested myself.

They detained you?

No. Carlos Aguilera was very clever. He told the pro-coup officers that I had come to take him under arrest to Fort Tiuna. They allowed Carlos to leave with me and when he got into the car he ordered me, 'Let's go, let's go.' We started going around Caracas, round and round and round, studying the situation, not knowing exactly what to do. At around that time, they called me asking me to appear in command headquarters – it was already around midnight or one in the morning of the 12th. They promised me there would be no reprisals, that they only wanted to talk to me.

Who called you?

Colonel Granadillo. I consulted with my friends and we decided to hand ourselves in to see what happened. We went up to the fifth floor of command headquarters, where the pro-coup staff officers were. They locked me up in the commander's bathroom.

A while later, the door opened and there stood General Enrique Medina Gómez. He is Venezuela's military attaché in the United States, who just happened to come to Caracas on the same day of the coup. He told me that this action had been in the pipeline for a long time and that the only way to prevent deaths was to proceed as they were doing.

That's when it dawned on me that, in effect, everything was very well organized and that they had planned a slaughter in Puente Llaguno to justify the mobilization of the Armed Forces against the President. If the high command could be convinced that there was no other option but to accept the coup, they would have no need to call out the troops. The leaders of the pro-coup faction did know that they would first have to kill a number of innocent people to get the upper hand and keep the military leaders loyal to the President under control.

How did you react?

When they started telling me all of these things, I assumed a passive attitude. It was to my advantage. I needed to know what their plans were, and I went along with them without committing myself to anything. 'Oh, okay, that's what you had planned.' I was also trying to get out of that mess.

About half an hour after my conversation with Medina Gómez, Vázquez Velasco came in with General Henry Lugo Peña, who had been chief of the household troops. I heard Lugo Peña tell

Vázquez Velasco, 'Shit, I thought you were going to take off.' 'How could I take off? No, it's been decided,' he answered. Pedro Carmona was already in the commander's office. When the two generals left the room, I went out behind them. Since they didn't see me assume any aggressive attitude, they left me alone.

What was the atmosphere like in that place?

Euphoric. Carmona was seated at the Comandante's table and most of them were sitting around him; some were telling stories, others laughing . . . all of them were celebrating, because, you see, they had accomplished their objectives.

Was the American military present?

Yes. There were two American officers.

Do you remember their names?

I don't remember their names, but I do their facial features, their hair cuts, the way they talked. One can recognize a gringo a mile away.

Were they in uniform?

No, they were in civilian clothes, but they carried rifles. It really caught my attention, because it was the first time in my life I saw a rifle with a grenade launcher mounted. I later found out they were M203s.

Lieutenant Colonel James Rodgers and Colonel Ronald McCammon are said to have been there, in the fifth floor of command headquarters, where they remained until the end of the coup . . .

Exactly, those were their names. I found out their true identities later, but that was the first time I saw them and I was certain that they were two Yankee soldiers.

Who were also celebrating . . .

Yes. They looked euphoric. I remember General Carlos Alfonzo Martínez, who was the National Guard's inspector general, showed up. As soon as he came into the room, he said, 'Well, he's on his way. You keep him here, don't take him anywhere else. He's going to be tried here, we have to try him here.'

Try whom, Chávez?

Chávez. So, I went up to General Martínez Vidal and said, 'Look, what you're thinking of doing is a mistake. Whoever underestimates the President's appeal is mistaken. You think the story's ended, but I think it's just beginning.' They paid no attention. In any event, that's when I went home.

What time was it?

A bit after three in the morning. Television channels were broadcasting the same message over and over again. 'García Carneiro, turn yourself in.'

Around that time, a neighbour of mine, Carmelo, who lives across the street, arrived. We started to talk about what was happening. One of my brothers was also there. My sisters arrived later. We stayed up until around six in the morning, and that's when I decided to return to Tiuna.

In the Eye of the Hurricane, Again

Was it your decision, or had they called you?

It was a personal decision, I was anxious to know what was happening in Fort Tiuna.

Were you able to get inside?

Without any problems.

Where did you go to?

To the Third Division.

Who had assumed command of the Third Division?

They had appointed now General Lameda Hernández, who was then colonel.

What did you do when you saw him?

Lameda warned me, 'Look, just so you know, they want to arrest you. They've asked me to assume command of the Division and they've told me they're going to promote me. But I'm not interested in their offer and I've decided to stick by you, whatever the consequences.' It was the morning of the 12th when we started to call all of the officers we thought loyal to the President.

Did you know Chávez was being held in Tiuna?

He was being held in the military police building, but I didn't know that at the time. They kept it absolutely secret. There was some suspicion surrounding that, but nothing certain. We continued to call the officers and battalion commanders from there that morning. Later, in the afternoon, Carmona swore himself in as president and the abolition of the executive, judiciary and legislature was decreed.

Which means, you had been officially dismissed . . .

Everyone was dismissed, and we took advantage of that disaster to speak with the officers once again. Carmona appointed the members of the high military command that same night, and that was even worse. When he appointed General Lugo Peña commander of the army, Medina Gómez was so offended that, on the morning of 13 April, he went to businessman Isaac Pérez Recao's house, took off his uniform and the two of them left for the United States.

General Vázquez Velasco was also left without a job.

Exactly. Taking advantage of the fact Vázquez Velasco was very angry, the officers at the Fort started ordering the pro-coup officers around, to tell them they had been deceived, because they hadn't seen the President's resignation. They also questioned the abolition of all civil institutions, that they weren't respecting any norms, that that was a dictatorship. The majors called Vázquez Velasco and proposed a meeting, and he, who was angry, agreed to have it on 13 April, at one in the afternoon, at the Ayala Battalion. Of course, they informed me he had agreed to meet and, a few hours before, at around eleven in the morning, I asked the commander of the military police permission to grant the troop leaders due to arrive restricted access to the Fort.

Held in Tiuna?

When did the people start to gather at Fort Tiuna?

From the evening of the 12th on, but especially on the 13th. They were yelling, 'I want to see Chávez, I want to see Chávez.'

That was their slogan. They were saying he was detained at the military police headquarters, and, in effect, in the afternoon of the 12th those rumours were confirmed and we began to plan his rescue.

Who told you Chávez was being held in Tiuna?

One of the officers. However, after two hours of planning the rescue, they informed us they had already taken him to Los Teques prison. So we put together another group of officers who were going to crash an articulated lorry through the prison gates and go in to look for Chávez, where he was supposedly being held prisoner.

A while later, another officer came around and informed us they had taken him to Turiamo and, after that, on the 13th, that they had transferred him to La Orchila. That's why we gave up on our rescue attempts. There was no point to waste our energies looking for Chávez when we didn't know with any certainty where he was.

On the morning of 13 April, when the officer came around and told me he had been transferred to La Orchila, I called the Cuban embassy. At that moment, I had a somewhat crazy idea. 'Hey, what if Fidel sends us a plane and we go get Chávez at La Orchila?'

What did they say?

That it would cause an international problem, something that had to be avoided at all costs.

And what was happening outside the Fort?

That morning around eleven, when I tried to get the troop commanders in here before the meeting at one in the afternoon, we were thinking that, with the people's help, we could also set a trap for the pro-coup faction and Carmona.

Were you in touch with Baduel in Maracay?

No, but I did know there was an uprising in Maracay, that the Paratroopers Brigade did not recognize the new government.

Where was Carmona?

In this same office.

How did you get to command headquarters?

At eleven in the morning, when I tried to convince the commander of the military police to let the troops in, the commander of the guard of honour's regiment, Colonel Jesús Morao Cardona, called me. 'General, I don't agree with what's happening and am at your orders.' I asked him to take the Miraflores Palace, to implement the defence plan and to put the pro-coup faction under arrest in the basement to start putting on the pressure. I assured him that we were working hard at our end.

I swear everything happened like that, without much thought. He called me again, about ten minutes later. He told me a helicopter was firing at them. I said to him, 'Well, shoot it down.' I was very clear. 'Shoot it down.' He called again, saying he had given the orders to the soldiers who had responded immediately, and that the helicopter had flown off. They didn't manage to hit it. They had taken the Palace but Carmona had escaped from them and had rushed over here, to Fort Tiuna.

How did Carmona get here?

He came escorted by a caravan his new household troops provided for him. That's when we started the meeting planned for one in the afternoon. Neither the generals nor the admirals knew that the Palace had already been taken and that Carmona was on his way to Tiuna. They didn't know anything; the only person there who knew that was me.

The Retort

What happened at the meeting?

They spoke about the need to recognize the constitution, because the people were determined to defend it. It wasn't a mere exercise in rhetoric. The ruckus the people were making at the posts could even be heard there. They were banging on the Tiuna bridge railings with sticks and pipes, and they were making a huge racket. Vice Admiral Héctor Ramírez Pérez, commander of a frigate, resigned as minister of defence at that juncture. 'No, I don't want to be responsible for the slaughter that's going to happen here, because the people are furious.'

The pro-coup faction wanted to convince the officers, all battalion commanders, that they hadn't lied, as the latter were claiming. A commander said, 'I haven't seen Chávez's resignation. I was lied to, they didn't tell me they were going to abolish all constitutional guarantees.' The truth is that the meeting got bogged down, and something very important happened. They began to draft the second coup pronouncement, in which they recognized Carmona as head of state but assured the people they would preserve the same social programmes of the previous government.

Taking advantage of Vázquez Velasco's anger over being excluded from the line of command, when he handed me the document I crossed out everything I deemed out of line or offensive that didn't have to do with the political situation. I took great delight in that.

Vázquez Velasco went out to have a word with General Antonio José Navarro Chacón, who was outside. The meeting was put on hold. We waited a while and, as we continued to hear the people in the streets, I told the battalion commanders, 'We're not waiting any longer, we're going to get the general and have him make the declaration for once and for all.' The officers came with me, we went and got Vázquez Velasco into the room. I said, 'Look, read the document. Look it over, because I'm going to let the press in.' When the journalists arrived, someone told the people in the room, 'There's no signal. All relay stations are down. There's no way of broadcasting the declaration live, and, if we don't do it this way, the facts could be distorted.' A journalist from *Globovisión* gave us one of CNN's phone numbers. She convinced CNN to air the story. 'This is a declaration from Caracas. All signals are down, we want to broadcast a live statement.' They gave us the signal, we put Vázquez Velasco on the phone. That's the story behind the communiqué recognizing all constitutional powers and where there's talk of restoring normal conditions around the country.

Why did that document not say anything about Carmona being president?

I had crossed that part out, and, in his nervousness, Vázquez Velasco didn't even notice.

From a Tank

Didn't Carmona know any of this was happening?

No, and, like I told you, neither did the pro-coup faction know what was happening in Miraflores. Then there was talk of a second pronouncement, this one to be made at the office of the minister of defence. They all came down here – where we are now. And so did I, to see what they said. They started arguing. 'How are we going to tell the people that the minister of defence is no longer Ramírez Pérez, but rather Navarro Chacón? The people aren't going to like it.' They were very nervous. I thought they were going to tackle something more significant and, seeing this was not the case, I returned to the Third Division, where they had warned me they were looking for me to arrest me. 'Well, let them arrest me at the guard post, with the people.' I picked up a microphone, I climbed onto a tank and I addressed the multitude . . .

I said that the Armed Forces did not recognize the authority of the government installed by the coup, that it did not accept Carmona as commander in chief, that it was a de facto government, that the army was going to fight to the death to have Chávez return to power.

What about Carmona?

Carmona was already with the generals. They knew Miraflores had been taken. At around seven at night, I ordered Colonel

Mantilla Pantoja, Colonel Granadillo and other generals to take the office of the minister of defence with the Caracas Battalion, to capture Carmona and the other pro-coup supporters. So they did.

Was there a confrontation?

No, they were demoralized. When they went into the office, they were told Carmona was in the minister's private quarters, but the door to the room was locked. An officer from the Caracas Battalion who knew the facility well went in through a different door and captured Carmona.

Did he resist?

No, not at all. He was terrified. He was in his ordinary clothes, and he didn't put up any resistance. The officer informed him he was under arrest, and he replied, 'For what crime?' The young officer answered, 'For violating the Constitution of the Republic.' I brought him into his office immediately. When everyone had been gathered – the generals, admirals and Carmona – Minister of Defence José Vicente Rangel was informed; he came here immediately and gave them all a good dressing down.

Were you there?

No, I was miles away, with the people, because, if they didn't surrender, the idea was to open the gates to let the multitude in and surround them. I already had complete control of the Fort.

Chávez's Return

General, at the beginning you told us that, had Chávez asked you to join the Movement in 1992, you wouldn't have known what to do. What motivated you, ten years later, to get on top of a tank and address the people?

We knew the pro-coup faction was afraid of the people, and that they were willing to do anything for their President. Chávez was my friend, to whom I owed loyalty, but, above all, a legitimately elected President, whose popular appeal was being demonstrated again at that moment. I knew Chávez's feelings, someone who was putting all his heart into a process that, for the first time, was attending to the needs of the people and fighting the vices and abuses of power in this country. I had served in the household troops and had been able to see, up close, the work he had been doing. All of that gave me great strength and I just mustered up my courage. If I was on Chávez's side, whom they loved so much, that would be obvious to the people there. And that's the way it went.

What did you feel at that moment, when you addressed the multitude?

One of the greatest satisfactions ever. The people had been waiting for a response from the Armed Forces, which is what we gave them then. There was a great show of support. We informed them that all commanders were with the people. That was put on television.

And after that?

When the generals and admirals were arrested at around seven at night, we were still out there with the people. We would play them music by Alí Primera and, every ten minutes, we gave them any news we got. For instance, we would say, 'Look, the Zulia, Cerúpano and Sucre garrisons have already recognized Chávez as the Constitutional President of the Republic.' The applauses, yelling and hugging would follow, and we'd play Alí Primera again. Then, ten minutes later, 'People, the Carabobo, Táchira and Mérida garrisons recognize President Chávez . . .' The same thing every ten minutes, 'People, such and such garrison . . .' The idea was to keep people awake. At around two in the morning on the 14th, we knew that Chávez had left La Orchila in a helicopter headed for Miraflores.

Who informed you of this?

I got a call from Maracay telling me that the commission had already left with a helicopter to get the President. That's what we told the people who had gathered there and whose numbers continued to grow. The people were hoping Chávez would arrive at the Fort, but we weren't certain where he was headed. A young man took out a mini television set he had installed in his car and there we found out he was heading for Miraflores, that he would be arriving in a few minutes. I yelled out to the crowd, 'Let's go and meet him!', and many asked us to find buses for the people. I answered, 'Find buses for 60,000 people at four in the morning? I can't.' But just look, the people, exuberant, set off down the highway on foot and walked all the way to Miraflores.

How many kilometres is that?

From here to there? Around 6 kilometres, but it's farther by the highway.

Did you also go there?

In the young man's car with the television set. When we arrived, Chávez was already inside the Palace. We hugged.

What did you say to one another?

He said, 'Comrade, I didn't expect any more support than that you showed me. You have been very loyal to me and I am grateful for that.' We hugged like brothers. We went on celebrating the return of the President, and that's where the morning found us.

The Pro-Coup Faction Gets Off Scot-Free

Did you see the officers who were arrested again?

They were detained here, but the public prosecutor intervened. There was talk that their rights had been violated, that this, that and the other. In the end, they let them go home, with a summons to appear in court.

What about Carmona?

He remained under arrest, and was later placed under house arrest, which he managed to evade.

A few days after the coup, you told the press that, on searching the homes of several pro-coup officers, evidence of a plan to assassinate Chávez had been found. What documents were found?

Searches were conducted and many incriminating documents were found, but there was also a lot of pressure from the media which torpedoed the decisions of the prosecution and prevented justice from being done.

The truth of the matter is that the pro-coup officers got off scot-free like nothing had happened. They would go in and out of Fort Tiuna. They went there to jog, to meet with people. They enjoyed real impunity and it got to one. We had the idea of putting up lists with the names of the pro-coup officers in the sentry posts, to restrict their access, and a court presented an appeal on grounds of unconstitutionality. They called the commander of the military police and told him he couldn't prohibit their access, nor curtail anyone's rights and who knows what else . . . In the end, we had to take the list down. So, the impunity continued. They boasted about things, jogged, ran and did dreadful things. That went on for over nine months. Then came the Supreme Court ruling, which established there had been no coup d'état.

This ruling emboldened them even more, as though recharging their batteries. They had a sense of entitlement and would come into command headquarters when they felt like it. We had to keep them posted as though they were on active service and had moral authority, and this was tolerated. Then, they would go and eat, have lunch, shave, visit friends. They started to provoke people.

What decision did you make?

We said, 'If we don't put the pressure on, this is going to end up in another attempted coup. Discipline is going to go out the window.' Nine months after the coup, I was appointed head of the ministry and one of the first things I did was meet with all officers in Caracas. I told them that if the pro-coup officers came into the Fort, we would be forced to kindly request them to identify themselves and, just as kindly, were going to ask them very nicely to get into a patrol car to be taken to the military police. If they resisted, we would shove them into the patrol car, or use machetes; what's certain is that they were getting into those cars, no matter what their rank. Of course, the officers spread the word. Some had friends, acquaintances, buddies among the pro-coup officers. That did the trick. Not one of them came back to Fort Tiuna. Truth is, if we didn't put our foot down, they were going to continue acting with impunity.

Every time there were rumours of a coup in the making, I placed two tanks next to every sentry post. We were very strict about the requisition of vehicles. We would set up additional, internal sentry posts in other parts of the Fort, would ask for ID and check on things regularly. In one of those checks we found Alfonzo in Madariaga Square trying to incite the National Guard to rebel. I went up to him and said, 'It's a shame to catch you like this, you who were one year ahead of me, who I called "general". Now, what I will tell you is that, if you so much as step out of line, I will kick your ass.' That's what I said to him, it's true, and he spread it around, that I had threatened to kick his ass. I did it, precisely, so he would spread it around, for them to know we were determined to have them respect us, no matter what.

Did they still have weapons in their possession?

They had weapons and vehicles in their possession. I mentioned the need to take away the vehicles and weapons they had at several meetings here. All of them had state vehicles, weaponry, license to bear arms.

What about salaries?

And their salaries, and they were even being given the basket-ticket, a food bonus given to people on the basis of days worked. It was shameless free-loading. An end was put to all of that.

And what about their weapons?

Some had a veritable arsenal in their possession. I signed a ministerial resolution notifying them that, if they did not hand in their weapons and other state property within an established period of time, they would be tried for insubordination and misappropriation.

Approximately how many weapons were in their possession?

An average of six or seven weapons of war per person, including machine guns, grenade-launchers and everything else under the sun.

And the Americans kept going into the Fort like they owned the place . . .

Yes, like they owned the place. They had a military mission here inside and offices in army buildings. An end was put to that. Where the American mission was, the Vuelvan Caras (Turning Faces Around), Identity and Barrio Adentro (Into the Neighbourhood) missions were set up.

What do the flyers we've seen in Fort Tiuna, offering a reward for information about officers wanted by law, mean?

They were pro-coup officers with ties to the paramilitary. People gave evidence against them during the investigation. With this evidence, we requested an arrest warrant, and, since they didn't turn up, I asked the President permission to put out those flyers, offering fifty million bolívares to anyone who could come forward with information.

The investigation has also revealed that they were planning to kill many of the people loyal to the President.

Plans to kill those people?

Yes, kill.

Did you find lists of people or something like that?

Yes, and also an operation order that, according to the analysis we've conducted, could only have been drafted by a member of the military. It has the five paragraphs all operational orders have, with the corresponding annexes. Among them was the fumigation plan – as they call the systematic killings – and a list of officers they were going to kill.

Were you on the list?

Yes. The President was the first on it; José Vicente was number two, and I was number three.

Did the list include your families?

Yes.

Why has none of this been made public?

Because that is still under investigation, and the media has no interest in making it public.

Speaking of the media, you have been severely criticized for having defended what you call the concept of Integrated National Defence.

Ah, that's a revolutionary concept. The President speaks of a new defence concept for the nation which we also support. It is based on three essential ideas or axes: the strengthening of the Armed Forces, the unification of the civil and military spheres and the popular movement. We've analyzed this concept a lot and there are a number of serious proposals that have been made available to the President.

In a nutshell, it envisages the defence of the entire people in the context of Venezuela's situation. Seeing the position the United States is in in Iraq, even with its highly powerful army and very sophisticated weapons, we're also getting ready for a completely asymmetrical and irregular type of war. We needn't think of it in terms of giving a rifle to everyone. The concept of integrated national defence recognizes the need to train reservists, teach the people how to defend itself and train it to respond to a difficult situation.

General, many Venezuelan military leaders studied in the United States and had a very prejudiced attitude towards Cuba. Is that still the case, or has it changed?

Governments prior to Chávez's fostered a deeply hostile attitude toward the Cuban government. I was lucky enough to go to Cuba a year ago. It was the first time I visited the island and I saw some very nice things, a sense of justice and living conditions which the majority of Venezuelans don't have. I realized it was not the hell that they had spoken about for so many years in Venezuela.

I was able to see, with my own eyes, what a revolution is and how a country with few resources can develop. People live in peace, have a good education system, a good network of hospitals, social justice; things that we really don't have here. You look at Venezuela, with so many resources, so much money, and see the majority of the people living in poverty. Eighty per cent of the population is beneath the poverty line. That has absolutely no justification.

There's another decisive element: profound hatred toward imperialism, wide-spread awareness of the power of the United States and what it can do. Don't forget the United States was behind the coup and had the gall to say that it did it so that not one more barrel of oil was sent to Cuba. Today, it's very common to see both Venezuelan and Cuban flags in a march. It's common.

What kind of Venezuela do you see in the future?

A country infinitely better than the one we have today. I have great hopes for our people. I believe that if the President is re-elected in 2006, in 2013 Venezuela will be a different, much better place.

And will you be with him up till then?

God willing.

Appendix Five

Power to the People

Evo Morales' Speech at 'In Defence of Humanity' Forum in Mexico City

Thank you for the invitation to this great meeting of intellectuals 'In Defense of Humanity'. Thank you for your applause for the Bolivian people, who have mobilized in these recent days of struggle, drawing on our consciousness and our regarding how to reclaim our natural resources.

What happened these past days in Bolivia was a great revolt by those who have been oppressed for more than 500 years. The will of the people was imposed this September and October, and has begun to overcome the empire's cannons. We have lived for so many years through the confrontation of two cultures: the culture of life represented by the indigenous people, and the culture of death represented by the West. When we the indigenous people – together with the workers and even the businessmen of our country – fight for life and justice, the State responds with its 'democratic rule of law'.

What does the 'rule of law' mean for indigenous people? For the poor, the marginalized, the excluded, the 'rule of law' means the targeted assassinations and collective massacres that we have endured. Not just this September and October, but for many years, in which they have tried to impose policies of hunger and poverty on the Bolivian people.

Above all, the 'rule of law' means the accusations that we, the Quechuas, Aymaras and Guaranties of Bolivia keep hearing from our governments: that we are narcos, that we are anarchists. This uprising of the Bolivian people has been not only about gas and hydrocarbons, but an intersection of many issues: discrimination, marginalization, and most importantly, the failure of neoliberalism.

The cause of all these acts of bloodshed, and for the uprising of the Bolivian people, has a name: neoliberalism. With courage and defiance, we brought down Gonzalo Sánchez de Lozada – the symbol of neoliberalism in our country – on October 17, the Bolivians' day of dignity and identity. We began to bring down the symbol of corruption and the political mafia.

And I want to tell you, compañeras and compañeros, how we have built the consciousness of the Bolivian people from the bottom up. How quickly the Bolivian people have reacted, have said – as Subcomandate Marcos says – ¡ya basta!, enough policies of hunger and misery.

For us, October 17th is the beginning of a new phase of construction. Most importantly, we face the task of ending selfishness and individualism, and creating – from the rural *campesino* and indigenous communities to the urban slums – other forms of living, based on solidarity and mutual aid. We must think about how to redistribute the wealth that is concentrated among few hands. This is the great task we Bolivian people face after this great uprising.

It has been very important to organize and mobilize ourselves in a way based on transparency, honesty, and control over our own organizations. And it has been important not only to organize but also to unite. Here we are now, united intellectuals in defense of humanity – I think we must have not only unity among the social movements, but also that we must coordinate with the intellectual movements. Every gathering, every event of this nature for we labor leaders who come from the social struggle, is a great lesson that allows us to exchange experiences and to keep strengthening our people and our grassroots organizations.

Thus, in Bolivia, our social movements, our intellectuals, our workers – even those political parties which support the popular struggle – joined together to drive out Gonzalo Sánchez Lozada. Sadly, we paid the price with many of our lives, because the Empire's arrogance and tyranny continue humiliating the Bolivian people.

It must be said, compañeras and compañeros, that we must serve the social and popular movements rather than the transnational corporations. I am new to politics; I had hated it and had been afraid of becoming a career politician. But I realized that politics had once been the science of serving the people, and that getting involved in politics is important if you want to help your people. By getting involved, I mean living for politics, rather than living off politics.

We have coordinated our struggles between the social movements and political parties, with the support of our academic institutions, in a way that has created a greater national consciousness. That is what made it possible for the people to rise up in these recent days.

When we speak of the 'defense of humanity,' as we do at this event, I think that this only happens by eliminating neoliberalism and imperialism. But I think that in this we are not so alone, because we see, every day that anti-imperialist thinking is spreading, especially after Bush's bloody 'intervention' policy in Iraq. Our way of organizing and uniting against the system, against the empire's aggression towards our people, is spreading, as are the strategies for creating and strengthening the power of the people.

I believe only in the power of the people. That was my experience in my own region, a single province – the importance of local power. And now, with all that has happened in Bolivia, I have seen the importance of the power of a whole people, of a whole nation. For those of us who believe it important to defend humanity, the best contribution we can make is to help create that popular power. This happens when we check our personal interests with those of the group.

Sometimes, we commit to the social movements in order to win power. We need to be led by the people, not use or manipulate them.

We may have differences among our popular leaders – and it's true that we have them in Bolivia. But when the people are conscious, when the people know what needs to be done, any difference among the different local leaders ends. We've been making progress in this for a long time, so that our people are finally able to rise up, together.

What I want to tell you, compañeras and compañeros – what I dream of and what we as leaders from Bolivia dream of is that our task at this moment should be to strengthen anti-imperialist thinking. Some leaders are now talking about how we – the intellectuals, the social and political movements – can organize a great summit of people like Fidel, Chávez and Lula to say to everyone: 'We are here, taking a stand against the aggression of the US imperialism.' A summit at which we are joined by compañera Rigoberta Menchú, by other social and labor leaders, great personalities like Pérez Ezquivel. A great summit to say to our people that we are together, united, and defending humanity. We have no other choice, compañeros and compañeras – if we want to defend humanity we must change the system, and this means overthrowing US imperialism.

That is all. Thank you very much.

(25 October, 2003)

Appendix Six

Hugo Chávez Addresses the United Nations 16/9/05 'ICH'

Your Excellencies, friends, good afternoon:

The original purpose of this meeting has been completely distorted. The imposed centre of debate has been a so-called reform process that overshadows the most urgent issues, what the peoples of the world claim with urgency: the adoption of measures that deal with the real problems that block and sabotage the efforts made by our countries for real development and life.

Five years after the Millennium Summit, the harsh reality is that the great majority of estimated goals — which were very modest indeed — will not be met.

We pretended reducing by half the 842 million hungry people by the year 2015. At the current rate that goal will be achieved by the year 2215.

Who in this audience will be there to celebrate it? That is only if the human race is able to survive the destruction that threats our natural environment.

We had claimed the aspiration of achieving universal primary education by the year 2015. At the current rate that goal will be reached after the year 2100. Let us prepare, then, to celebrate it.

Friends of the world, this takes us to a sad conclusion: the United Nations has exhausted its model, and it is not all about reform. The XXI century claims deep changes that will only be possible if a new organization is founded. This UN does not work. We have to say it. It is the truth. These transformations —

the ones Venezuela is referring to – have, according to us, two phases: the immediate phase and the aspiration phase, a utopia. The first is framed by the agreements that were signed in the old system. We do not run away from them. We even bring concrete proposals in that model for the short term. But the dream of an ever-lasting world peace, the dream of a world not ashamed by hunger, disease, illiteracy, extreme necessity, needs – apart from roots – to spread its wings to fly. We need to spread our wings and fly. We are aware of a frightening neoliberal globalization, but there is also the reality of an interconnected world that we have to face not as a problem but as a challenge. We could, on the basis of national realities, exchange knowledge, integrate markets, interconnect, but at the same time we must understand that there are problems that do not have a national solution: radioactive clouds, world oil prices, diseases, warming of the planet or the hole in the ozone layer. These are not domestic problems. As we stride toward a new United Nations model that includes all of us when they talk about the people, we are bringing four indispensable and urgent reform proposals to this Assembly: the first, the expansion of the Security Council in its permanent categories as well as the non permanent categories, thus allowing new developed and developing countries as new permanent and non permanent categories. The second, we need to assure the necessary improvement of the work methodology in order to increase transparency, not to diminish it. The third, we need to immediately suppress – we have said this repeatedly in Venezuela for the past six years – the veto in the decisions taken by the Security Council, that elitist trace is incompatible with democracy, incompatible with the principles of equality and democracy. And the fourth, we need to strengthen the role of the Secretary General; his/her political functions regarding preventive diplomacy, that role must be consolidated. The seriousness of all our problems calls for deep transformations. Mere reforms are not enough to recover what 'we', all the peoples of the world, are waiting for. More than just reforms we in Venezuela call for the foundation of a new United Nations, or as the teacher of Simón Bolívar, Simón Rodríguez said: 'Either we invent or we err.'

At the Porto Alegre World Social Forum last January different persons asked for the United Nations to move outside the United States if the repeated violations to international rule of law continue.

Today we know that there were never any weapons of mass destruction in Iraq. The people of the United States have always been very rigorous in demanding the truth to their leaders; the people of the world demand the same thing. There were never any weapons of mass destruction; however, Iraq was bombed, occupied and it is still occupied. All this happened over the United Nations. That is why we propose to this Assembly that the United Nations should leave a country that does not respect the resolutions taken by this same Assembly. Some proposals have pointed out to Jerusalem as an international city as an alternative. The proposal is generous enough to propose an answer to the current conflict affecting Palestine. Nonetheless, it may have some characteristics that could make it very difficult to become a reality. That is why we are bringing a proposal made by Simón Bolívar, the great Liberator of the South, in 1815. Bolívar proposed then the creation of an international city that would host the idea of unity.

We believe it is time to think about the creation of an international city with its own sovereignty, with its own strength and morality to represent all nations of the world. Such an international city has to balance five centuries of imbalance. The headquarters of the United Nations must be in the South.

Ladies and gentlemen, we are facing an unprecedented energy crisis in which an unstoppable increase of energy use is perilously reaching record highs, as well as the incapacity to increase oil supply and the prospect of a decline in the proven reserves of fuel worldwide. Oil is starting to become exhausted.

For the year 2020 the daily demand for oil will be 120 million barrels. Such demand, even without counting future increments – would consume in 20 years what humanity has used up to now. This means that carbon dioxide levels will inevitably be increased, thus warming our planet even more.

Hurricane Katrina has been a painful example of the cost of ignoring such realities. The warming of the oceans is the fundamental factor behind the destructive increase in the strength of the hurricanes we have witnessed in the last years. Let this occasion be an outlet to send our deepest condolences to the people of the United States. Their people are brothers and sisters of all of us in the Americas and the rest of the world.

It is unpractical and unethical to sacrifice the human race by appealing in an insane manner to the validity of a socioeconomic model that has a galloping destructive capacity. It would be suicidal to spread it and impose it as an infallible remedy for the evils which are caused precisely by it.

Not too long ago the President of the United States went to an Organization of American States' meeting to propose Latin America and the Caribbean to increase market-oriented policies, open market policies – that is neoliberalism – when it is precisely the fundamental cause of the great evils and the great tragedies currently suffered by our people: the neoliberal capitalism, the Washington Consensus. All this has generated is a high degree of misery, inequality and infinite tragedy for all the peoples on this continent.

What we need now more than ever, Mr President, is a new international order. Let us recall the United Nations General Assembly in its sixth extraordinary session period in 1974, 31 years ago, where a new International Economic Order action plan was adopted, as well as the States Economic Rights and Duties Charter by an overwhelming majority, 120 votes for the motion, 6 against and 10 abstentions. This was the period when voting was possible at the United Nations. Now it is impossible to vote. Now they approve documents such as this one which I denounce on behalf of Venezuela as null, void and illegitimate. This document was approved violating the current laws of the United Nations. This document is invalid! This document should be discussed; the Venezuelan government will make it public. We cannot accept an open and shameless dictatorship in the United Nations. These matters should be discussed and that is why I petition my colleagues, heads of states and heads of governments, to discuss it.

I just came from a meeting with President Néstor Kirchner and well, I was pulling this document out; this document was handed out five minutes before – and only in English – to our delegation. This document was approved by a dictatorial hammer which I am here denouncing as illegal, null, void and illegitimate.

Hear this, Mr President: if we accept this, we are indeed lost. Let us turn off the lights, close all doors and windows! That would be unbelievable: us accepting a dictatorship here in this hall.

Now more than ever – we were saying – we need to retake ideas that were left on the road such as the proposal approved at this Assembly in 1974 regarding a New Economic International Order. Article 2 of that text confirms the right of states to nationalize the property and natural resources that belonged to foreign investors. It also proposed to create cartels of raw material producers. In the Resolution 3021, May 1974, the Assembly expressed its will to work with utmost urgency in the creation of a New Economic International Order based on – listen carefully, please – 'the equity, sovereign equality, interdependence, common interest and cooperation among all states regardless of their economic and social systems, correcting the inequalities and repairing the injustices among developed and developing countries, thus assuring present and future generations, peace, justice and a social and economic development that grows at a sustainable rate'.

The main goal of the New Economic International Order was to modify the old economic order conceived at Breton Woods.

We the people now claim – this is the case of Venezuela – a new international economic order. But it is also urgent to develop a new international political order. Let us not permit that a few countries try to reinterpret the principles of International Law in order to impose new doctrines such as 'pre-emptive warfare'. Oh do they threaten us with that pre-emptive war! And what about the 'Responsibility to Protect' doctrine? We need to ask ourselves. Who is going to protect us? How are they going to protect us?

I believe one of the countries that require protection is precisely the United States. That was shown painfully with the tragedy caused by Hurricane Katrina; they do not have a government that protects them from the announced natural disasters, if we are going to talk about protecting each other; these are very dangerous concepts that shape imperialism, interventionism as they try to legalize the violation of national sovereignty. The full respect towards the principles of International Law and the United Nations Charter must be, Mr President, the keystone for international relations in today's world and the base for the new order we are currently proposing.

It is urgent to fight, in an efficient manner, international terrorism. Nonetheless, we must not use it as an excuse to launch unjustified military aggressions which violate international law. Such has been the doctrine following September 11. Only a true and close cooperation and the end of the double discourse that some countries of the North apply regarding terrorism, could end this terrible calamity.

In just seven years of Bolivarian Revolution, the people of Venezuela can claim important social and economic advances.

One million four hundred and six thousand Venezuelans learned to read and write. We are 25 million total. And the country will – in a few days – be declared illiteracy-free territory.

And three million Venezuelans, who had always been excluded because of poverty, are now part of primary, secondary and higher studies.

Seventeen million Venezuelans – almost 70% of the population – are receiving, and for the first time, universal healthcare, including the medicine, and in a few years, all Venezuelans will have free access to an excellent healthcare service. More than one million seven hundred tons of food are channelled to over 12 million people at subsidized prices, almost half the population. One million gets them completely free, as they are in a transition period. More than 700 000 new jobs have been created, thus reducing unemployment by 9 points. All of this amid internal and external aggressions, including a coup d'état and an oil industry shutdown organized by Washington. Regardless of the conspiracies, the lies spread by powerful media outlets, and the permanent threat of the empire and its allies, they even call for the assassination of a president. The only country where a person is able to call for the assassination of a head of state is the United States. Such was the case of a Reverend called Pat Robertson, very close to the White House: he called for my assassination and he is a free person. That is international terrorism!

We will fight for Venezuela, for Latin American integration and the world. We reaffirm our infinite faith in humankind. We are thirsty for peace and justice in order to survive as a species. Simón Bolívar, founding father of our country and guide of our revolution swore to never allow his hands to be idle or his soul to rest until he had broken the shackles which bound us to the empire. Now is the time to not allow our hands to be idle or our souls to rest until we save humanity.

Index